Out
of the
Rabbit Hole

A Memoir

Kathy Wilson

Fulton Books, Inc.
New York, NY

First originally published by Fulton Books 2015

ISBN 978-1-63338-035-6 (paperback)
ISBN 978-1-63338-036-3 (digital)

Printed in the United States of America

For my mother

I attribute the vividness of my early memories to the stories told to me by my mother in her frequent states of inebriation and to the many hours I spent alone, waiting, thinking, pretending and dreaming.

Acknowledgments

From 2001 to the present I've been in a New York City writing workshop funded by *Poets and Writers*. Thank you to Bonnie Rose Marcus, the Director of Reading and Workshops, for having been our guardian angel and to Veronica Golas, the workshop's original teacher, who encouraged and motivated me to begin writing this memoir. I must also thank the members of this group for their helpful critiques as I read many of my chapters in class.

Many thanks to Elena Alexander, our current teacher, for her constant guidance and support and for introducing me to my editor, Frazier Russell. I am most grateful to Frazier for his insightful editing suggestions that gave me the inspiration for final touches.

A special thank you to Cathi Stoler and Terry Jennings, my other writing group partners, who read and re-read many chapters and offered their helpful perspectives.

I am also grateful to Mirga Girnius, who generously offered her valuable assistance with all of the Lithuanian translations.

My largest debt of gratitude goes to Catherine Gibran who has lovingly and passionately formatted, researched and copy-edited my entire memoir, not once but twice.

I am honored to have had artist Johanna Gillman, design my cover including her painting *Over the Ramparts*. Thank you Johanna, it's perfect.

Thank you to all my early readers for their comments and suggestions and to Frank and the many others for their various kinds of support and assistance.

My compliments and appreciation to all at Fulton Publishing for designing my book and especially to Jason Murray for his endless guidance and valued advice.

Finally, I must acknowledge my family, whose stories are woven into the fabric of my life and writing. My love and gratitude to my mother, who did the best she could. My warmest thank you for the support of all my wonderful friends whom I love and feel loved by. Most of all, I thank my beautiful daughter Christina for the sunshine she has brought into my life.

Part I

CHAPTER 1

Kathy with a K

From the moment my mother became pregnant with me, she and my father were locked into an angry, bitter war.

Perhaps the combination of my mother, Eva Tomalavage, a former actress, second generation Lithuanian and Russian, and my father, Joseph Persico, a dance hall and restaurant owner, second generation Italian, contributed to my becoming absorbed in the world of music, movies, and theatre. Without that world to escape into, I can say most definitely I would not have survived my mother and father.

Even my name caused controversy. My mother was enchanted with the operetta *The Student Prince* and was determined to name me Kathy, after the heroine. In the Italian culture, out of respect, I should be named after my paternal grandmother. Miraculously, my grandmother's name was Catherine with a C. For once a battle was averted and I became Katherine with a K, but have always been called Kathy. I don't know for whom my half brother Ronald was named, probably a movie star, or perhaps for his father, a man neither he nor I ever met. He was my mother's son and was six years old when she married my father. Since he often stayed with my aunts or my grandmother, I was often the "only child" in the house.

One of my earliest recollections is that of the big brown box in our living room called the radio. Actually, we referred to the living room, where our radio was the focus, as "the parlor." Gathering around that beloved brown box is the only memory I have of my immediate family doing something together. My mother and brother Ronnie listened to what it said—funny things that made them laugh, like *Fibber McGee and Molly*, and scary things that made them upset. On December 7, 1941, it told us that Pearl Harbor was bombed; I imagined all the pretty pearls black and ruined. Ronnie and I started to play hide and seek at night when we heard the loud wailing of the air raid drill sirens. We'd shut off all the lights and stay in the parlor so the Japanese could not bomb us. With only the tiny light from my dollhouse, we would wait for the "all clear" signal. At the sound of the sirens, our dog Mugsy would bark and howl. Mugsy was a spitz and terrier mix weighing about thirty-five pounds. Predominantly black, he had a brown strip across one eye and a tail curled like a pretzel. He was from Tiny's litter, my father's dog that always lived at the bar. I have a picture of my father with his brother, my Uncle Tony, holding Tiny.

Our apartment was in the Bronx on Mosholu Parkway, with the bedroom windows facing the park. The parlor was the middle of three rooms, with windows level with the elevated train tracks on Jerome Avenue. The trains passed frequently, drowning out our voices. From the kitchen window over the rooftops, you could see the garden in the back of my father's bar and grill. It was called the Venetian. The neighborhood was a really nice mix of predominantly middle class Jewish and Catholic families of mostly German, Irish and Italian descent.

From the radio we could hear our favorite singers. Mine was Frank Sinatra, Ronnie's was Bing Crosby, and my mother loved the Ink Spots. Ronnie and I would have heated arguments; he would insist that Bing Crosby was better. It seemed so very important to me that he agree that Frank Sinatra was the best. We would keep debating who was better.

"Bing Crosby is the best."

"No, Frank Sinatra is the best."

"No, he isn't."

"Yes, he is."

We would do this over and over until I would scream and cry; then he'd call me a crybaby and sometimes whack me with a newspaper.

As early as I can remember, I sang along with Frank Sinatra. I knew all the lyrics to his songs. My mother would also play his records for me on our Victrola. I can see myself in the parlor singing along with Sinatra to *Nancy with the Laughing Face,* passionately involved in the lyrics with the radio at top volume. A cacophony of sounds accompanied us—the elevated train passing near our apartment window, the loud angry voices of my mother and father coming from the bedroom, and Mugsy frantically barking at the thuds from behind the closed bedroom door.

I'd also sing along when I visited my father's bar and grill, spending hours putting nickels in the jukebox, singing Sinatra's words of love and pain. My father kept a little red velvet box behind the bar. He called it "a magic box" because whenever I came back to get more nickels, he'd hand me the box and it would once more be filled with nickels. I would clap my hands with joy, the customers applauded, and my father would stand there smiling. Sometimes he even smiled at my mother. I don't ever remember him smiling at home. I hardly remember him at home at all, except for sleeping or fighting. The most enduring picture I have of him is slumped over black coffee at our kitchen table in a thin-strapped tee shirt, his bloodshot eyes staring straight ahead. I never spoke to him during those times.

At the Venetian he was always cheerful. It felt good being there because it was one of the few times my parents were in the same place without arguing. As you entered, my father would usually be standing behind the long oak bar on the left. Across from it, right in the middle of the opposite wall, was the jukebox. In the rear were eight booths, four on each side, with red and white checkered tablecloths. Empty Chianti wine bottles stuffed with candles served as centerpieces. In the summer, the back door opened into the small wine garden that we saw from our kitchen window. At the Venetian I could hear Frank Sinatra any time I wanted just by inserting a nickel and pressing the right button. When a record was playing, I was mesmerized by the glow of the changing colors the jukebox produced—reds, blues, and yellows fading from one to the next creating new colors as they overlapped. I remember eating *Pasta e Fagioli* after watching my father cook the beans with the ditalini macaroni in the bar's tiny kitchen. This dish always reminds me of him. I spent many hours of my childhood at the

Venetian, while my mother drank her beers and my father charmed his customers, tended bar, cooked, and served food and drinks.

My mother was very beautiful; she could have been one of the movie stars in the MGM musicals I saw at the Tuxedo Movie Theatre. She had an oval face with high cheekbones and shiny brown hair turned under just below her neckline in the style of the Forties. Her soft flowered dresses complemented her statuesque figure. She seemed to know everyone in the bar and laughed a lot while there. The more she laughed, the less my father did; the more she drank, the more she laughed. Just when we would be having a really good time my father would tell her, "It's time you took your daughter home and put her to bed."

She never answered. She'd just finish her beer, take me by the hand and leave, barely nodding goodbye to anyone. I'd wave to those who waved to me. Sometimes she'd take me to another bar called the Golf. It was one block up on the corner of Jerome Avenue and Gunhill Road; it was our "secret" that we were going to the Golf. "Daddy will be very angry at us if he knows." (I never told. I knew he would hit her.) I would also play the jukebox at the Golf; however, I did not have the endless nickels from the "magic box" so my playing was limited. Sometimes my mother's friends (they were all men except for my mother's drinking buddy, Kathleen) would give me as much as a quarter. I also knew I should never mention being with Kathleen to my father. "If I catch you with that tramp Kathleen, I'll give the both of you black eyes," I remember him shouting to my mother. The Golf had a separate back dining room where I, when hungry, would be served a small seventy-five cent pizza; I ate many pizzas there. In the Forties there wasn't anywhere you could buy just a slice except maybe at Coney Island. The Golf was also where my mother went many nights when she left me alone in the apartment after putting me to bed.

I would wake up and listen for sounds in the frightening darkness. Nothing, nothing, but the trees blowing in the park across the street and occasionally the sound of a passing car. It was the reflection of the trees in the mirror that created giant moving shadows on the walls. I'd reach for my beloved black and white stuffed panda bear, Poochie, and clutch him close to my chest.

"Mommy?" No answer. "Mommy?"

I told Poochie not to be afraid. I would protect him from the shadow monsters. I was three years old when these nights of being left alone began. Some nights the sound of the air raid sirens would awaken me. I'd reach for Poochie and assure him I would save him from the Japanese if they broke into our apartment, took us prisoners and tortured us by dripping water on our heads until our heads exploded. Sometimes I got up and checked all the rooms, my heart pounding against Poochie for fear of being pounced upon at any moment. When I found no one, I'd run back to bed and once again reassure Poochie that we were safe. Other nights I was just too terrified to move at all. I would not let Poochie know how afraid I was, afraid of the shadow monsters, afraid of the Japanese, afraid my mother might never return.

I would talk to Poochie waiting for him to answer. I knew he could answer if he wanted to, because my mother told me that the candy and gum I found on the coffee table each morning were bought by Poochie in the middle of the night when I was sleeping. When she first told me this, I was so excited.

"Mommy, when will Poochie walk and talk for me?"

She hugged me and said, "When you are a good girl."

Well, I thought I *was* a good girl but I would try to be better. During the nights when I would lie awake, I pleaded with Poochie to talk to me. I told him how good I was, how good I would be. I told him how much I loved him…but he did not respond. I tried pretending I was asleep so I could catch him getting up to go shopping. I'd wait and wait until sleep finally conquered me.

In the morning, I would wake up with Poochie still next to me. I'd peek to see whether Mommy was home safe, sleeping and recovering from her night at the bars. She always was. I'd then run into the parlor to see if the goodies were on the coffee table. They always were. I'd hug Poochie and thank him for all the treats. This caused very mixed feelings. I was thankful for the candy but angry that he had left me alone at night. I was so angry that one morning while my mother was still asleep, I locked us in the bathroom, filled the sink with water and through gritted teeth demanded that Poochie speak to me. I didn't drown him; instead I asked for his forgiveness and told him how much I loved him. Now I'd shown him how bad I was and felt he'd never walk or talk for me. But I guess he still loved me because he continued to bring me goodies for several years to come.

One night, when my mother had only run out to get cigarettes, she left the light on in the parlor. I woke to the air raid sirens screeching and the air raid wardens banging on our door to have us put out the lights. I grabbed Poochie and hid behind the couch, thinking for sure the Japanese had come to get me. Mugsy, who would otherwise be curled asleep on my bed, barked and finally scared them away. As soon as the "all clear" sounded, my mother came home. I remember her always telling the story and quoting me as saying, "Mommy, I hid behind the couch and did NOT let the Japanese in." For years, whenever she would tell this story, I would cringe as the listener would laugh and say how cute I was.

I especially remember waking up on summer nights in my junior bed at the foot of my mother and father's. I must have been at least four. With the light from the street, I could see their empty bed reflected in the large round mirror of my mother's dressing table positioned cater-corner in the room. The dreaded silver-plated "spanking brush" waited there. During the day this same big mirror would reflect my image for hours on end as I changed from pretending to be Dorothy Lamour in a makeshift sarong to Deanna Durbin, Judy Garland or Betty Grable. These movie stars were my babysitters and I knew them well, as I was often deposited at the Tuxedo Movie Theatre where my mother would periodically check in on me; the Golf bar was only a few doors away. I would watch these films over and over; I even got to know all the songs. I'd sing and dance with my leading men like Dan Dailey, Van Johnson, or, of course, Frank Sinatra. I'd pretend we would kiss, fall in love, get married, then sing and dance about how happy we were, and when we'd push buttons, beds would come out of the walls. Sometimes I would try to hold Mugsy up by his two front paws and dance with him. He would tolerate this for a short time then pull away.

On summer nights, I'd often stand on a chair and carefully climb out onto our second floor fire escape from the bedroom window that overlooked Mosholu Park. The section outside our window, although somewhat precarious, was on the opposite side of the fire escape ladder and was enclosed, so I felt safe. Sitting there with Poochie, I'd watch for my mother to turn the corner and come back home. Our building was just a few doors in from Jerome Avenue. These waiting sagas occurred frequently and went on from the time I was four until I was six years old. Sometimes for hours, I would picture my mother leaving the Golf bar two blocks north on Jerome Avenue, swaying as she headed home, then turning the corner onto Mosholu Parkway where she would come into view. I'd carefully imagine her passing by all the familiar places along the way, like the Tuxedo Movie Theatre, Woolworth's Five-and-Ten Cent Store, Schweller's Delicatessen, and the chocolate store which was right next to my father's bar and was about the halfway mark. I'd visualize her waiting at each corner for the lights to change green and even have her stop to light up a Pall Mall cigarette.

When the time came for her to turn the corner of our block and she didn't, I would start imagining her homecoming all over again from the Golf bar, past the landmarks, but walking more slowly each time. I don't recall ever seeing her actually turn the corner during this waiting game. I wasn't afraid of being alone on the fire escape; it was better than being in the apartment with the shadow monsters. Interestingly, no one ever noticed me up at my look-out station. My memory is that the park was quite picturesque. From my perch, I looked over hundreds of trees that sloped downhill to meet the Grand Concourse. On clear nights the moon and stars would add to the glow of the streetlamps. However, I can still feel the intense loneliness and longing for my mother's return. I don't think I ever told my mother about these nights of waiting. Until this day when I am waiting for someone who is late, I get an ache in the pit of my stomach; the more meaningful the someone, the greater the pain. I always arrive early—too early.

CHAPTER 2

You Mustn't Hate
My Mother

Somehow, as long as I can remember, I knew my mother's story. She told it to me over and over in bits and pieces during her drunken monologues, or perhaps I absorbed some of it overhearing both sides of the family talk about her; the Lithuanians were much less sensitive to what a child should hear than the Italians.

My great grandparents, Eva and Pete Bononis, and their two daughters, Mary, age thirteen, and Elizabeth, age ten, arrived in America from Vilnius, Lithuania in the early 1900's. They settled in Pottsville, Pennsylvania, where my great grandfather Pete found work as a coal miner. I am not sure of the exact year. Their daughter Mary, my grandmother, was married at fourteen to a coal miner named John Tomalavage. He was in his late twenties and had also come from Lithuania but was half Russian on his father's side. My grandmother Mary had a total of fourteen children by three different husbands, and had a baby or a miscarriage almost every year. Of the fourteen, my mother and three aunts were the only ones who survived to adulthood. Most of the others were stillborn or died as babies or as very young children from common colds, fevers, and influenza. I only remember two that were ever talked about: While swimming in a river with his friends, Eddie drowned at nine when pulled away by the current, and Agnes died of consumption at nineteen. Years later, I would lie awake at night looking at Agnes among all the other sepia photographs of family members hanging on my grandmother's bedroom wall. The pictures took on a ghostly appearance seen through the flickering of the vigil light candles adorning the makeshift altars my grandmother dedicated to Jesus, Mary, Joseph, Saint Anthony, Saint Teresa and Saint Agnes. In front of each of the two dressers on which the altars rested, there was a little padded stool to kneel on while praying.

My mother was born in Minersville, Pennsylvania, on November 15, 1911. She was named Eva after her grandmother, whom I would come to fear and dislike. My mother's two older sisters were Helen, born in 1907, and Mae, born in 1909. Their father, John Tomalavage, was burned to death in a coal mine when my mother was four.

My grandmother went on to marry two more coal miners, both named John. None of the children from her second marriage to John Luksis survived; this John was killed in a mine collapse. My Aunt Jean, the fourth of Mary's surviving children, was born of the third marriage to John Gallagher. I am not sure when Jean's father died; he fell down the cellar steps and broke his neck. He must have lived long enough for her to become really attached to him, because when planning her own funeral seven decades later, Aunt Jean wanted to be buried in Minersville near his grave.

I remember hearing my aunts and mother, while sitting around the kitchen table drinking pitcher after pitcher of beer, laughing about my grandmother having three Johns and always shopping for a new John on the way back from the funerals. My understanding was that each time my grandmother found a new husband, the existing children were put out of the house if they were old enough. At eleven, my Aunt Helen was considered old enough to work and was sent to Newark, New Jersey, to board with my grandmother's sister, Elizabeth. Helen started working in a factory skinning rabbits. My mother, then age seven, and Aunt Mae, age nine, were left behind with the ill-fated younger children, including Agnes and Eddie. Being the oldest in the house, it was my Aunt Mae who had to take care of all the younger siblings. My grandmother always gave her attention to her new husband and new children.

Coal miners did not make much money, and with all those children, what they did make didn't stretch very far. My grandmother would bake many loaves of bread, sometimes with borrowed flour, or pies with fruit from the local blueberry bushes or apple trees, and give one to each family member. That was their only food allotment for that day and sometimes the next. They could choose to eat it all at once or divide it up to last longer. In the winter, the children hunted for coal that fell from the freight cars onto the railroad tracks, or their father brought coal home in his pockets. It was all they had to heat the house. Their dresses were sometimes made from flour sacks.

Once when the local priest came to take up his "Easter collection" from the parishioners, my grandmother was so embarrassed at "being poor" that she borrowed a dollar from a neighbor. A dollar was a lot of money in those days! At the time her husband was in the hospital with third degree burns, but she did not want the priest to think her an uncaring Catholic. In Newark, my Aunt Helen was earning fifty cents a week working in the factory. Twenty cents went to her Aunt Elizabeth for weekly board, ten cents for her food, and another ten for her clothes, but somehow she managed to put the remaining ten cents into savings. A few years later, those savings actually bought her a share of a beauty parlor.

When she was twelve, my Aunt Mae left Pennsylvania and joined her sister Helen in Newark, taking my mother, who was only ten, with her. Mae was more like a mother to her than my grandmother had been. Left to her own devices at such a young age, Mae resorted to using manipulation to control her younger siblings. She would tease and ridicule them until they cried. Then she'd hug and kiss them as a consolation. Because I, too, experienced Aunt Mae's tactics when I was a little girl, years later I kept her well away from my own daughter.

After her last husband—John number three—died from the fall on the cellar stairs, my grandmother also moved to Newark, taking Jean and Agnes with her. At that time, Helen, Mae, my mother Eva, Jean and Agnes were the only surviving offspring. They also paid board to live with my grandmother's sister Elizabeth. This was in the Ironbound section of Newark, also referred to as "Down Neck," which was and still is a nice area. Even with three in a bed and two beds in one room, they felt their standard of living had improved. My great grandmother and grandfather were also living nearby. Having survived the mines, my great grandfather Pete was working two shifts in a factory, saving all the money he could. His dream was to go back to visit Lithuania before he died.

The physical contrast between my grandmother Mary and her sister Elizabeth was remarkable. My grandmother looked exactly the same from as early as I can remember until the day she died, when I was twenty-seven. Even in the pictures of her as a young woman, she looked the same as I had always known her. She was about five feet two inches, with straw-like blond hair, parted in the middle, cut straight just below her ears and fastened by two blond bobby pins to keep it away from her face. With her pock- marked face and bulbous nose, I always thought she looked like a cross between George Washington and W.C. Fields. She was quite heavy and wore old lady print house-dresses with buttons down the front adorned with pop pearls. In fact, because of her weight, many of her children were not always aware she was pregnant. After a night of commotion—screams and neighbors running in and out of their cramped house—a new baby would appear in my grandmother's arms the next morning. While nursing, the infant would sleep with my grandmother and then be shifted to share a bed with several others. While living in Minersville, the family only spoke Lithuanian. My grandmother learned only a few words of English from her children, who were taught English at school.

My grandmother's sister Elizabeth, on the other hand, was only five feet tall with a petite figure. She had style in a Norman Rockwell sort of way, wore small glasses and kept her dark brown hair in a neat bun at the nape of her neck. Elizabeth married a Navy man, moved to West Virginia and they had three sons. It was always rumored by the family that a lover was the father of one of her sons. After her husband died, I don't know how or exactly when, she moved to Newark. Certainly she had a better life than my grandmother, spoke English well, and actually had acquired a charming West Virginian accent. She dropped the g from words like "darlin'" and often said "y'all" stretched out like the beginning of a yodel. All three of her sons went through high school and later joined the Navy.

My mother was Elizabeth's favorite niece. With her Russian heritage dominant, little Eva had an oval face, high cheekbones, a long neck, and glossy dark brown hair, giving her a very classic look. She looked very much like Natalie Wood both as a child and as an adult. In my scrapbook, I saved pictures of Natalie Wood; you would swear they were photographs of my mother at about nineteen. My mother's eyes were brown and soulful. In contrast, her sisters were blond and blue eyed, very Slavic looking. Next in line for looks were Aunt Helen, then Aunt Jean and last Aunt Mae. My favorite was my Aunt Helen who was like a second mother to me. She had the kindest deep blue eyes, was soft-spoken, even tempered and very pragmatic. Mae had sharp features, bleached blond coiffed hair and always wore blue eye shadow. Her beak nose made her look like a witch when she got angry. She always commented about herself, "I may not be the prettiest, but you have to admit I certainly am the most attractive." I was caught under Aunt Mae's possessive wing for many years. Jean was the youngest, simple and modern in dress, her blond hair always very contemporary. They were all slender; fortunately, none of them inherited my grand-mother's physique.

My mother Eva was a bright, gentle child. She wrote poetry, kept journals, and loved to read novels and plays. Some of her artistic ten-dencies probably came from her grandfather. Before he and my great grandmother moved to Newark, she had been very close to him. In Minersville, he told her stories as they went for long walks together; he also read her poems and sang to her. I remember her telling me that the poetry he wrote in Lithuanian made the language seem lyrical. Lithuanian is not a lyrical language; I always thought the sound of it was very harsh. She used the word "flowery" to describe the way her grandfather wrote and spoke. Their close relationship probably began during the time my Aunt Helen had moved away to Newark and my Aunt Mae was busy taking care of the younger children. When he moved to Newark, little Eva was devastated. She was thrilled when she later moved there and could be close to him once more. With working two shifts, he could not spend much time with her but did manage to help her with schoolwork, and she helped him to learn English. Her schooling through eighth grade far exceeded the education of Helen and Mae, who both only finished grade two. The only sister to graduate from high school was my Aunt Jean.

While Helen and Mae worked in the factory, my mother accom-panied her Aunt Elizabeth wherever she went, to the library or shopping for clothes or food. They often went to the movies together. When I think about it, to Elizabeth, then a widow with three grown sons, my mother must have been like the daughter she never had. Eva learned to cook, sew and keep house well, and also learned to smoke. She and my Aunt Elizabeth were the only two who ever smoked in the family, until my mother introduced me to smoking at age fourteen. I was sitting on the rocking chair near the parlor window when my mother came into the room and offered me one of her Pall Malls. The first drag hurt my throat and caused me to choke. We both laughed—but I was flattered that my mother saw me as her peer. That day started twenty plus years of my smoking, which I stopped during my pregnancy, then again for my daughter's sake when she was four.

When my mother was almost thirteen and entering eighth grade, her grandfather planned to make his long awaited visit to Lithuania. Working the two shifts for about five years had taken its toll. He felt he had to go while his health endured and bring his only sister Libby back to America with him. During their correspondence over the years, he was aware his sister had never married in order to care for their mother and father through long illnesses that eventually caused their deaths. His attempts to send money were futile; apparently, it was intercepted and stolen. He thought his savings were now sufficient for his round trip on the ship, his sister's passage, and the under-the-table fees he would need to bribe the authorities to allow her to leave the county. Without payoffs, no passports were issued. It was also very important that he be back when his sweet grandchild Eva graduated from the eighth grade. "I would never miss such a momentous occasion," he told them all.

Everyone in the family was excited about his trip, knowing not only that he would have many stories to tell, but also that they would finally meet Libby, whose letters had arrived for years. They all went to the port in New York City to see the ship off. These were treacherous times to travel in steerage class; there was a lot of thievery on the ships as well as in Lithuania. Coming from America, you were a good prey.

In his wallet he would carry very little, another smaller amount was in a purse pinned to the inside of his underwear. For safety my great grandmother sewed his entire savings into the lining of his over-coat to be unstitched when he finally arrived in Lithuania.

After about twenty-four days of traveling on rough seas with most of the passengers seasick, then on trains, and finally by horse and carriage, he arrived at his sister Libby's. When he opened the lining of his coat he discovered that his wife had substituted cut newspaper instead of money! He was devastated. She had kept all of his savings. He would not be able to return to America. He wrote and wrote and begged her to send money for his return; his letters went unanswered. I don't know exactly when or of what, but he died in Lithuania.

"He died of a broken heart," my mother would tell me through her tears. My mother's heart was also broken; she hated her grandmother for what she had done, and disliked her own mother for accepting it. Although she asked them both, no explanation was ever given to her for the cruel behavior of her grandmother. Because I had heard this story, I always hated my great grandmother. Aunt Mae often took me along to visit her. I dreaded those visits in her dark apartment and later in a nursing home. My recollection of her is a stern, wrinkled old lady with big bunions on her feet.

My mother lived at home long enough to graduate from the eighth grade; it was her tribute to her grandfather. Then she took a job as a live-in cook and housekeeper for a family in an affluent community in North Newark. She would be fourteen that coming November.

By this time, my Aunt Helen had a share in the beauty parlor in downtown Newark that she called the Greenwich. All four sisters now spoke English and worked there in some capacity. Until the shop built a client base, they ate peanut butter and Ritz crackers for lunch every day for months. Both of Aunt Helen's partners were of Russian ethnicity and both were named Eva. With my mother also working at the Greenwich part-time on weekends, there were now three Eva's. Aunt Helen would later marry Bill, the man she was dating, an American of Scottish descent. The shop became so successful that she was able to pay for Bill to go through law school.

One day when my mother was sixteen, she left both jobs without telling anyone and just disappeared. Everyone was frantic. My Aunt Mae could not sleep or eat for weeks. They all searched for her and even reported her missing to the police. The only reason they didn't think she was kidnapped or murdered was because she had packed and taken all her belongings with her.

Finally, after two months, she came to visit on a Sunday. Eva Tomalavage had renamed herself. "I am now Sonia Thomas," she declared. She was dancing in New York City at a Second Avenue Burlesque Theatre on the Lower East Side. In those days burlesque was made up of mostly vaudeville skits, with a few dancing girls. Her family thought of it as shocking and it made them relate to her as a "wayward woman." Aunt Elizabeth pleaded with her to come back home, go to high school and become an English teacher. Mae, who could be mean, very sharp tongued, and domineering, told her if she didn't quit and come back home that she would never be welcome again.

Before Sonia Thomas returned to her dancing job, she announced to them all, "I am going to be an actress."

CHAPTER 3

The Actress

I regret that I am unable to fill in all the details about my mother between the burlesque engagement and when my brother was conceived. Her four years in New York City, during which time she worked as a waitress and then as a live-in domestic helper while studying acting, are rather sketchy. At first she shared small apartments on the Upper West Side with two or three young women. Reminiscing about the city, she'd tell me about taking a light blanket and walking to Central Park to escape the intensity of the midsummer night's heat, sleeping on the grass when New York City was still safe. These were the stories my sober mother would tell as we sat in our parlor in the Bronx. She on the couch, me on her lap, I would put my head on her shoulder and share her reverie; these blissful moments were few but treasured memories. I would picture her happy, see her then as I wanted her to be now and always. She would speak fondly of her acting years, telling me she would walk from the Upper West Side to her classes and rehearsals which were in midtown.

At some point she began working as a live-in housekeeper and cook for a prominent family who owned and occupied an entire brownstone in the West 70's just off of Central Park West. The most wonderful part for her was having a lovely room to herself on the fourth and top floor with the privacy to study, write and dream of her future. She was peaceful, far from the coal mines. Being off every evening after the dinner dishes were washed and put away, and all day Sunday, the job allowed her time for acting classes and rehearsals. Life was sweet, and the future promised success and happiness.

The family she worked for consisted of a husband and wife in their early sixties and their only son whom I shall call James since I never knew his name. The entrance of the brownstone opened into a large foyer. To the left, in the main room, a baby grand piano sat nestled into a plush carpet. James, a concert pianist with a promising future ahead, was in his late twenties. He was tall, good looking, with sandy brown hair and twinkling brown eyes, and was his mother's pride and joy.

My mother fell deeply in love with James. They spent romantic nights in her room, reading and writing poetry to each other, passionately making love, then lying contentedly together until the sun would peek into the window sending James back to his downstairs room before his parents would wake. "This is our secret for now," James whispered.

Within the first year that my mother worked for them, James's father died suddenly of a heart attack. His mother now became totally dependent on James; her whole world revolved around him. Apparently, the feeling was mutual. When my mother told James she was pregnant with his child, his main concern was not to hurt or embarrass his mother. "It would destroy her," he said.

He offered to arrange and pay for an abortion, but this was not an option for my mother. In the 1930's, abortion was not only illegal but also very dangerous. It was also an unforgivable mortal sin, an act of murder for a Catholic. She flatly refused, and could not believe that this gentle, loving man would ask her to have his child cut out of her body. He said he could not give her any support if she chose to have the baby. His mother controlled all the funds, and if she ever revealed that this was his child, he would be compelled to deny it. He told my mother that the best thing for her to do was to leave immediately, go back to her family and not tell anyone he was the father. The new world she built crumbled in that instant. She felt shattered and very much a fool.

This is all I know about that time in her life. More importantly, this is all I could ever tell my brother about his father. My mother hardly told him anything at all. However, I vividly remember a cold winter's night when we were living with my grandmother in Newark. Ronnie was almost sixteen when my mother gave him the diary she had kept during that time in her life. Ronnie, obviously only a teenager at the time, didn't pay close attention and only skimmed through most of the chronicles leading to his conception. Afterward, Mommy took the diary and threw it into the flames of the coal stove. The story of her time with Ronnie's father and his birth turned to ashes.

He would never know very much about his father, only the bits and pieces that I could share with him—the ones our mother frequently seemed in need of telling me during her teary times. When I was a young adult, she told me she wished I would have read the diary and very much regretted having burned it. Other than the highlights I mentioned, she seemed unable to speak about it in detail. There remained a big gap in information about Ronnie's father and that period. Ronnie never even knew his name.

There was an old movie titled *Not Wanted,* the first film that Ida Lupino directed. My mother said the story was so close to her own life, it was as though the script had been written about her. When I was a teenager she insisted I go to the movies to see it with her. She wept through the entire movie. It haunts me as I wonder how much of my recollection of Ronnie's father is what she actually told me, or how much I filled in from seeing the film. The most I know for a fact is that my brother was born on May 23, 1932; nine months earlier takes us back to August of 1931. My mother would have been nineteen at the time. How long did she work for the family? How long were they having an affair? I don't know, but I do know that James was the love of her life. I know this from hearing it over and over as a young child and through the decades that followed. She confided that her fantasy was that when the baby was born, James would change his mind. She would bring him this precious infant, and they would resume their passionate relationship that would culminate in marriage.

Pregnant, she left New York and her dreams behind. Thinking her Aunt Elizabeth would understand since one of her sons was conceived with a lover, my mother approached her first. Elizabeth was far from understanding; she threw her out, called her a tramp, and told her to get an abortion. She never forgave Elizabeth and kept distant from her for the rest of her life. My grandmother and my Aunt Mae were just as condemning and offered no help. Aunt Mae took it personally, since everything was always about her.

"After all I did for you! How could you do this to me? Get out and don't ever show your face again."

Aunt Helen was now married to Bill. My mother went to them. In secret Bill offered to help if she bedded down with him. "What harm would it do, you're already pregnant and who has to know?" This she confided to me when I was already an adult. It was too late. Uncle Bill had already approached me sexually when I was only eleven.

Confessing to the priest at Saint James only magnified her guilt. "You have committed a grave mortal sin. You are out of God's favor," he bellowed. "How could you commit such a shameful sin?" She told me upon leaving the confessional she was so embarrassed she ran out of the church, not even going to the altar to say the penance that the priest had given to her. In the years to come, the only time she would enter church was for a special event: our baptisms, communions, confirmations or weddings.

She fled from Newark. Boarding a bus at Penn Station to Buffalo, New York, she went to a home for unwed mothers. These homes were mostly for "wayward girls" whose family had disowned them. They were run down and very depressing, having just the bare essentials. This is where she stayed until her son was born.

Tears would stream down her face when she would tell me, "During those months I had to decide if I was going to keep the baby or give it up for adoption. A very wealthy family was waiting hopefully to adopt my baby."

I couldn't have been more than five, I always felt so sorry for her, and I'd hold her tight.

"My final decision was to keep him," she wept, "even before I fell in love with his sweet little face." Ronnie's birth certificate reads, "Ronald James Thomas; Mother, Sonia Thomas; Father, unknown." She had honored James's wishes.

Returning to New York City, she brought Ronnie to his father, James. He whispered at the door, "My mother is now very ill and any awareness of our affair or the child's birth would kill her. I am so sorry but that is the way it has to be, at least for now."

Each time she repeated these words to me, it would rip her apart again. Leaving her fantasies behind, she brought Ronnie back to

Newark. Once my grandmother saw her grandchild her heart melted. Mae also fell in love with her sweet little nephew. Mae had since married a man named Pete. She suggested that Ronnie stay in Newark with my grandmother while my mother went back to New York to work and live. My grandmother was now living on Elm Street in Newark with only her thirteen year old, my Aunt Jean, and she welcomed and cherished Ronnie. She bestowed more love and attention on him than she was ever able to give to any of her fourteen children. Ronnie lived with her until he was six years old, when my mother and father married.

Once again, I am at a loss to describe exactly what happened during the next few years. I know through my mother's beer-evoked repetitions that she visited James once more when she heard his mother had died. Ronnie was now two. It took that visit for her to realize James hadn't been torn between her and love of his mother; he just didn't care about my mother or their son.

Ronnie was a contented little boy living with his grandmother, always smiling. There are pictures of him beaming, holding his cat, or holding his grandmother's hand looking like the happiest boy in the world. As an adult, when he looks at these pictures, he has asked me on several occasions, "What ever happened to that happy little boy?"

My mother started working six days a week as a practical nurse at Montefiore Hospital in the Bronx and was only able to visit Ronnie once a month. She was an unfamiliar figure to him. Instead of helping the relationship between Ronnie and his mother, Aunt Mae visited frequently and got her claws into him. She would tease him when my mother came to visit, "That's not your real mother, I am your real mother."

How confused he became! He would run to Aunt Mae thinking that my mother, this stranger, was going to kidnap him. These stories of Ronnie's confusion would be retold by my aunt years later and also described as "cute." Obviously she didn't realize how much that teasing affected Ronnie. As a little boy, he did wonder just who his real mother was. My grandmother was the only person he loved and really felt secure with. To him she would always be his true mother. He would weep bitterly at her funeral, which was one of three times that I had ever seen Ronnie cry.

It was during the time she was working at Montefiore Hospital that my mother met my father. The hospital staff would often eat lunch or dinner at my father's bar and grill. Although he was not especially good looking, only five feet five with black hair, a moustache and large round eyes, my father exuded enormous charisma and charmed everyone—especially my mother. My father often entertained his customers by singing Neapolitan love songs and was an excellent dancer. He also owned a dance hall in Harlem where he frequently sat in for a set on the drums. A really sharp dresser and a very romantic figure, he was highly sought after by the ladies.

From the first moment he saw my mother, he knew he wanted her for his own. "Own" was the right word for he would come to think of her as his beautiful possession. With two failed marriages and one child in his past, he thought this lovely young woman would be the perfect wife. He was twelve years her senior. Though she frequently went to the Venetian, my mother drank only ginger ale then. It wasn't until after I was born that she began to drink beer.

While working at Montefiore, my mother had resumed acting. She was accepted as a member of *The Little Theatre Players,* a group located at 145 West 45th Street in Manhattan. In the 1930's, this artistically excellent company was very well-regarded and being a member was a great achievement. I have a program which lists my mother as playing two of the lead roles in three one act plays that were presented. She received excellent reviews. The director of the company dedicated a great deal of time to her development as an actress. He thought she was exceptionally talented, so much so that the group offered to pay for her to go to Russia and study at Constantin Stanislavski's Moscow Art Theatre. Another lament I would hear over and over and over was, "My bags were already packed. The night before I was to leave, your father closed the Venetian early. While *How Deep is the Ocean* was playing on the jukebox, he came to my table, got on his knees and begged me not to go to Russia, to stay and marry him.

"I stayed, I married him," she'd sob.

CHAPTER 4

The Italians

My paternal grandparents were Italian Catholics from Naples, Italy. When my father Joe Persico was born, they were renting a house on East 116th Street in Manhattan. It was predominantly an Italian neighborhood for the first part of the twentieth century with its own Italian church, Our Lady of Mount Carmel. Joe was one of eight children, four brothers and three sisters named Terry, Tony, Joe, Arthur, Johnny, Ola, Bridget, and Mae. I would come to know all of them except Arthur, who was killed in World War II the year after I was born. In the 1930's, when 116th Street started to change demographics, the family moved to Fteley Avenue in the Bronx. This avenue consisted of two or three blocks of identical sets of attached two family brick houses occupied by Italians. Over the years as the Persico family expanded with marriages and births, they stayed on Fteley Avenue. Moving from one house to another, upstairs or downstairs, we could pretty much visit everyone. When Ola married, she moved the farthest away to Southern Boulevard. I liked visiting her because we would always go across the street to the Bronx Zoo. The older generation stayed married to their respective spouses and lived in these apartments until their deaths. Their sons and daughters moved to Queens.

My father was the exception when it came to marriage. He married and divorced four times; my mother was wife number three. His first two wives were beautiful Jewish women. He was the first in the family to marry outside of his faith; however, his family was very supportive. This was not the case with his first wife's family. The shame of their daughter Ruth marrying out of the Jewish religion was so great to them that the family sat Shiva for her as though she had died. Becoming pregnant early in the marriage, Ruth gave birth to a baby girl who was named Louise. In the Italian tradition, the baby was named after the paternal grandfather Luigi. When she was three weeks old, her mother abandoned both her baby and my father to return to her own family permanently. It was rumored that Ruth once came to look at Louise from a distance when she was a toddler but never attempted to make contact. Louise learned that Ruth died only fifteen years later. Louise never got to know her real mother.

Joe's sister Bridget and her husband Tom lovingly raised Louise as their own from the time Ruth abandoned her. Bridget and Tom already had four children ranging in age from ten to four: Alvera (nicknamed Tootsie), Stella, Helen and Arthur (nicknamed Sonny). Louise always called Aunt Bridget and Uncle Tom mother and father, and her cousins would forever be referred to as her sisters and brother. Joe was "Daddy" and came to visit often, especially for the family dinner on Sunday since it was a very important tradition. Early Sunday mornings the smell of the Sunday gravy (or meat sauce) drifted through all of Fteley Avenue. The pot of gravy sat simmering on the stove in preparation for the macaroni while the women went to mass at the local church. Even the church smelled of the meat sauce. Not having macaroni with meat sauce as a first dish on Sunday was almost as sacrilegious as not attending mass. After church they would rush home to prepare the next course, a special cut of meat or fish. No matter how tight the budget, good food always managed to be on the table for Sunday dinner. These family dinners typically began at one in the afternoon and lasted for hours. First served was an antipasto, then the macaroni, followed by a second course, the meat or fish. After dinner, Bridget's husband Tom would play the piano and the family would join in song while still sitting at the long table, eating fruit, nuts and pastries and drinking espresso. It was a happy family life for Louise.

No one really knew much about my father's second marriage since the entire relationship, marriage and divorce was over in less than a year. During that time he was absorbed in establishing and running both the dance hall in Harlem and the Venetian.

The first time my mother came into my father's bar, she was with co-workers, two men and two women from Montefiore Hospital, one of whom was her closest friend Eva Prokapchak. Eva often told me this story. My father was short of help and happened to wait on their booth himself. They were regulars and knew him by name.

"Joe, this is Tommy," Eva said while introducing my mother.

The booth sat four and my mother sat on a chair, which was added to accommodate them all. He was standing right next to her so it was necessary for her to turn and look straight up at him.

"It's a pleasure to meet you, Joe." Each time she turned, her shiny shoulder length hair threw off a faint scent of gardenias.

"Likewise. Tommy?" he questioned.

"At the hospital they nicknamed me Tommy, short for Sonia Thomas and the name stuck. Joe, what is Eggplant Parmigiana?"

She felt flushed from his intentness, and to keep her composure, she looked back at the menu. He threw his arm over the back of her chair, leaned over and found himself explaining in great detail.

"First I peel, thinly slice, salt and press the eggplant so any bitterness drains out. I dip it lightly in flour, then in egg and brown each side in an iron pan that is bubbling with hot olive oil. Afterward I layer it in a baking dish, putting my homemade tomato sauce and fresh pieces of mozzarella cheese on each layer. I bake it for about a half hour or until the sauce thickens and is absorbed by the eggplant. The cheese must be fully melted and browned on top."

She listened attentively then looked directly into his eyes. "I'm salivating! You make it sound so delicious. I'd like to try it, Joe."

The way she said "Joe" made him want to hear her say it again and again. He noticed her speech had no trace of a New York or Bronx accent. She obviously was not local; most locals were familiar with the Italian dishes. He took all their orders and wished it wasn't so busy. When he put the eggplant in front of her, he waited for her to take the first bite.

"This is wonderful! It tastes just like veal! If I didn't know I was eating eggplant, I would swear I was eating veal."

Suddenly he felt like the best cook in the world. "Dessert is on the house," he told everyone at the table.

Whenever my mother came into the Venetian for lunch, he would make it a point to wait on her table personally. He was very attracted to her and began inviting her to come in for dinner. In the beginning she came with co-workers. Later, on the nights she wasn't working or performing, she'd come alone, spending many evenings there. As the owner, he would need to stay until closing at four a.m., but would join her in a booth and they'd talk for long intervals; his brothers Tony and Terry were bartenders and they'd cover for him. During their talks together, they discovered the similarities they had in their pasts. Each had a child that was abandoned by the other parent and was being brought up by a family member.

Their early dates consisted of going dancing at his dance hall in Harlem where he would also play the drums for her. Both were excellent dancers. They had fun together. He would sing to her and she would read poems she wrote to him. When he went to see her in a production at the *Little Theatre Players* on West 45th Street, he was mesmerized seeing her play two entirely different characters in an evening of three one act plays. Joe was crazy about her. He had never met anyone as exciting and was falling in love.

While dating, my mother liked my father and they certainly had a very good time together, though she often told me, "I never loved your father."

I think she told me this in an attempt to have me understand that marrying my father was the sacrifice she made, first to make a home and be a mother to Ronnie, later to give birth and raise me. After all, my father had professed his love for her, claimed he could not live without her, begged her not to go to Russia, pleaded with her to marry him, and asked to please allow him to take care of her and Ronnie. Financial security was not easy to come by in 1938 since the country was feeling the aftermath of the Great Depression. In the 1930's, it was a stigma to not be married at her age, and worse yet, having an illegitimate child. There had been long intervals between her visits to Ronnie in Newark since she worked long hours six days a week at Montefiore Hospital. Originally, she thought as soon as she got on her feet financially Ronnie could join her; now he was already six and she knew it would be impossible to take care of him on her own in the near future. She wanted to raise her son; she also wanted a protector, a person she could count on, someone who loved her. Joe seemed to be that someone.

My father wanted to be her savior and said he wanted to take care of her. He met Ronnie once and thought him to be a very nice little boy. He also loved the romance in the relationship. He liked her to be at the Venetian with him, showing her off endlessly to his friends and customers. After closing, they would go back to his apartment on Mosholu and listen to records on the Victrola. *Paper Doll, You Made Me Love You, Night and Day,* and *You Always Hurt the One You Love* were some of the songs they loved. My father's all time favorite was *Sentimental Journey.* He had an extensive record collection, especially big band music. They would talk and dance and spend the rest of the night making love. Both were able to awaken late. He would open the Venetian in the early afternoon, and she worked the afternoon to evening shift at the hospital. He had the reputation of being a fantastic lover, and he took pride in this. He loved her looking up to him, admiring his success, his ability to cook, his drum playing, and his singing. He wanted to be the center of her universe. He wanted her love.

After several months of dating, he wanted her to meet his mother; she was a very strong woman and now, as a widow, the matriarch of the family. Her opinion was not only valued but also law. She adored her son Joe, but with two marriages behind him she was skeptical of this new woman. Both of her sons, Tony and Terry who worked with Joe at the Venetian, knew Tommy for many months and genuinely liked her. They assured their mother she would like her as well.

Joe's daughter, Louise, was twelve when she met my mother for the first time. She has often described my mother's entrance into the garden on Fteley Avenue. "How pretty she was. I'll never forget how beautiful she looked in her beige summer dress and large brimmed straw hat. She looked like a movie star."

Joe's mother was also taken by her beauty, but remained reserved on her final opinion. By the end of the family dinner, she, the aunts, uncles and cousins said goodbye to Tommy, kissing both cheeks and giving her warm embraces. They agreed this good looking, intelligent, warm person would finally make Joe the perfect wife...and she was a Catholic!

So Sonia Thomas and Joe Persico were married in the Bronx by a Justice of the Peace. Louise chose to continue living with her Aunt

Bridget and Uncle Tom. Ronnie would come to live with them in the apartment my father had on Mosholu Parkway. For my mother, life was finally taking a turn toward normalcy. Her new husband seemed to adore her. In addition, he had two very lucrative businesses and she wouldn't need to work. She now had a warm and welcoming extended family, and also had established many friendships since she worked in the neighborhood at Montefiore Hospital. The decision had been made not to study acting in Russia but to give it up for a while in order to fulfill her other dream, to be a full-time mother to her son.

In Newark, six year old Ronnie had already settled into the first grade at Saint James School and had begun religious instructions for his First Communion the following May. All of this was disrupted by his moving to the Bronx at the end of 1938. He transferred from a parochial school to a public school, PS 80 on Mosholu Parkway. He would have to continue his religious instructions at Saint Ann's Sunday school. It is always difficult to change schools, but even worse to do so in the middle of the school year; not only was he leaving his friends behind, but he was also leaving the only family he had ever known to move in with virtual strangers. The most traumatic change was leaving his grandmother, who to him was his real mother.

Newark was quite a distance from the Bronx. He had also become very close to his aunts, Mae, Helen and Jean. Jean was the youngest, still single and living at home; she brought Ronnie to the park and movies and played games with him. As the only young child in the family, he was the center of attention. From stories my aunts would tell me, he was always laughing, singing, very affectionate and very happy as a little boy. While in Newark, Mae visited him every weekend and was so attached to Ronnie that her husband Pete was often jealous of her affections toward him. After Ronnie moved to the Bronx, Aunt Mae would bring him back to her house and to visit my grandmother in Newark as often as possible. They all visited the Bronx occasionally. Helen and Bill never had children, so Ronnie was their focus as well. They bought a country house near the Jersey Shore in Belmar, New Jersey, which they named Picky Pine, and Ronnie spent his summers and most of his vacations there with Aunt Helen and Uncle Bill.

I can't even imagine Ronnie's feelings during his first few years in the Bronx. Even now, just thinking of the longing he must have had for all those he loved makes me feel such empathy for him. He says he doesn't remember very much of that time at all. I must assume Ronnie needed a lot of time to feel comfortable with his mother, stepfather and new surroundings. He did, however, tell me that my father was very decent to him, but my mother was extremely strict.

I was born on July 15, 1939. Did my mother and father know she was pregnant when they married or was this discovered in the first month or two? Whenever the discovery was made, the reality was that my father had made an appointment for her to have an abortion. Somehow, as long as I can remember, I knew this. When did my mother start telling me, was I three, four, five? For decades she told me, "Your father wanted me to have an abortion." She never said "Joe" or "my husband," just "your father." I believe this was her way of trying to make me feel secure in how much she loved and wanted me. Instead, I would feel unwanted by my father and that my birth was the primary cause of her drinking and of their relationship ending. As a child, I wanted to love my father but loving him seemed a betrayal to her.

My mother could not believe that her husband, an Italian Catholic, could possibly want her to have an abortion. After all the sacrifices she had endured to give birth to Ronnie illegitimately, she was certainly not going to undergo this horror as a married woman. My father was still waiting for her to agree to abort me and she was still hopeful he would have a change of heart. This became their ongoing argument until abortion was no longer a possibility.

She played the role of a good wife and mother, immersing herself in redecorating the apartment, cooking (she, too, was a good cook), and caring for Ronnie as much as he would allow. It certainly was not a very nurturing environment for him. Having only moved a few weeks before, Ronnie was still feeling she was a stranger. What made it even more uncomfortable were the silences and unspoken hostility between Ronnie's mother and stepfather. I also remember those silences. They were sometimes even more terrifying than their physical battles.

Meanwhile, she tried to be the mother to Ronnie she had dreamed of being, settled him in school and religious instructions, helped him with his homework, bought him new clothes, and made him dinners. She also wanted to prove to my father that Ronnie and the new baby would be no trouble, so she kept punishing Ronnie for small things, like not washing his hands or being a few minutes late for dinner. Ronnie never rebelled. If asked to sit on a chair for an hour he would just sit there. Being a very congenial child, if she asked him to bend over to be spanked when he had been disobedient, he would just submit. My mother saw this as a virtue.

My father placed no value on my mother's attempts to be domestic and provide a happy home life. "Your father only wanted a beautiful woman to sit on his barstool and be admired, not a housewife and mother. When I would cook dinner, your father would sweep the dish off the table. I never really loved your father; I just thought I was doing the right thing to marry him. Your father never forgave me for not having the abortion." When I was older, I wondered if my father really couldn't forgive her for never loving him.

He stayed at the bar all day and then until three or four in the morning while she tried to make a life for herself, Ronnie, and her expected child. Once again, her fantasy was that as soon as the baby was born, Joe would have a change of heart. He was crazy about his daughter Louise and always looked forward to seeing her. Louise would spend an occasional weekend with them; she and my mother got along well. On those weekends he would be his charming and loving self with both of them. In fact, years later as adults, when Louise and I spoke of our father, she would always laugh fondly and roll her eyes, "Our father who art not in heaven." While Louise saw him as a charismatic, four times married ladies' man, I remembered the beatings my mother had gotten. We both knew two entirely different men.

During my mother's pregnancy, as far as his family knew, this was a good marriage. With Louise next to him at the Sunday family dinners, he again played the part of a caring father and husband—my mother acted the part of happy wife and expectant mother. After the usual goodbye hugs and kisses from the family, they would drive back home in my father's Chevy. My mother would attempt conversation about how cute Louise looked, how good the dinner was, or how well Tom sang, only to find my father would revert back into his punishing silences. He would let her off at the apartment and go to the Venetian until closing.

Christmas time came and they actually shopped together for Louise's and Ronnie's gifts. This was the first Christmas with both Joe and Ronnie; she was hopeful it would be a happy one for them all. Joe thought they should spend Christmas Eve with him at the bar; she thought they should be home together decorating the tree. She thought he agreed to close early. Wanting to please him, she had gotten recipes from his mother and made him a traditional Italian Christmas Eve fish dinner. When it became late and he didn't arrive, she tried to hide her disappointment from Ronnie as they began dressing the tree together. Before he went to sleep Ronnie prayed to keep his grandmother, aunts and friends safe; he also prayed that Santa Claus would find him in the Bronx. Joe closed the bar early at two a.m. and came home around three, slamming doors and drawers. She pretended to be asleep, unable to bear another argument.

Ronnie's prayers were answered. Santa did find him and left the train, sled and skates he asked for; however, Christmas was awful. They dressed early to go to his new grandmother's for Christmas dinner, he in his suit and his mother in her new maternity dress, but Joe left without them. Storming out Joe yelled, "You wanted to stay home with your tree last night? Well you can spend all day with it thinking about your decision regarding the baby." The door slammed.

"How could he be so mean, especially on Christmas?" My mother repeated this to me many Christmas Eves. "No wonder he already had two divorces." She had always thought of Louise's mother as heartless for abandoning her three week old baby; she was now seeing her husband in a different light. She wondered about the other side of the story. Did he treat his first wife Ruth the same way when she was pregnant? My mother told me she also had thoughts of leaving him as soon as I was born, but where would she go with two children?

Snow started to fall over the park but Ronnie knew not to ask his mother to take him out on his new sled. He spent the day playing with his train, pretending it was taking him back to his grandmother, and listening to his mother's intermittent weeping; she could no longer contain herself. The highlight of the day was the peanut butter and jelly sandwich she let him make himself for lunch. He did not eat much dinner since she served the fish not eaten the night before. He hated fish! As he looked down at his plate yearning for the fresh ham and mashed potatoes his grandmother would cook for Christmas, he wondered what she was doing right this minute. He remembered her laughter when he had said, "Granny, I love these potatoes more than anything."

After an endless day, Ronnie welcomed the suggestion of saying his prayers and going to sleep early. He slept in the parlor on a fold up bed kept behind the door. As he lay there, he could still see the snow falling softly through the window; the multicolored lights of the tree cast a soft glow in the room. It looked like Christmas but it didn't feel like it. His eyes scanned the Christmas tree for the ornaments that he put on it. He searched for his very favorite, a little blue glass bird, and then he realized it was not here but on his grandmother's tree. Aunt Mae would be coming to take him to Newark for a few days over this holiday vacation. He wanted to see that little blue glass bird again so badly. Only an occasional elevated train passing and the sound of his mother weeping in the bedroom broke the snowy silence.

CHAPTER 5

Menus and Mexicans

By January 1939, when abortion was out of the question since my mother was in her fourth month, my parents' relationship remained an angry one. My mother escaped by decorating the apartment while listening to her records. Ronnie also enjoyed records and began listening over and over to Al Jolson's *Sonny Boy* and *Swanee* until he learned to pantomime the words exactly. My mother tried to make the apartment homey for Ronnie. She had painted the bottom half of the kitchen yellow and left the top half white, separating the two with a three inch border that had different sized Mexican sombreros on it in reds, yellows, and greens. Ronnie had picked it out. The kitchen décor would remain this way for years, and I vividly remember those colorful Mexican hats. I can even recall using them as atmosphere for my four year old rendition of *You Belong to My Heart* from the movie *The Three Caballeros.*

Ronnie made some friends and began adjusting at school. Spending many weekends and school vacations with his aunts and grandmother in Newark was a welcome relief from the household tension. My father was involved with his business and spent all of his time there. He sold the dance hall and concentrated on the Venetian, which he had expanded and built a wine garden in the back. He would get up very late each morning, have coffee and leave, not returning until after closing the bar. Once my mother's pregnancy started to show, he did not want her coming to the bar any longer. They barely saw each other except on Sunday.

The family Sunday dinners continued, as well as their charade of being a happy couple. Joe's mother was always pleased when my mother admired her culinary skills and asked for the recipes of dishes she served. She'd watch Joe eat with gusto, smile and laugh as his mother served dinner, and his sisters, brothers and in-laws caught up on each other's events of the week. After dinner he'd sing with the family, sometimes solo with Louise on his lap. The family would constantly hug and kiss him; he loved being the center of attention. Tootsie and Stella, Louise's cousins, whom she called her sisters, had married Stu and Kangroo. They all were only a few years younger than my mother and were great company for her on those Sundays. She thought about confiding in Tootsie or Stella but there never seemed to be any privacy or an appropriate moment. Also a piece of her knew Joe would not want her talking about their relationship with his family. She liked his family; she even liked him when he was with them. Joe would throw his arm around her shoulder and give her an occasional hug, the way he used to before she was pregnant. He was so convincing that she could see the family watching and admiring their relationship. In those moments it even made her hopeful that all the anger would just vanish. However, the smiles and laughter disappeared when they were driving home in the car in silence. She dared not speak. His icy silence frightened her. One of those times when they were driving home, she asked, "What would your family think if they knew you wanted me to have an abortion?"

Without saying a word, he just whacked her hard on her face with the back of his right hand and kept on driving looking straight ahead. (She told me this story many times for years, always shaking her head while weeping.) "He smacked me across the face and just kept looking straight ahead." Her cheek stung and she was quite stunned. No man had ever struck her before; now she was angry as well as hurt. After this incident, she started her own punishment in the form of silences. When he would ask her the simplest question like "What time is it?"

she would not answer. He stopped taking her with him to the Sunday family dinners.

Other than Joe's family, no one knew she was pregnant. Once she was starting to show, she told her friend Eva Prokapchak. In addition to working together at the hospital, they were also roommates prior to Eva's marriage to a male nurse twenty years her senior. Eva's husband absolutely adored her and they remained very happily married. I believe that part of my mother's decision to marry my father was looking at them as role models.

Eva would occasionally stop up for coffee before she started her night shift at the hospital. Ronnie would be in school and Joe at the bar. My mother confided in Eva that she was pregnant and Joe wanted her to have an abortion. She told her how unbearable the last few months had been. It was now too late for an abortion but Eva thought it might have been the better option; it would have given her more choices. She could have lived the life Joe and she thought they would have, or if that didn't work out she could have left him and gone back to living the way she did before she married him. Eva liked Joe and had known him from the bar even before she met my mother. He always spoke affectionately about his daughter Louise, and when Louise visited the bar, Eva saw how loving he was toward her. She felt it wasn't so much that he didn't want a child, it was that he wanted my mother to be the way she was before. Eva thought that once the baby was born, he would probably mellow.

Eva Prokapchak took the reins now; it was important to get good prenatal care. At Montefiore the doctors would have treated her gratis but my mother was too humiliated to go there. She didn't want anyone to know her new husband's attitude toward her pregnancy. My father refused to pay for anything to do with the baby nor would he accompany her to any appointments. Eva went with my mother to the Bronx Maternity Home and Woman's Hospital on the Grand Concourse. Though it was very small and the prenatal fee, which Eva paid, was minimal, it offered good care and specialized in childbirth. From what I can gather, the relationship between my mother and father never improved for the rest of her pregnancy.

At the end of June, Ronnie left to spend the summer vacation in the country with my Aunt Helen and Uncle Bill. Early on the very hot morning of July 15, 1939, my mother went into labor. She woke my father and asked him to drive her to the Bronx Maternity Home. She told me he slept for two more hours then got up, took a shower and then insisted she make him coffee. When she could barely stand the pain and felt she was ready to give birth, she claims he kicked her in the stomach and sneered, "I hope both of you drop dead in the delivery room." He finally dropped her off at the maternity home about noon. She was alone when I was born at 1:37 p.m.

CHAPTER 6

Born

I recall seeing a $61.00 receipt from the Bronx Maternity home dated July 17, 1939. It was for payment in full of my birth expenses made out to my grandmother, Mary Luksis. My grandmother must have come from Newark to bring my mother and me home to Mosholu Parkway. My Aunt Mae, Aunt Jean, or both of them would most likely have accompanied her since my grandmother only spoke Lithuanian. It was a long trip for them; first a local bus to Penn Station in Newark, then the Hudson Tubes (now called Path trains) to Fulton Street in New York. After a three block walk, they took the No. 4 Subway for a ride of about one hour to the Bronx. This would make the round trip travel a total of four to five hours.

I know that no provisions were made for my arrival other than a crib added to my mother and father's bedroom that was also bought by my grandmother. For the entire time we lived in the Bronx, I only remember having either my crib or my junior bed and two drawers of a dresser that I shared with my parents. On the bedroom closet floor was a cardboard carton where I kept my "pretend dress up" clothes.

My earliest memory was of opening my eyes while in my crib to see many adults smiling down at me. They were all gathered for a house party to celebrate my baptism. The baptismal certificate from Saint Ann's Church is dated October 1, 1939, naming my father's brother Johnny as my Godfather and my mother's sister Jean as my Godmother. Years later when I told my mother I remembered a group of people at my crib, she said the only time many people were at our apartment was for my baptism. She also said since I was only two and a half months old, I could not possibly remember. However, I do vividly recall this. I have very definite early recollections from my infancy and early years. I can remember being in my carriage, riding through the park. I remember taking a chocolate bunny to bed at Easter time and waking up to its having melted all over my crib. I was probably two and a half at the time because, by age three, I was already in my junior bed.

One of my most traumatic memories is that of a "Terrible Two's" tantrum. I don't know why I had the tantrum, but my Aunt Mae was visiting and to teach me never to act-up again, she locked me in the closet. I can remember exactly where I was standing in the parlor. It was the far end by the foyer that separated the bedroom, parlor and bathroom. I can see myself, standing in the doorway to that foyer very angry about something and screaming. My Aunt Mae pulled me by the hair and thrust me into the closet, slamming the door shut. It was summertime and very hot and dark in there and it was packed with winter clothes. Woolen coats rubbed against my head, I was sweating, there wasn't any room, wasn't any air. I was afraid. My aunt yelled from the other side of the door.

"That will teach you."

Then I heard her tell my mother, "Eva, that will teach her."

The name Eva sounded so strange. My mother's whole family refused to call my mother by her chosen names either Sonia or Tommy. My father, his family and most of her friends called her Tommy. I was kicking and punching the door.

"Mommy!"

"Never mind Mommy. You were scaring your mother to death, don't you ever try that again, young lady."

I was crying and banging on the door.

"Stop banging or you will stay in there all night."

I feared she meant this and after a time I stopped screaming. Stifling my sobs, I thought my mother would rescue me, but she didn't.

"Mommy…Mommy!"

"Don't you answer her, Eva," I heard her say. My mother obeyed; she didn't answer.

For years my Aunt Mae would tell this story. "She was screaming and turning blue, scaring her mother to death. I just took Kathy by the hair and put her in the closet, I told her she couldn't come out until she stopped screaming and kicking at the door; finally she stopped. That taught her a lesson; she never had a tantrum again."

My mother would nod in affirmation through her beers, agreeing with the course of action my aunt had taken. Each time I heard the story, I hated my aunt and again felt betrayed by my mother. I resented their stupidity, resented the emotional scar that they created in me. All of my life I have had a difficult time telling anyone how I really feel about things because the "lesson" Aunt Mae taught me still restricts me from showing my real feelings. Did I ever confront her on this behavior? No. Later I would learn that my mother was even more afraid of Aunt Mae than I was. Domineering Aunt Mae always influenced the rest of her siblings about how they should feel about someone or something. Especially my mother, who saw herself as "a bad woman," since she had given birth to Ronnie illegitimately and felt guilty about drinking. With her self-esteem quite low, any criticism by Aunt Mae would send her into a state of depression and guilt. I assume when my mother was a child, my aunt also taught her a few "lessons."

When Aunt Mae finally let me out of the closet, I ran into the bathroom and did not come out for a very long time. They didn't seem to care. I was so angry with my aunt for what she had done to me, and with my mother for not rescuing me.

A better memory of both the bathroom and my mother was taking bubble baths. I'd soak in the tub while my mother left the door open—the music from the record player filled the apartment with the *Ink Spots* or the *Andrew Sisters*. All baths were accompanied by a serving of little green Spanish olives. I'd sink down into the warm bubbly water until it touched my chin. When I sat up to reach the olives in the dish my mother had tucked into the corner where the tub met the wall, my wet hair sent water trickling down my back and the cool air caused me to submerge to my shoulders once more, except for the hand holding the olive. First I sucked out the little red pimento keeping it in my mouth until the tangy flavor no longer existed, then using my tongue as a tool, I'd stick the tip into the hole tilting my head backward balancing the olive as long as I could. When one fell into the water, I tried to retrieve it through the bubbles as quickly as possible, and then wiped it off on my forehead. And if the taste of apple blossom bubbles was too strong, I'd put the discarded olives into my ears, using them as plugs, taking them in and out to hear the change in the volume of the music.

My mother popped her head in now and then still singing words from whatever tune was playing. She'd occasionally add more hot water. The hot water flooded over my feet then up my body till it warmed my shoulders. These baths lasted a long time. Afterward when my mother would lift me out of the tub, my body shivered as the cool air hit it. Within a few seconds she'd wrap me in my large pink towel and twirl another color towel high on my head to dry my hair. Looking at myself in the full length mirror behind the bathroom door, I thought I looked like Carmen Miranda.

Other early memories are still very vivid. I definitely remember the radio announcement about the bombing of Pearl Harbor on December 7, 1941. During the war years, 1941 through 1945, I recall fenced in Victory Gardens appearing in every vacant lot, where I would watch our neighbors plant vegetables, fruits and flowers. A variety of uniformed men and women walked the streets and came into my father's bar. Sailors, soldiers, marines and others; I especially loved the sailor uniforms; they made me think of Frank Sinatra in *Anchors Aweigh*. Air raid drills became routine and ration books were issued to families to restrict purchases of meat, sugar and other items that were scarce.

Betty Grable became the GI's "pinup girl," offering her "gams" (as her legs were called) for them to drool over. Even Ronnie had a picture of her hanging behind the parlor door near his pull out bed. This was a view of her from the back, looking flirtatiously over her shoulder, inviting all her admirers to look at her long shapely legs jutting out of her very short costume. Her legs were so famous that Twentieth Century Fox insured them with Lloyds of London for one million dollars. President Eisenhower was even quoted as saying, "Betty was the girl who helped us win the war!" During those years I saw her in many lush Technicolor musicals, *Sweet Rosie O'Grady*, *Footlight Serenade*, *Spring Time in the Rockies*, and *Song of the Islands*. She was beautiful; I wanted to be her, the blond, blue eyed all-American girl. All the leading men instantly fell in love with her and they always lived happily ever after.

Instead, I was the little "Guinea-Wop."

"Are you my Little Guinea-Wop niece?" my Aunt Mae would affectionately ask, while hugging and kissing me as I sat on her lap. She'd tell me how much she loved me. She'd often get weepy and sad while squeezing me, rocking me back and forth, telling me about the many stillborn babies my grandmother had. She said she would sit on the rocking chair singing to the dead babies until the undertaker arrived. The story would make me cry and then she would comfort me. "Don't cry, my sweet little Guinea-Wop." When I was older and discovered that Guinea-Wop is a derogatory term, I felt even more anger toward her.

My mother never had to ask twice whether I would like to go with her to the bar or to the movies. When given the choice, I always chose the movies. Each time, in anticipation, I'd sit on the edge of my seat as the lights dimmed, the curtain opened and the music blared introducing the newsreels. They showed the progress of World War II and other major world events. Then a film short played for about ten to fifteen minutes. In the Forties, there were many patriotic films. One, *The House I Live In,* featured Frank Sinatra. "Hello, I'm Frank Sinatra," the film began. Sinatra himself talked right to the audience about how wonderful America was, how proud we should be to be an American and how thankful we should be for all we had. I felt that he was talking right to me, looking straight at me with his very blue eyes. I fell in love! This short is still one of my favorites.

A "B movie," as well as the coming attractions, would precede the feature film and an intermission. Feature films ran from one and a half to two hours. The total screen time would be anywhere from four to four and a half hours. For twelve cents admission, my mother would have many hours of babysitting. I was more than happy to be sitting in the movie theatre rather than on a barstool. The feature movie ran from Sunday to Wednesday, and then changed starting Thursday through Saturday; at least this was the schedule at the Tuxedo. So you could spend all day Saturday and Sunday in the movies (and I usually did) and see four films and two different shorts.

Most of the ushers knew me and would keep an eye on me. Only once do I remember an usher going to get my mother at the Golf bar because I said I had a very bad stomach ache. It is a wonder that I didn't have a stomach ache more often. With the ten cents my mother gave me for candy, I would buy two big fat dill pickles from the wooden barrel at the deli next door and save the other nickel for either a Hershey Bar or Jujubes that I'd buy at the candy counter at intermission. Jujubes lasted longer and I loved sucking slowly on the tiny gummy candies and trying to figure out what flavor I had in my mouth. Sometimes I would take one out of my mouth and hold it up to the light from the screen to check the color.

From ages three to five before I started kindergarten, I would sit in the movies from the early feature at noon until two or three o'clock, when Ronnie would be getting out of school from PS 80 on Mosholu Parkway. My mother picked me up and on the way home we'd buy food for dinner. When Ronnie got home he would play records and sometime pantomime to Bing Crosby songs, entertaining me while my mother cooked, then the three of us would eat together. My mother was a good cook when she made the effort and Ronnie and I both loved everything she made, except on Saturday she would make pigs knuckles for her and me. Ronnie would have a hamburger, which they called a Salisbury steak. On Saturdays, we looked forward to our favorite sandwiches as a lunch treat. My mother and I loved liverwurst, so did our dog Mugsy, and Ronnie loved bologna. Starting at four years old, I would be sent around the corner to the butcher shop with a note and the ration book to pick up a quarter pound of liverwurst and bologna. One Saturday, before I reached the butcher store, I somehow lost the ration book. I ran home crying and got a spanking by my mother with her silver hair brush, then had to sit in a chair for two hours. Mugsy came and sat beside me. Ronnie consoled me and told me it was okay, he did not need to have his "baloney" sandwich that day.

I looked up to him; being seven years older, he was my "big brother." I thought he was so handsome with his blond hair and fair skin. We did not look like brother and sister at all. He looked Lithuanian and I looked Italian. He was definitely the favorite on my mother's side of the family and was very well liked on my father's side. My father's sister Ola had three boys. Her stepson Joey was much older, but Louis was Ronnie's age and Albert was one year younger than Ronnie. They got along well and had a lot of fun together. When they would come to our house to visit, or we would go to theirs, I was left out. The boys didn't want a little girl around. Some Saturdays when Ronnie would go to the movies with his friends, my mother would tell him to keep an eye on me. He wouldn't let me sit near him and his friends. I would squeal on him and then he would be punished. Feeling guilty that he was punished, I would become very afraid that he wouldn't love me anymore. But he still loved his little sister, at least most of the time.

When Ronnie was away for the summer or the weekend, my mother didn't bother to cook for just the two of us. I would either have a quick bite at my father's bar or my mother would escort me diagonally across the street to Schweller's Delicatessen and pick me up in about an hour. I liked going there. The smell of pastrami, pickles and other deli food made me even hungrier as I strolled past the display case of sumptuous desserts on the way to my favorite booth. The waiter Sam looked like someone's grandfather with his gray hair and wire glasses. He'd bow to me and ask, "Your order, my sweetheart?" I felt very special, like a little princess, Shirley Temple in *Poor Little Rich Girl*. I loved talking to Sam. He was very funny and he knew what I wanted to eat. I always had the same thing: chopped chicken liver for an appetizer, an open hot turkey sandwich on rye with mashed potatoes and peas, a chocolate egg cream and rice pudding for dessert. I ate a lot and was a little chubby from age four.

At other times for dinner, if my father had already sent my mother home for drinking too much, she would take me with her to the Golf bar. These were neighborhood bars where everyone knew everyone else. Sometimes my mother would ask me to sit on the barstool and tell the jokes she taught me. One was:

> *Mr. Wood and Mr. Stone were standing on a corner.*
> *They saw a pretty girl go by.*
> *Wood turned to Stone. Stone turned to Wood.*
> *And they both turned to Rubber ("Rub her").*

I could not understand why their turning to rubber was so funny to everyone, but they would laugh and my mother would wink at them. I enjoyed making them laugh and being the center of attention. Usually they would give me nickels to play the jukebox. I would run off to play my favorite Frank Sinatra records, *Blue Skies* or *Night and Day*, while my mother continued to socialize and drink more beer.

Staying at the Golf was better than going home. I hated going home when my mother had been drinking too much because she would start her repetitive speeches about how awful my father was to her and how she tried to be a good wife and mother and she'd cry and cry. I would pat her hand, tell her not to cry, and tell her that I thought she was a very good mother. Even our dog Mugsy seemed to be sympathetic and would snuggle next to her on the couch with his snout on her lap, where she would sometimes fall fast asleep. As far back as I can remember, my mother had two personalities: with beer and without beer. When my mother fell asleep, I would go into the bedroom with my little bear Poochie and escape into sleep myself.

After my birth, my mother began going to my father's bar again. Her usual drink of ginger ale was passed up for beers, many beers. My father once again would show off his pretty wife and, now, his cute new daughter. I have a few pictures of myself from that period dressed stylishly in clothes my mother told me she made. He loved having the customers compliment him on his "beautiful wife and cute little girl." I told my jokes here as well. Another was:

> An American man is at the cemetery putting flowers on his wife's grave.
> He sees a Chinese man throwing a handful of rice on a grave.
> The American says to him, "When do you expect your loved one to come up and eat the rice?"
> "The same time yours come up to smell flower!"

I would say this last line in an imitation of a Chinese accent and everyone would howl. My father would throw his head back and laugh. I felt important at the bar; at home my father hardly spoke to me. I always thought he was angry with me; he didn't want me to love my mother so much, since he was always angry with her. Their relationship at home remained strained and silent. Although he wanted her drinking with him at the Venetian, he would get furious when she drank one too many beers; he would send her home before she got drunk. She would just leave, as ordered. Hitting her when he got home had become more frequent. Sometimes he'd just punch her in the face when she least expected it.

In those early years of my life when we went to the Sunday dinners at my paternal grandmother's, the family hugged me and sat me on their laps, while telling my father how cute I was. I always wished that my father would do the same thing. He loved being the center of attention with his family and loved a good time. Sometimes he'd arrange and pay for family parties at restaurants on City Island in the Bronx where steamed clams were eaten by all. I can still smell the melted butter and feel it dribbling down my chin as I enjoyed eating those clams. I'd run around, going in and out onto the decks where you could see Long Island Sound. I'd look out at the water and sing songs to myself, pretending Frank Sinatra was singing to me.

My father loved social gatherings so much that on Sundays in the warm weather he would organize a block party on Fteley Avenue at least once or twice a year, especially to celebrate his birthday on July sixteenth, one day after mine. Somehow I do not remember celebrating my birthdays in the Bronx, but I must have because my mother was always big on birthday celebrations. Or did mine begin when we moved away from the Bronx?

My father would cook and supply most of the food. Other families would bring their food specialties and, with communal tables and chairs, everyone would eat, sing and dance until dark. He would bring his drums and others their instruments, an accordion, trumpet, mandolin or whatever they played. I can remember dancing and having fun at these parties. The growing violence in our household, however, far outweighed the good times.

CHAPTER 7

Granny's and Aunt Helen's

We started visiting my grandmother when I was quite young. I hated going there. It was a very long trip to Newark by public transportation. She lived in railroad rooms on the first floor of a four-story, wooden walk up. I thought they were called "railroad rooms" because she happened to live one house away from the railroad tracks of the Jersey Central Railroad. I later learned that the reason they were called railroad rooms was because the only way you could get from the front to the back of the house was by walking through the rooms with doorways that led to the next room like railroad cars. There were only three rooms, the kitchen, the bedroom and the parlor. The middle room, the bedroom, was very dark; toward the ceiling there were large interior windows on each side for ventilation. That room was scary. My grandmother had altars of various saints on both the dressers, and with the vigil light candles constantly flickering, it appeared that the statues and yellowing family pictures on the walls were alive.

The building had two apartments on each floor separated by a long hallway that went from the front entrance to the backyard. You could enter an apartment from this hallway by one of two doors, the first going into the parlor or the second into the kitchen. In the backyard, each of the eight tenants had rectangular mounds of dirt for planting vegetables or flowers. My grandmother had arranged her garden with four old car tires circling beds of marigolds.

On the right, a wooden fence separated her yard from the yard of the attached four-story house next door. The inhabitants were African-Americans, very politely called "colored people" in the Forties. In Lithuanian, my grandmother referred to them as *"juodukas,"* the little black ones. Actually, my grandmother's side of the railroad trestle was mostly an African-American neighborhood. The black family on the first floor next door operated their own wood cutting business out of their backyard. In the warmer months, the electric saw was always screeching. The trains passed overhead on each street via a little bridge, and the steam engines blew a loud whistle that alerted walkers who might be using the tracks. Directly in the back of my grandmother's yard was the rear of an old red brick building. To the left was a building with two windows belonging to the banquet hall of the bar and grill on the corner. Wedding receptions and parties were held there; you could hear loud music and see people dancing the polka and other Slavic dances through those two windows. On weekends, the festivities usually lasted until three or four in the morning. All this could be viewed from my grandmother's kitchen window.

We would sit in the kitchen for the entire visit. Usually my three aunts would come to visit as well, everyone crowded into the small kitchen. They'd all drink beer and speak and sing in Lithuanian. It sounded so very strange to me; I didn't understand a word. The kitchen had only a white enamel table, three chairs of dark wood with spindles and a fourth, which was my grandmother's rocking chair covered with many throws and extra cushions. A little matching wooden chair with a spindle back had been Ronnie's when he lived there. I would usually sit on it, stroking the small pieces of rabbit fur, dyed in pastel colors that Granny gave me to play with. She brought them home from the factory where her job was to skin rabbits. The furs were then dyed and used to make good luck rabbit's foot key chains. She gave me a pink one.

In addition to the refrigerator and a coal stove, there was a kitchen cupboard with many compartments, including one for the "ice box" to hold a block of ice and another for bread. It was only a few years before that my Aunt Helen bought my grandmother a "Frigidaire."

Next to the kitchen sink was a door, which opened to the toilet. There was nothing in this tiny little room except a toilet bowl, with its tank overhead and long chain hanging from it for flushing; even my knees touched the wall in front. The coal stove provided all the heat for the entire three rooms. The supply of coal, which was delivered once a month, was kept in individual bins in the cellar. During one of my visits, my grandmother took my hand and led me down the slanted wooden stairs on the dirt floor to show me her bin. It was dimly lit with a bare bulb overhead, and smelled musty. Everything was so strange and old fashioned. Without even a fan, the kitchen was extremely hot in the summer since part of the coal stove always had to have coal burning on one side in order to cook. The kitchen was even hotter in the winter because the stove heated the whole apartment.

I especially recall going to my grandmother's early in June when I was one month away from turning four. The reason for our visit was to drop Ronnie off so that my Uncle Bill and Aunt Helen could come by and take him to their summer house, Picky Pine, where he would spend his entire school vacation.

My grandmother had a male boarder who paid her by the week to sleep in her parlor on the studio couch. It was popular in these Slavic communities for families to have boarders in their apartments. While everyone was sitting in the kitchen drinking draft beer from a pitcher, refilled many times at the corner bar, the boarder sat me on his lap. Rocking back and forth on my grandmother's chair, he had one hand under my buttocks cupping me from behind touching me with his finger between my legs. The other hand alternated between being around my waist and picking up his glass of beer. He kept swinging back and forth in the rocking chair. Every once in a while he would bounce me on his leg and say "Horsie, horsie," tapping his finger firmly. It felt kind of good, but it made me feel bad! I kept looking to see if anyone knew what he was doing. They all were very involved in their conversation, laughing and drinking beer. No one seemed to know I was even there. Each time I tried to get off his lap he would tighten his grip around my waist. I was frozen. I turned to look at him; I wondered if he really knew he was touching me or if his hand was just accidentally in the wrong place. He just kept talking to my mother and grandmother. I was so relieved when we left to go home to the Bronx. I looked away as he gave me a big hug and a wink. I didn't like him at all but everyone else seemed to. I was too ashamed about being touched to tell my mother, I just wished I would never have to see him again.

I would miss Ronnie over the summer. When he was home and I woke up at night, it was comforting to know he was sleeping in the parlor with Mugsy curled up next to him. Without him, I was alone; the only good part was that Mugsy would curl up in bed with Poochie and me. These were the summer nights I played the "waiting game," waiting for my mother on the fire escape.

I don't really remember what I did all summer. Of course there was going to the movies and to the bars, feasting at Schweller's, eating endless pizzas at the Golf bar, and playing with the superintendents' granddaughter, Gretchen, who lived with them. I also remember often asking to be crossed to the park and spending hours accumulating granite powder in a jar. I would take a rock in my hand and hit it against a large piece of granite and get great satisfaction filling up those jars. I had quite a collection. I don't know why I started this activity. It was during the war and I vaguely remember seeing boys pretend they were making "gun powder." I always sang songs as I hacked away at the rocks. The introduction to Frank Sinatra's *Night and Day*, "Like the beat, beat, beat of the tom-tom," was my favorite accompaniment to this activity.

One day when I was at the playground swinging on the large swings, several boys were singing, "You're in the Army now. You're in the Army now. You'll never get rich, you son of a bitch…you're in the Army now."

I went home singing the song at the top of my lungs. My mother was horrified and not only gave me a big smack on my hiney with her hairbrush, but also washed my mouth out with soap. I never sang that song again.

We went to visit Ronnie for one week during that summer at Picky Pine. The house was tucked away in the woods seven miles from the Jersey Shore. It was very tiny, a bungalow really, with only an out-house for a bathroom. The outhouse seemed more of an adventure and not half as old fashioned as my grandmother's cramped kitchen toilet. It had two wooden holes cut out of the bench, one smaller than the other in order for an adult and child to eliminate together. Even at four, I was modest and insisted on using the outhouse privately while my Aunt Helen waited outside the door. After you made your "deposit," you shoveled sand from a pail down into the hole. This kept flies from swarming around, but it didn't help the smell. Once a week my Uncle Bill would go though the ritual and "bury the body," as he referred to the unpleasant task of digging a big hole and disposing of all the waste. The outhouse was kept a distance from the house, so at night my aunt and I would just go outside the kitchen door and lift our nightgowns while we wet the grass. This caused me to get mosquito bites on the cheeks of my behind, which my aunt would treat with calamine lotion.

Picky Pine had two tiny bedrooms with only a curtain over the doors. One bedroom had bunk beds where my aunt and uncle slept, and the other, where Ronnie slept, could barely fit a twin bed and dresser. The tiny parlor had a maple love seat with a green brocade cover that Aunt Helen made on her Singer sewing machine. The parlor also housed a three-quarter size pull out bed. This is where my mother and I slept. There were also two matching maple armchairs and an end table. To me it seemed like a mansion. The interior walls were all knotty pine; I guess that was why my aunt and uncle named their little bungalow "Picky Pine."

The small porch, which served as the dining area, was screened half way. From the porch, you could see the little road leading to the house, which was lined by two sets of umbrella trees and Aunt Helen's prized blue and white hydrangeas. Fresh cuttings from her hydrangeas were always in vases throughout the house. The umbrella trees had robins' nests tucked in their branches. As Aunt Helen lifted me up to peek in, she whispered, "Baby birds will come out of these little blue eggs." She brought me to the back of the property where an old renovated chicken coop, which was made into one large room, served as a storage place for odds and ends. In it was an old wind up RCA Victrola with a handle that turned and a large horn to send out the music. We played the brown 78 records together. She had some of Al Jolson's records and I sang the songs I knew for her. She talked to me all day long and showed me what other things she had sewn on her Singer.

"I made all my own curtains and bedspreads from material which I keep in this large suitcase. If you shop for material on Orchard Street in New York City, you could get a real bargain," she'd say. She told me stories of how she grew up, about working in the factory and her beauty parlor, as well as visits to the World's Fair and Coney Island's Luna Park before it burned down. Now, she said, they built the Steeplechase at

Coney Island. My favorite stories were her detailed description of the rides at the amusement parks. "Tell me again," I would say, and she would tell me as many times as I asked. I loved being with Aunt Helen, it was peaceful and fun.

Every day we would eat breakfast, lunch and dinner on the porch. I would wake to the enticing smells of coffee, Taylor Ham, bacon and sausages. For breakfast, she would serve all the meats on a large red and white checked platter with a stack of toast; you just took as much as you wanted. We also had eggs any way we liked them; I loved mine sunny side up. I would dunk the Taylor Ham into the yolk and follow the example of my uncle making little sandwiches on buttered toast. The Fisher Bakery truck would come into each driveway every morning and Aunt Helen would buy fresh coffee or crumb cake. At lunchtime she would put out various sandwich meat, ham, cheese, liverwurst, tomatoes, lettuce, mustard and mayonnaise and Fisher's white and rye bread. Dinner was the best. Every night Aunt Helen cooked potted meats with potatoes, rice or noodles with fresh vegetables and we always had coleslaw that was even better than Schweller's. We'd pick blueberries from the local bushes and she would make blueberry pie, pudding or muffins.

At night we would sit outside on the glider swing. It was painted orange and had two slated benches facing each other. My aunt, uncle and mother would drink beer and talk while we swung and sang, listening to the crickets and the whippoorwills. Most nights a neighbor or two walked over and joined them for a beer. It was very peaceful, no one got drunk, not even my mother. My mother would spend her days reading and Ronnie would run off with his friends. When my mother and I were preparing to leave, I asked to stay. My aunt said we would try it. I was fine during the day, but when it got dark a great loneliness would overtake me and I yearned for my mother. I could not bear to be without her. So after crying for two nights, my mother came back by train for me. I didn't stay for the whole summer at Picky Pine until I was five.

At the end of that summer, we went back to my grandmother's in Newark to pick Ronnie up. Aunt Helen and Uncle Bill always brought him back to my grandmother's to spend a few days with her. After the boarder episode, I dreaded returning. To my relief, he was no longer there. My mother asked, "What happened to that nice man that was living here?" "*Rupūžė*" my grandmother said very angrily. *Rupūžė* refers to someone as being the lowest form of life; it is just about the worst curse word in Lithuanian. Translated literally it means frog. She said she caught him stealing some of her money and told him to leave. My mother shook her head in disbelief. I was too embarrassed to ever tell anyone about what I thought he did, but I felt I was right in not having liked him.

CHAPTER 8

Pretending

There is an old movie called *The Human Comedy* (1941) with Mickey Rooney and Van Johnson. I'm not sure what year I actually saw it; however, it made quite an impression on me. Mr. Grogan, the old telegraph master, is this very endearing character, liked by the whole town even though he was always drunk. I remember the scene when he told Mickey Rooney, "I feel much better when I drink." My mother was so unhappy, and I knew she felt much better when she drank, so I silently accepted and understood my mother's need to drink.

This became my secret. When I would overhear the family talking about how awful it was that my mother drank, I would feel gratified that I was the only one who understood that she *had* to drink. In fact, years later, perhaps when I was ten, my Aunt Mae sat me down in my grandmother's house and told me, "You should speak to your mother. Ask her to stop her drinking; she'll listen to you. You're the only one who can get your mother to stop."

I was very angry that she wanted me to be the one to ask her to stop the only thing that seemed to make her happy, so I said, "You leave Mommy alone; she has to drink."

When did the roles reverse for my mother and me, at age three or four? When I was alone, I would often rummage through my "dress-up box" and find one of my mother's discarded dresses to wear, remove the ribbons from my brown shiny braids and let my thick wavy hair fall onto my shoulders and down my back. I'd pin the dress above my chest and look into the large round dressing table mirror. I would apply my mother's lipstick and put on her high heels. Strutting around in my makeshift sarong, I thought I looked quite beautiful. Bing Crosby and Bob Hope were dying to dance with me, I'd tell the mirror, "I am Dorothy Lamour!"

I recall one time when the loud slam of our apartment door jarred me back to reality. I heard the irregular tapping of my mother's footsteps as she staggered to the bedroom and watched in the mirror as she appeared behind me in the doorway. I thought she looked so lovely, tall, and slender with her shoulder length hair slightly messy. Her soft flowered dress seemed right out of a magazine ad.

"Hi, Sweetie!" (I loved it when she called me Sweetie.) "Clean off your face and come talk to me," she slurred. I looked back in the mirror and now saw only the four year old chubby Italian girl, wiping the lipstick off. My mother had already thrown herself across the bed and was crying. I went to her and sat on the bed.

"What's wrong, Mommy?"

"I try to be a good wife; I try to be a good mother," she cried with tears rolling down her face.

"Mommy, I think you are a very good mother," I'd say once more, as I'd pat her hand, knowing this would make her feel better. When she cried, Mugsy would come over and put his snout on her hip and whimper, I would keep patting her hand and Mugsy and I would just stay there with her; she would often fall asleep. Sometimes I'd grab Poochie and lie down next to her and the four of us would nap. On other days, I would tiptoe out and go downstairs to play with Gretchen. My mother didn't want me to play with her because she was four years older than me, but who else was there to play with?

There were just a few other children I would see occasionally. My mother and I would sometime visit the Ridbergs. It was so nice there. My mother knew Mrs. Ridberg from my father's bar, where she would sometimes come to have a drink with her husband or to eat with her whole family. They had four children and the oldest, June, was my age, then Gay, Joy, and baby Danny. It was just a short walk to their house, which was surrounded by red and white rose bushes in front of a white picket fence around a little lawn. They also had their very own backyard. We would play hopscotch out front or throw a ball back and forth in the yard while our mothers talked. They did things like the families did in the movies; ate peanut butter and jelly sandwiches all together or played Monopoly. I loved it there. When Mr. Ridberg came home everyone would run to him; he would give each one a kiss on top of their heads, he even kissed the top of my head. I didn't tell anyone, but I would pretend he was my father too.

The most exciting event was when they bought a television set. The very first time I saw a television was at my father's bar. Televisions were mostly in bars and were coin operated. A good deal of the time only the station's broadcast signal was present on the screen because there were very few shows, but even looking at the signal was exciting with the anticipation that a program would come on the screen eventually. Reception was not very good, there was a lot of static and snow on the screen and the only thing I remember seeing at the bar were sports events. The Ridbergs were the one family we knew who had a television right in their own parlor. We were invited to watch *The Lone Ranger*. Mrs. Ridberg drew all the curtains shut and turned on the ten inch console. The program began! She adjusted the rabbit ears until the picture was clear. What a thrill it was to see the Lone Ranger riding his horse, shouting "Hi Ho Silver!" All of us kids sat on the carpet with our backs against the extra crib that was kept in there for baby Danny. Our mothers crouched forward on the velvet couch puffing on their cigarettes. I'm not sure why but we nibbled on orange skins, which tasted great. Eating orange skins and watching *The Lone Ranger* made this one of the best days of my life so far. Often the smell of oranges, and especially chocolate covered orange rinds (my favorite candy), bring this memory rushing back. Unfortunately, we did not go to visit the Ridbergs very often.

Winnie, another one of my mother's friends, had a daughter named Barbara, who was also my age. My mother also knew her and her husband from the bar. When we went to their apartment, Barbara and I would play hopscotch and jump rope right outside her street level parlor window so her mother could keep an eye on us. Inside we played regular checkers and Chinese checkers. We also cut and dressed paper dolls. My mother had the record *Paper Doll* that I loved to listen to. I knew all the words and would sing it to Barbara as we dressed the dolls. After she learned it, we would sing it together.

There were two girls living in my building, Debbie and Helen; both were Jewish. At some point they stopped playing with me. I don't know if it was because during the war Jewish families were more protective of their children or because my mother and father both drank and their mothers wanted them to keep their distance. I do, however, remember being invited and going to both of their birthday parties. I also remember once walking with Debbie and her mother and father to the synagogue they attended. I felt very special to be taken there and I pretended I was Jewish, too.

So my only friend was Gretchen. Her grandmother was a huge cheerful woman with a raspy voice, she had curly short hair and glasses; her grandfather was a very gentle, scraggly, slender man, tall and gray. Gretchen herself was chubby, fair and blond. Her face would often redden when she was angry or frustrated with me. She was eight, four years older than I was.

Our building had a dumbwaiter. Every apartment in this six floor walk up (we were on the second floor) had a small door that opened into the dumbwaiter. It was located in the foyer between the kitchen and the parlor. Tenants would put their trash on its shelves and then use a rope on a pulley to send it to the basement. My mother often discarded pretty clothes that had gotten stained and Gretchen would retrieve them for dress up clothes. I don't know when I began going down to the basement to play with her. They lived in an apartment located at the end of the basement. We'd play "dress- up" in her grandparents' bedroom using my mother's or other tenants' discarded clothing. She would put make up on me and I would be the mother. Putting on her grandfather's shirt and jacket she would always be the father. There was an area separated by a long dingy foyer between their apartment and the alley entrance where there were a few washing machines for the tenants. It was dim and the old plaster walls smelled musty. It was against these walls between two washing machines that Gretchen would pretend that the father was "doing it" to the mother. She would pull down my underpants and thrust her pelvis against mine, grunting with each thrust. I would listen for approaching footsteps, terrified of being discovered. I felt like I was doing something "dirty." She told me if I told anyone she would hit me. This was the beginning of a form of blackmail she would use to get me to do other things that I knew were "bad," like stealing little things from Woolworth's or stealing money from my father's pocket to give to her.

My father would always have a huge roll of money in his pants pocket, held together by a money clip. I guess much of this was from the bar. His routine was that he would come home about four or five in the morning and drape his pants over the chair by the bed. He usually slept until late morning or early afternoon. While he was snoring I would hold my breath and quietly tiptoe into the bedroom, go into his pants pocket, take one or two dollars, and then clip and return his money, thinking he'd never notice. I would then give the money to Gretchen. She began to expect it every day, in return she would not tell of our games or of my stealing from Woolworth's. If a day went by that I could not get the money, she would kick me in the shin. When my mother questioned the bruises I would tell her I fell on the stairs. Other times she might demand that I give her one of my dolls or a toy. When my mother would ask where it was, she'd go down to get it from Gretchen. Most times she'd wind up having a cup of coffee or a beer with Gretchen's grandmother and no one would be the worse for it. I was glad when my mother got my doll or toy back, even if I got kicked again. Once Gretchen even had Poochie for a day, but I cried so much she gave him back without my mother's intercession. Sometimes Gretchen and I just colored with crayons or played Chinese checkers, Parcheesi, or cards and I had a nice time. We also went to the movies together. I would like to play "pretend I am that person" in the movie.

"I'm her," I'd say watching June Allyson who was part of a singing and dancing sister act in the MGM musical *Two Girls and a Sailor*.

"No, I'm her," Gretchen declared.

"Oh, please let me be her, you can be the other sister, anyway I said it first. Please!"

"Okay," she said, "you can be her." She agreed to be Gloria DeHaven instead.

One time in *Anchors Aweigh* when Frank Sinatra sang *I Fall in Love Too Easily*, I whispered, "I'm going to marry him."

"Okay, then I'll marry the other guy," she whispered back.

The other guy was Gene Kelly. Because it was so much more fun to sit next to Gretchen and watch the musicals, I liked treating her to the movies.

I later found out that my father noticed that his very neat bankroll had been tampered with. He thought it was my mother and she received many additional smacks across the face for it. He had begun hitting her quite regularly. When she had really bad bruises, especially on her face, we would not go outside until they faded. Somehow he always seemed to hit her when Ronnie was not there. He would yell very loudly and get red in the face. She would say, "Joe, please!" when he would start to hit or punch her. I would run in between them and scream at my father, "Don't you hit my Mommy." He never hit me but he would get even redder in the face, and if he was dressed, he'd just turn and leave the apartment, slamming the door behind him.

It was unknown to me that my mother thought Ronnie must be the one taking the money. She gave him several spankings for it and others for lying about it. Finally, one day I was caught in the act by my mother.

"Here's for all the smacks your father gave me, and here's more for the ones I gave to Ronnie," she screamed as she hit me not with the brush, but with my father's belt.

I felt very guilty about the fact that my mother and Ronnie had been blamed. It was one of the few times I didn't run through the house as she swung the strap at my behind. In spite of a heavy-duty spanking, I was so relieved to be able to tell Gretchen that they knew what was going on and I couldn't take money anymore. However, the stealing from Woolworth's still continued. I never got caught there, but Gretchen used this to make me do other things I knew I shouldn't do. Nevertheless, our friendship, if you could call it that, lasted until we moved away.

CHAPTER 9

Perception

If my Aunt Mae was still alive and you asked her why she did what I perceive to be hurtful things, I believe she wouldn't have had any idea that her behavior was anything but loving. Some weekends I would stay at her apartment with her and Uncle Pete. They rented the top level of a two family house on a tree-lined street in a very upscale neighborhood in North Newark. She had china and silver and very plush furniture. I would sleep cozily nestled in two small burgundy velvet armchairs that when pushed together formed an oval. Her apartment was cheerful, sparkling clean and sunny; I remember waking up to her singing *Oh, What a Beautiful Morning.*

However, Dorothy, also age four, lived downstairs from my aunt and would often come to visit. We would both compete for her attention. Aunt Mae would tell us whichever of us loved her more, would be the one she would love the best. We would kiss and hug her; longer and longer kisses; tighter and tighter hugs, each trying to outdo the other.

"I love you, Auntie Mae," Dorothy would say.

"I love you more, Auntie Mae," I would say.

Each of us worried that she would not love us if we didn't win. After we worked ourselves up emotionally and were both crying in desperation, she would tell us she loved us equally. I always felt she loved Dorothy more because she lived downstairs and got to spend a lot more time with her. I only visited a few times a year. To be her favorite became all important; I learned to play the game of conditional love.

In all fairness, there were also very nice times with Aunt Mae. She always let me play with her costume jewelry and sent me home with a few treasures that I would add to my dress-up collection. When she came to visit us in the Bronx, she would take Ronnie and me to Radio City Music Hall. Radio City always featured major new movie releases. We saw *Lassie Come Home*. I cried hysterically and thought of Mugsy. "I would die if anything happened to him," I wept. I was absolutely dazzled by my first live stage show, the orchestra coming up from the floor, the booming music of the lavish gold organ, and the beautiful costumes of the Rockettes. Their tap dancing and kicks made me want to learn to dance like that. It was just like in the movie musicals, but for real. It was breathtaking. I saw myself up on the stage dancing with them. "When I get home, I'm asking Mommy to send me to dancing school," I told Aunt Mae. "When will we come back to Radio City?"

I could hardly wait until the next time. She promised to take me, and she did, to the Christmas show and the Easter Show many times over the years. We also went to the Roxy Theatre, which was on the same block as Radio City and had feature films and live shows on a slightly smaller scale. She took me to the ice show at Madison Square Garden several times to see Sonja Henie. She was an Olympic champion ice skater. This was most exciting because she was the star of many movies I had seen, *Sun Valley Serenade*, *Iceland* and *Wintertime*, and now to see her in person...what a thrill! As she went whizzing by us on the ice, I was almost able to touch her. There wasn't anywhere else you could see a star, except maybe in the movie magazines because television wasn't popular yet.

Aunt Mae would always take me out to eat, sometimes on 42nd Street to an Italian restaurant called Romano's. I always ordered Veal Parmigiana with ziti on the side, and I loved to dunk the heavily buttered bread into the tomato sauce. Aunt Mae would compliment me on my appetite and then affectionately call me "Puddin'," which referred to my being overweight. Other times we went to Horn and Hardart's automat. I marveled at viewing the various selections through little glass windows. When you deposited the correct amount of coins, a window snapped open and allowed you to pull out your dish of food. As soon as you took your dish out of the glass window, it snapped shut and another dish of the same selection would spin into place. If it was out of anything, you tapped on the glass with your coin, and some unseen person would miraculously fill the compartment. I always got the baked macaroni and cheese; it was so nice and creamy, it was the best ever! The servings were small, so I ate two or three. We would find a seat by the large window facing Broadway from which you could see a giant screen with little white lights forming animated cartoons, like *Felix the Cat.*

Later we would walk and look up at the neon signs that created the magical world of Broadway. The "Bond" clothing store sign was my favorite. A waterfall cascaded over a huge billboard with a giant figure of a man and woman on each end adorned in neon lights. Next best, I liked the "Camel" cigarette sign; the smoker slowly blew out giant smoke rings. I looked up in awe of the many movie theatres lining both sides of the street, with their marquees displaying the names of the movies and large posters of the stars on display in glass panels. I wished I could live there and go in and out of each theatre, seeing movies all day. In Penny Arcades, for a nickel the machines would spit out an autographed postcard of different movie stars. Each time I would go home with a treasure of five. I was especially excited to get Frank Sinatra and June Allyson postcards, which I still have.

Aunt Mae didn't have any children of her own and enjoyed taking me out. She called going out "stepping." "We're going stepping," she'd say. She told the family she wanted children, but Uncle Pete loved her so much he didn't want to share her with anyone. Supposedly, he did everything for her.

"He adores her. Waits on her hand and foot, even washes the floors," my aunts would comment.

Aunt Mae's husband was jealous of the little girl Dorothy downstairs because Aunt Mae would also take her "stepping." He was also very jealous of her affection for Ronnie and me. At some point, the family started to refer to him as "the goose." They continued to call him that whenever they spoke of him through the years.

"Why do you call him the goose?" I asked my Aunt Mae.

She said, "Because he *is* the goose that laid the golden egg."

That was the only answer I could ever get. Years later, I learned he had been caught seeing another woman. He left my aunt, got a divorce, and had two children with his new wife. Even though my Aunt Mae claimed he said he didn't want children, I overheard her tell my Aunt Helen that she was too fearful to ever have a child. The idea of childbirth terrified her. At eleven, when I began to menstruate, she insisted we celebrate; yet she told me that when she was twelve and saw blood, it horrified her, she thought she was dying. She cried and cried, and prayed that it would go away. She claimed God answered her prayers and she did not start to menstruate again until she was sixteen.

Meanwhile Aunt Jean was getting married to a man also named Pete, Pete Delisky. I went to Newark for their wedding with my mother, father and Ronnie. I still remember my Aunt Jean dressed in her white satin wedding gown and Aunt Mae, who was her matron of honor, in a lavender satin gown. I never saw gowns before except in the movies. It was my first wedding, held in a very crowded banquet hall, with people dancing to a band playing polkas. There was the smell of kielbasa, sauerkraut, beer and whiskey. I never saw a tiered wedding cake before; it had thick white butter cream flowers and a bride and groom on top. I watched them cut it and feed each other a piece. It was so delicious, I ate a big slice. My mother told me I had to wrap a crumb in a napkin and put it under my pillow, and then I would dream about the man I was going to marry. The most fun of the day was running back and forth to a candy store directly across the street with some other children. I remember we made quite a few trips to buy little wax bottles for a penny a piece. They were filled with different colored syrups and we exchanged our favorite flavors with one another.

The wedding was one of the rare times my father went with us to Newark. He danced a lot with my mother and even with my aunts. Everyone seemed to have a very good time. I remember the long ride home that night; I fell asleep in back of the car. Ronnie had stayed in Newark to leave the next day for Picky Pine with Aunt Helen. When we got back to the Bronx, my father carried me upstairs and put me into my bed. I was half awake and asked my mother for my napkin with the wedding cake. Apparently, it had gotten misplaced. I started to cry, "I really wanted to know who I'm going to marry."

"You're better off if you don't marry anyone," my mother said.

A shattering loud crash startled both of us. My father had heard what she said to me. He had kicked the bedroom door so hard it broke off the hinges. Lunging at her, he punched her in the face. "Maybe that will teach you to keep your mouth shut," he shrieked and stormed out of the apartment, slamming the front door with great force. A short time later there were loud knocks on the door and she wouldn't open it. I was afraid Daddy had come back and there would be more hitting, I guess she was too. Then we heard, "Police, open this door."

When she opened the door, two policemen entered. Mugsy was barking and I was crying: we were both afraid of the police. One went to look in the other rooms, while the other sat at the kitchen table with us. "What happened?" he asked. Holding ice to her swollen cheek and dabbing at her bleeding lower lip, she told him it was just a domestic quarrel.

"I'm fine," she winced as she tried to smile.

I knew she wasn't, but she would never press charges against my father, it would only make things worse. Besides, in the Forties, domestic violence was treated much more leniently.

"Are you sure?" She nodded. He got up, patted me on the head and joined the other cop who was now petting Mugsy by the door.

"Call if you need us," he said.

When they left, she spent the rest of the night crying while I huddled with Mugsy and Poochie in my bed. I thought the argument was my fault since I made a fuss about the lost wedding cake. I told Mugsy we should go to sleep, things would be better in the morning.

The next day someone came and fixed our bedroom door. My mother's face was badly bruised, so we stayed in all day. On long days like this I spent a lot of time in the kitchen. Under the window there was a square metal door that had vents to the outside. This small compartment was used for cooling additional perishable items, a holdover from the days of the icebox. I would pretend that it was my jukebox. I would open the door, deposit a coin, and when I shut it imaginary music would start and I would sing and dance for hours. When my mother came into the kitchen, I asked her, "Mommy, can I go to dancing school?"

"We'll see," she said.

All her life she always said, "We'll see," when she definitely didn't mean no. I was excited, because I knew that this meant, "Maybe."

A few days later, she took me to the Tuxedo Dance School on Jerome Avenue to sign me up for a class. I remember the excitement of seeing the mirrored room with girls in leotards. I already saw myself doing pirouettes. But that night my mother and father had a screaming fight and he forbade her to allow me to go back. It seemed anything my mother wanted he put a stop to. I was angry with him and very disappointed. My mother told me she thought he just didn't want to have a daughter in show business. He seemed to know how upset I was and tried to make it up to me by buying me a small maroon three-wheeler bike with a little bell on it. This was nice but it wasn't dancing school. They weren't speaking at all. I would ride my bike to his bar and go in to spend some time with him. He was nicer to me when my mother wasn't around. He had a lot of steady customers. One older man had a large Boxer dog named Fritz. Fritz would actually smoke a cigar. My father would always ask the man to light the cigar up so I could watch the dog smoke. My Uncle Tony and Terry were often bartending and would make a big fuss over me and give me money to play the jukebox.

Next door to the bar was a candy shop where two old Austrian ladies made their own chocolates and marzipan. The enticing smell of melted chocolate would seep into the back door. Their backyard met the Venetian's. Daddy would take me through the back way to watch the ladies make chocolate. The ladies would give me freshly made chocolates and I would always leave with a little basket of marzipan in the shape of different fruits.

Everyone seemed to like my father and everyone liked my mother; they just didn't seem to like each other. When she was at the bar, I would feel guilty about being affectionate toward him. I felt like I was betraying her. He hated her drinking and to insure that she didn't, he began to leave her only one dollar a day for food. He would actually throw the dollar at her when he left for work. If she needed any additional money he would want to know exactly how she planned to spend it. The butcher and the grocery store kept a tally when she bought food, then he would pay the bill. Somehow she still managed to go to other bars and drink. We frequently spent many hours a day in bars other than my father's. She always asked me to promise not to tell my father where we went. I promised.

Other days I would go to the movies instead. My mother was comfortable about me going there alone so she now let me stay at the movies longer, and of course I wanted to. Sometimes I would see the whole show twice. I still preferred the movies to the bars. Looking back it was a strange mix—bars and movies for a five year old.

During that time, there were many war pictures and I didn't like them as much as the musicals. Movies like *Neptune's Daughter* with Esther Williams swimming in spectacular swimming pools, accompanied by bathing beauties doing underwater ballet, was what I really enjoyed. On Saturdays they would also show cartoons like *Bugs Bunny*, *Sylvester the Cat,* or *Porky Pig*. I liked these but not as much as the musicals or a good love story. An episode of the *Three Stooges* was very frequently shown as the short. You can certainly understand why I did not like them. All that hitting was not a bit funny to me, and besides they were all ugly. I would choose this time to go to the bathroom or to the candy counter.

That year my mother took me to see *Snow White and the Seven Dwarfs* at the beautiful Paradise Theatre on Fordham Road. The Paradise was very special; it had little stars and clouds all over the ceiling. It was enchanting. I felt like this was what heaven must look like. It was my first Disney movie and I loved it. However, that night and many other nights I had really awful nightmares. I kept dreaming that Snow White's stepmother, in the form of the witch, was jealous of me and kept chasing me to cut my heart out because the prince loved me more than her. I never told my mother or anyone that I was afraid; I didn't want to be thought of as a baby. I don't recall any other movies causing fear or anxieties, only Disney. Later when I saw *Dumbo*, I could not bear his mother being taken away, and in *Bambi* his mother's death was just too sad and scary. This sadness stayed with me for a long time afterward.

CHAPTER 10

The Accident

Life stayed pretty much the same. The war was still on with its air raid drills and rationing, our visits to the bars, movies, the fights between my father and mother, and the long trips on trains and buses to visit my grandmother in Newark continued. What was new in my life was my then favorite record, a Christmas present from my mother, a 78 LP album of Lewis Carroll's *Alice in Wonderland* performed by Ginger Rogers, whom I had seen in many movies dancing with Fred Astaire. This oddly wonderful tale enchanted me. I couldn't wait to listen to it; I played it over and over. I would sit in the parlor at the corner of the couch with Mugsy curled up next to me; I'd memorize the lines, saying them in the same voice as Ginger Rogers. Sometimes I would say them to Mugsy and he would look up, tilt his head and think I was really talking to him, but if I did it too much he would look annoyed and jump off the couch, so I tried not to bother him. The clatter of the elevated trains, although muffled in the winter by the closed windows, made it necessary to keep the volume high. In a loud voice I took on the personalities of my favorite characters like the Mad Hatter and the March Hare. "No room, no room." I especially loved joining Ginger Rogers' melodic voice saying, "Down, down, down, down,

down, falling, falling, falling, falling, falling," as she fell down into the rabbit hole. Little did I know this record would be my refuge for quite some time.

One night after waking with no one at home, I waited for Mommy to come back from the bars. Sometimes while waiting, I would sing my favorite Frank Sinatra songs and watch the shadows of the trees dance on the bedroom walls. I no longer saw them as monsters. I would give the trees men's and ladies' names and make up a whole story about them. Mommy always came home before Daddy. I very rarely heard him come in because as soon as my mother was home, I would drift off into much needed sleep. It was Easter vacation, Ronnie was visiting with Aunt Mae in Newark, and on this particular night when I heard the lock in the door at 4 a.m., I was surprised that it was my father coming home before her. He, too, would have had many drinks but somehow he always seemed steady on his feet and did not slur his words like Mommy. He came into the bedroom and seeing that I was awake said, "Where the hell is your mother?" I started to cry because I thought Mommy would be in big trouble and he would give her an awful beating.

She should have come home first, I thought, because now Daddy is very angry. I don't really remember what happened in the next few hours, I just remember being worried about my mother. In the Forties, not many households had a telephone; we certainly didn't. She did not come home the whole next day. Daddy told me he would drive to Newark to get Aunt Mae and Ronnie so they could come and take care of me. He took me to my mother's friend, Eva Prokapchak, to stay with her while he was gone. I liked Eva but didn't like to stay alone with her. She was very strict and made me sit on her couch a lot. "You be a good girl and stay there." When I was smaller, I always used to touch her stuff; she had a lot of glass knick-knacks on shelves, end tables and the coffee table, all of which were draped with lace doilies that she crocheted herself. She would warn me, "Keep your little hands off." But I couldn't help touching them; there were so many interesting little characters. I was especially fascinated by the large collection of small crystal animals. She would sit me on the chair and warn me, "If you don't stop touching, I will tie your hands." Then I would forget and touch again. Eva did tie my hands with one of her colorful babushkas. "Now you can't touch," she would say. Then I would stamp my feet on her shiny wood floor. "Don't you stamp your feet in my house, young lady." If I did it again she would tie my ankles together with another babushka. She always said this in a calm voice; she never seemed angry, only very bossy. This became a game, but after a few times, I didn't touch anymore. "See, now you listen," she would say. She had no children and I really don't think she knew how to talk to us. One nice thing was that every time I went there, she always had chocolate pudding in her refrigerator. We'd have a chocolate pudding party in her tiny bright pink kitchen. We'd have two puddings each, which she served in little pink flowered dessert dishes with real silver spoons.

Daddy came back that night to get me; he had Aunt Mae and Ronnie with him. It was Ronnie who came up to the apartment to wake me. I had fallen asleep on top of the soft gold satin comforter on Eva's bed. I was very glad to see him. We went down to the car and Aunt Mae hugged and kissed me and we all went home, but Mommy still was not there. I started to cry. Daddy told me to stop crying and go to sleep; he seemed very angry with me too. I could hear them through the bedroom door; I heard Aunt Mae and Daddy say they thought Mommy was probably with her friend Kathleen; they were very angry with her. Daddy kept saying Mommy was with that no good tramp. "I'll kill them both when I find them." He said no one knew where Kathleen was either.

Waking up in the late morning, I was so relieved to see that Mommy was in her bed. Daddy was sitting in the chair by her side, just looking at her. Then I saw that her head and face were all bandaged up. I thought Daddy had beaten her really badly this time. "Mommy, Mommy…what happened to Mommy?" I said. He put his finger to his lips and said, in a very quiet voice that sounded like he was crying, "Shush, she's sleeping, don't wake her." I ran out to ask Aunt Mae what happened. I was so scared I thought she was going to die, especially since Daddy looked so sad. Aunt Mae told me that Mommy was very drunk when she started for home at about 3:00 a.m. the night before last. She took a short cut through a gas station and fell head first into a twelve foot deep pit where they lowered cars. The mechanics found her when they opened several hours later. Still conscious, her chin was split wide open and all her teeth were broken or pushed up into her nose. An ambulance took her to Montefiore Hospital where they extracted most of her teeth and sewed up her chin. It was Eva Prokapchak who discovered that my mother was in the hospital. She then went to inform my father at the Venetian.

My mother didn't get out of bed for days and kept moaning and crying. She was unable to eat without teeth and could only sip milk-shakes Aunt Mae would make. I'd sit next to her on the bed and hold her hand. It was too painful for her to speak so she would just give my hand a squeeze. I felt she really needed me to be with her. She kept her eyes closed. I'd sit there for long periods trying to look at her face in the dim shade drawn light; the parts I could see that weren't bandaged were all purple and blue. Mugsy would stay at the foot of the bed. Then Aunt Mae would come and wave Mugsy and me out, "Let your mother sleep." She would close the door and I would have to go into the parlor. I didn't mind because I would have the Victrola all to myself. Ronnie was at school or out with his friends, so he would not insist on playing his records. Mugsy would stay curled up next to me on the couch, while I played *Alice in Wonderland* over and over without interruptions. I'd be immersed in the tale of this odd Wonderland until Aunt Mae would call me to lunch or dinner. The thing I liked most was knowing what Alice didn't know; that she would wake up very relieved and say, "It was only a dream."

At the end of the day when Ronnie came home, the three of us would eat dinner together. Ronnie was not his usual talkative self, it was Aunt Mae who did most of the talking and I did most of the eating. She kept telling Ronnie to eat more. "Look how Puddin' is eating," she said of me. I ate and ate. She made real dinners, like baked chicken, mashed potatoes and peas, and different colors of Jell-O for dessert. While she stayed with us, Ronnie slept on the couch and Aunt Mae on his folding bed. Since my bed was in my parents' room, I'd lie there listening to my mother weep and moan. Daddy did not come home for a few days. Aunt Mae cried a lot also. She kept kissing me and telling me she loved me. "How could your mother do this to you?" She said that my mother was a bad mother. I wanted to tell her that she should be nice to my mother, she should not be angry with her, yet I understood why Aunt Mae was angry. I didn't tell her that I was angry with Mommy too. Aunt Mae kept sitting me on her lap and calling me her poor little Guinea-Wop niece.

On the weekend, Ronnie took me with him to the movies. I was so glad to get away from Aunt Mae for a while. He usually never let me come with him and his friends; on the way there, he held my hand and let me walk next to him. I had to promise to be quiet. I sat in between him and his best friend Putchie, who was very nice to me and bought me candy and popcorn. I was quiet because we saw *National Velvet* with Elizabeth Taylor and Mickey Rooney, and it seemed like the best movie I had ever seen; the story was so good. Ronnie and I stayed to see it twice. Putchie said he had to get home. On the way back from the movie, we stopped at my father's bar to say hello. He was cheerful, as he always was at the bar and acted like nothing had happened. He gave me a handful of coins and told me to buy some candy for Ronnie and me. We went to the candy store and picked out some of our favorites, mine was Nestlé Crunch bars and Jujubes; Ronnie's was Milky Ways and Hershey Bars. I liked the silver wrapper on the Nestlé Crunch almost as much as I liked the chocolate; I would smooth it, flatten it down, and save it as a treasure in a cigar box. I had collected a large stack of them. I let Ronnie have more candy because he was older and also because I was so happy that he took me with him to the movies. Ronnie said we should not eat our candy until after dinner.

Aunt Mae was angry when we got home because it was late and dinner was waiting. She dabbed at her tears, saying. "Isn't it enough that I have to worry about your mother?" Ronnie took out one of his Hershey Bars and gave it to Aunt Mae. He said, "We bought this for you, Auntie Mae." She gave us both a kiss and stopped crying. I was smiling at him and he winked at me. Suddenly, I felt a huge surge of love for my brother. I kept thinking about how beautiful Elizabeth Taylor was in *National Velvet* and how she pretended to be a boy. I thought, "When I'm older and taller, I'll cut my hair and wear a hat. Then I can always hang around with Ronnie and his friends."

Aunt Mae left and Aunt Helen came to stay with us for a little while. I loved Aunt Helen; she was always humming and cooking. She spoke with a soft voice and always seemed to have a smile on her lips. She would talk to me all the time and always explain what she was doing when she was cooking or cleaning, or she would tell me stories about her life. I liked just hanging around with her. She showed me how to wax the furniture and wash the dishes. "You are my real big helper," she would say. My mother was getting better but still weeping a lot and spending a lot of time in bed. There were many visits to the dentist. It was difficult to understand her. She always kept her hand over her mouth and said she wouldn't be able to talk right until they made her new teeth. Her hand was also covering the thick red dent in her chin where all the stitches had been.

The apartment would smell wonderful from Aunt Helen's cooking. She was a great cook, even better than Aunt Mae, and she made a lot of dishes I had never had, like stews and pot roasts with cut potatoes and carrots, and tapioca or butterscotch pudding for dessert. She also baked bread, muffins or cakes that were always around for a snack. Our house was sparkling; even all the windows were washed. I thought, "It would be so nice if Aunt Helen could stay forever to take care of all of us." However, soon she had to leave. "Uncle Bill misses me," she nodded. "It's time to go home." She told me I could come to stay in Picky Pine with her and Uncle Bill for the whole summer if I wanted to.

The next few weeks were very lonely. My mother and I didn't go out to the bars, to the movies, or even to her friends' houses; when we did go anywhere, it was on boring bus rides to her dentist. Since my mother stayed in bed a lot, I'd listen to my records, especially *Alice*. Or I'd be in the kitchen with my favorite toy, that little metal door, under the window—my pretend jukebox. I'd drop a nickel into the top of the door and then imagine a record would start to play, choosing whatever my favorite song was from the radio program *The Hit Parade*. I would sing low if my mother was sleeping or at the top of my lungs when I knew the Number 4 elevated train would drown out my voice. I especially enjoyed singing *Don't Fence Me In,* pretending I was in the West, riding a horse in some location I had seen in a movie. Bing Crosby sang it with the Andrew Sisters. Although I didn't like Bing Crosby, I liked that song. If it were a torch song like one of Sinatra's, I imagined myself abandoned by a lover. *Full Moon and Empty Arms* comes to mind, and I'd actually cry. At other times I'd act out falling in love, climb on a chair, close my eyes, and kiss myself in the little mirror that hung on the wall. I spent many hours singing in our kitchen with my "jukebox" until we moved when I was six and a half.

Sometimes my mother would even suggest that I go downstairs and play with Gretchen. Since we didn't go anywhere, Gretchen was the only one I had to play with for a while. Gretchen had gotten nicer and didn't hit me much anymore. We mostly played cards and Chinese checkers. But we still took walks to Woolworth's where she made me steal little things for her, like a barrette or nail polish. I was always so afraid I was going to get caught and put in jail. My heart kept racing until we turned back onto Mosholu Parkway from Jerome Avenue and I knew we were home safe.

On the weekends, I would still go to the movies, but Ronnie wouldn't let me go with him anymore; he wanted to be alone with his friends. I would just have to go around the corner and ask, "Someone please cross me," then continue up Jerome to the Tuxedo Movie Theatre. With my usual pickle bag in hand I'd be one of the first in line to wait for the theatre to open. I liked to get there early. I would pay my twelve cents and then run to get the seat in the sixth row on the end—this was my seat. It was usually free, but if not I would sit directly in front or in back of it. Sitting on the end let me go in and out to the bathroom or to the candy counter without someone yelling at me. It also allowed me to eat my juicy pickles leaning over into the aisle.

One movie I really liked was *The Dolly Sisters*. Betty Grable and June Haver played Hungarian sisters who became very famous singers and dancers. They wore the most beautiful dresses. Every time they had to ride on a train they took out a make believe jelly apple and lollipop and pretended they were younger so they didn't have to pay the full ticket price. The eating of the artificial jelly apple made such an impression on me that for years and years, every time I ate a jelly apple, I would visualize Betty Grable. I came home singing *I'm Always Chasing Rainbows*, and this would remain a favorite song for a long time.

Another movie that really stayed with me was *Meet Me in St. Louis* starring Judy Garland. I kept remembering her in a long pale blue dress with her red hair swinging as she sang the catchy lyrics of the *Trolley Song*. At home I would loosen my braids, swing my hair, and belt out the tune. When out on the street, the *Trolley Song* played over and over in my head. "Clang, clang, clang went the trolley, ding, ding, ding went the bell...." Now I looked forward to what had been very boring bus rides to the dentist with my mother. I would pretend I was Judy Garland on a trolley and sing the *Trolley Song* in my head.

Eventually, my mother got her new teeth. I thought they looked very nice but she didn't. Now she could talk much better and her chin was not as red as it used to be, but her face was no longer oval—the deep scar squared off her chin. I often saw her eyes well up with tears when she made up in the mirror. She and Daddy did not seem to fight as often, but they didn't really talk to each other much either. He would just come home, go to bed, get up and go to work. I would go around the corner to visit him at his bar, but I didn't like to stay there long without Mommy.

We never went to visit Daddy's mother or my other aunts on Fteley Avenue anymore. Once in a while his sister, my other Aunt Mae, would come to visit with her two boys, Louis and Albert. They were older so they would only play with Ronnie. Ronnie really liked Louis but told me, "Albert is a spoiled little brat." I know my mother was always glad when Albert left because she said he broke everything. One year he knocked over our Christmas tree. I thought maybe Mommy should try tying him up to teach him a lesson like Eva did with me.

I was very surprised one day when Eva and Mommy were having coffee in our kitchen and Mommy was telling Eva how bad Albert was. Eva said, "You should tie his hands, that will teach him a lesson." She looked at me. "Right? That's how you learned your lesson," and she gave me one of her big Russian bear hugs. Somehow I had always thought I shouldn't tell my mother that Eva had tied me up because it might cause them to be angry at each other, but my mother wasn't angry at all. Each time Eva told this story (and she told it many times in the years to come) she always made it sound so comical. I was relieved that my mother now knew and started to giggle and giggle at the thought of Albert being tied.

It was Eva who got my mother to finally go out again. We went with her to the Golf bar to meet Eva's husband. I called him Mr. Pearls but everyone called Eva by her whole maiden name, Eva Prokapchak. Mr. Pearls was half Eva's size; she was large for a woman and he was small for a man. He was a nurse at Montefiore Hospital; it had been Mr. Pearls who discovered Mommy was there after her accident. They were telling the bartender the whole story; the way Mr. Pearls spoke reminded me of the popular movie actor, Peter Lorre, except Peter Lorre was always evil and Mr. Pearls was always so sweet and gentle. Eva and Mr. Pearls were very affectionate with each other, hugging, kissing and smiling; he called her "Honey" and she called him "Sweet Pea." The two of them got Mommy laughing and she seemed happy again, drinking her beer, smoking her Pall Malls and being with them and her other bar friends.

This was the first time I had been to the Golf in a long time. I played the new jukebox. It was bigger than the other one and had even more colors swirling up and down the sides and front. I was excited to discover my two current favorites, *The Trolley Song* and *I'm Always Chasing Rainbows*. I kept playing these two songs all night; life was getting back to normal.

CHAPTER 11

Picky Pine

A week before Ronnie graduated from eighth grade, my mother informed me I would be going with him to spend the summer with Aunt Helen and Uncle Bill at Picky Pine. "Sweetie, it will be so wonderful for you to spend a few months in the country."

I loved Aunt Helen and Picky Pine but…a whole summer without my mother! Mommy assured me she would come to visit, especially for my fifth birthday. During the next week, instead of going to the movies or playing with Gretchen after school, I stayed with her at the bars. The day after school ended we went shopping. My father gave her money to buy summer clothes for me; he must have given her a lot because we went downtown to Sterns on Fordham Road. We bought shorts, tops, playsuits, summer dresses, two bathing suits, pajamas, sneakers, and sandals. My favorite purchase was the every day of the week panties in different colors with the day embroidered on each. "I don't want Aunt Helen to have to do your wash too often," she said, squeezing my hand.

This shopping day was very special because, until now, I never had a day where I bought a lot of different things, and I spent the whole day with my mother other than in bars. We only stopped in a bar once for her to have one quick beer. Both of us had such a good time; Mommy smiled a lot more than she did since the accident. I was so happy when she was happy. She still looked pretty even with the deep scar across her chin. Her hair was now cut in the style of Claudette Colbert's, short and curly with bangs.

In the evening Mommy made me my favorite dish, meat loaf. At night we put all my new things into her old suitcase. Mugsy kept sniffing the suitcase and getting in our way. I insisted on packing my cigar box of Nestlé Crunch silver wrappers, my paper dolls and my *Alice in Wonderland* record. Mommy said she would ask Aunt Helen to hold my record. I refused to put Poochie into the suitcase; I would carry him. Aunt Helen and Uncle Bill were going to come and get Ronnie and me on Saturday, and Mugsy was coming, too. How I wished Mommy was coming!

My aunt and uncle arrived about ten in the morning. They had an old 1930's Ford. Both were on the heavy side, he much more so than she, they could barely fit in the front seat. Passersbys stopped to look; you didn't see too many of these old cars in the 1940's, certainly not in the city. What looked like a trunk on the back opened into a rumble seat. Mommy lifted me up and Ronnie and I climbed into the seat. Mommy put a collar and leash on Mugsy and tied it to the hinge so he couldn't jump out. Mugsy had never been leashed; he whined and squirmed between Ronnie and me. Uncle Bill was getting very impatient. We all kept attempting to calm Mugsy down. Then Uncle Bill said, "Why do we have to take this damn dog, anyway?" I was afraid of Uncle Bill's bellowing, and Mugsy must have been too. He quieted down and with an abandoned sigh rested with his snout across Ronnie's lap. So much was going on, I had hugged and kissed Mommy before jumping into the rumble seat, but I expected more goodbyes. Uncle Bill, however, was now bellowing again, "Let's get going or we'll never get there." He slammed the door and we were off. As the car moved away, I started to cry, "I don't want to go. I want to stay with Mommy. Mommy! Mommy!"

Mommy was waving and saying, "Don't cry, be a good girl." I think she was crying too.

"Mommy!"

Then we turned the corner and I couldn't see her any longer. By now I was sobbing and clutching Poochie to my chest, my heart was pounding so hard I thought it would break. Ronnie put his arm around me and Mugsy switched his snout to my lap. Uncle Bill was mimicking me and sticking his head out the driver's window. "Mah! Mah! Crybaby, a real Mama's Mah! Mah!" I hated him doing that; it made me very upset. I made myself stop crying so he couldn't tease me anymore. Through the back window of the car, I saw Aunt Helen give him a poke, but I couldn't hear what she said to him. I always noticed that my mother didn't like Uncle Bill and I didn't like him much either, but I wanted him to like me.

After a while Ronnie got me singing. I joined in when he sang the *Trolley* song, and we sang together for a while. Mugsy began to like the ride and stretched his front paws up to look over the back of the rumble seat, his ears blowing in the wind. The weather was nice, but with the wind constantly blowing, we sometimes got a little chilly so we put a blanket over us. But when we were stuck in traffic and the hot sun beat down on our heads, we put our hats on, only to take them off again while in motion so they wouldn't blow away. When traffic was slow or at a standstill, people from other cars would talk to us. One time we were stopped so long that we actually played catch ball with a boy from another car. Uncle Bill made us stop playing when Ronnie hopped down to retrieve the ball. He never yelled at Ronnie, he just said, "That could be dangerous, so don't do that again, Ronnie."

With heavy weekend traffic, the drive from the Bronx to Picky Pine took six hours. There were no highways then; once in New Jersey, we took Routes 1 and 9 all the way down. We stopped at gas stations to go to the bathroom and to walk Mugsy, but that was it. Aunt Helen had made sandwiches that we ate in the rumble seat while moving. She even brought liverwurst and water for Mugsy.

In South Jersey when we turned onto Highway 34, Uncle Bill yelled back to us, "We're almost there." Off Highway 34 we turned onto a very narrow gravel road surrounded by woods. This was Hurley Pond Road, which led to a little sign pointing left, "Carmersville." This little village, not yet on the map and deep in the woods, barely could be found. It was named after George Carmer, who first settled here at the turn of the century. Uncle George, as everyone called him, would soon become a very dear person to me.

We turned on Carmersville Road, which was little more than a sandy path, wide enough for only one car. When another car came in the opposite direction it would honk and one or the other car would have to pull into woods. Just about a quarter of a mile in, we hit a clearing in the woods with a few houses. There were only about twelve in the whole village. If you went to the end of the road and turned left, the last house belonged to Uncle Bill's sister, Aunt Jessie, and her husband, Uncle Andy. Turning into our driveway framed by the two large white wagon wheels, two sets of umbrella trees, and rows of dappled hydrangeas, the little white bungalow sat like an enchanted cottage in the forest. Aunt Helen helped me down from the rumble seat. Freed from his leash, Mugsy jumped down and ran off sniffing at trees.

"Well, Puddin'," Aunt Helen smiled, "here we are at Picky Pine."

When she called me "Puddin'" it was filled with affection, not like Aunt Mae, who always made me feel fat when she said it. She took me by the hand. While she unlocked the door, Ronnie and Uncle Bill took the suitcases from the car. Then Ronnie went to the back house to retrieve the hammock and set it up between two trees that had hooks waiting to support it from a previous summer. As we stepped into the tiny kitchen, the smell of damp wood was present. Once Aunt Helen rolled up the straw shades and opened all the windows, fresh air and sunshine came streaming into the house.

"Ain't it purdy?" Aunt Helen always said pretty that way.

I nodded in agreement. It was! It was so pretty and cozy.

"Over here your little bed is waiting for you; you'll sleep snug as a bug in a rug," she purred as she pointed to the pull-out love seat in the parlor.

"And remember, Ronnie will be in this little room right next to you, and you know that Uncle Bill and I sleep in the bunk beds in the other bedroom. I'm on the top bunk, so if you call me I can look over the top of the wall and see you." I sat little Poochie on the cushion and told him where we all would be sleeping. I glimpsed into the only remaining room, the small glassed-in porch where I recalled eating delicious meals during my brief visit the summer before. Aunt Helen pointed to the green dresser in Ronnie's area, "Why don't you put your clothes away, then you can go outside and play while I make dinner."

I chose to change into one of my new playsuits, and then went outside. As I roamed around on the property, I heard Ronnie belting out Bing Crosby's hit, *Swing on a Star* as he lay swinging in the hammock. On tiptoe I stretched to peek up into the umbrella trees hoping to catch a glimpse of a robins' nest, but I wasn't tall enough. I wished

Mommy were here to lift me up. I wondered what she was doing, and pictured her sitting at the Golf bar laughing and drinking. I smelled the hydrangeas and stood fascinated in front of a little silver maple tree; its leaves actually looked like real silver on one side. Everything was still and peaceful. All I heard was the chirping of birds, my aunt humming and the occasional clank of a pot from the kitchen. Wagging his pretzel tail, Mugsy came running over to me. It seemed he was telling me he was having a good time and was happy to be here. I told him I was having a good time, too.

Aunt Helen's dinner was great. "How is little Mah-Mah?" Uncle Bill asked, looking at me with a chuckle. Ready to say fine, I braced myself for the tease. I didn't have to answer because he started talking to Aunt Helen. "Ducky (they called each other Ducky all the time), I think I'll repair the lattice work around the shower tomorrow." It was an outdoor shower right next to the kitchen.

After dinner Aunt Helen let me be her helper by wiping the dishes dry. Then we sat in the little parlor. Climbing on her lap, I asked, "Tell me about the World's Fair and Luna Park." Her blue eyes would twinkle, I knew she liked telling me, and I was always enthralled. Uncle Bill, who had been reading the newspaper, put it down and said, "I think I'll get some Z's" and went off to bed. After many stories of rides and fun houses, Aunt Helen and I had a cracker and milk party before bedtime, and then she tucked me into the pull-out.

I could hear the squeaking of the ladder as she climbed to her top bunk. With all the lights out, I was very scared; there were strange noises. I thought I saw someone evil looking at me through the window. The terrifying image of the witch in Snow White came flooding over me. Uncle Bill was snoring loudly, and I could hear Ronnie's quiet breathing.

"Aunt Helen! Aunt Helen!" I whispered because I didn't want Uncle Bill to wake up and make fun of me. "Aunt Helen!" Afraid to get up but more afraid to stay by myself, I clutched Poochie and tiptoed to Aunt Helen's bunk bed. I silently climbed up the ladder and touched my aunt's arm. She slapped her arm and opened her eyes. We were both startled for a moment and then she smiled and said, "I thought you were a mosquito eating my arm for dinner." Patting the bed she said, "Hop in." I climbed over her and snuggled under the blanket, between her and the pine wall. I peeked over and could see Ronnie and my bed just below. "I miss my mommy, I think I want to go home," I said as my lower lip started to quiver.

"Well, tomorrow if you still want to go home tell me and we will take a train."

"Can I stay here and sleep with you?" I pleaded. She said, "Yes, but we have to sleep fast, because we have a lot of work to do tomorrow." She proceeded to tell me in great detail the chores we would need to accomplish; somewhere in the middle of the description of painting the lawn chairs, I fell asleep.

Aunt Helen would always assure me, "Ask me during the day and I will take you by train. The trains don't run at night." When I was older my aunt would love to tell this story of how I behaved the first few summers. "During the day you had such a good time, but when night came, you would ask to go home and cry for your mother. Yes, ask me tomorrow, when the trains are running, I'd say. By the third or fourth night you never asked to go home, you were having yourself a good old time." And a good time I did have every summer until I was eleven years old.

CHAPTER 12

Almost Paradise

Lying in my bed at Picky Pine, I loved to hear the sound of the crickets and the whippoorwills. On clear nights the moon and stars cast their light on trees blowing gently in the breeze. Once asleep, I didn't open my eyes until the morning sunlight streamed into the bungalow. Aunt Helen would be humming in the kitchen and the delicious smells of breakfast drifted into my nostrils. Mugsy was waiting for me to wake up, ready to jump, wag his tail, and lick my face at my first stirring. During the weekdays, Ronnie, now twelve, already would have left at 5:00 a.m. to caddy at the golf course, which was about a two mile walk. Uncle Bill worked in Newark as a district manager of Social Security. He would leave early on Mondays, sharing a ride with his brother-in-law, Uncle Andy. They wouldn't return until Friday evening. The Ford would be left for Aunt Helen to use. When no one else was visiting, I had Aunt Helen all to myself during the day.

Our mornings were filled with chores: sweeping, dusting, washing clothes, planting, weeding, and raking. After detailed instructions, I was always assigned a task. Painting was my favorite; I was allowed to give first coats to all the lawn furniture and various odds and ends. This became a ritual. Every summer Aunt Helen would refurbish just about everything. "You have to take good care of things so they last and look purdy," she'd say. Each year she even painted the old Ford with outdoor maroon high gloss enamel.

After lunch, I would put on my bathing suit and we'd walk down the road to visit Mr. Carmer. An occasional Army tank or jeep from the local base would cause us to step aside into the woods. Mr. Carmer and his wife owned a lot of property that had a natural spring. A number of years before, he hired a bulldozer to dig a large pond for the kids, many of whom were his relatives. But everyone in Carmersville was welcome to swim there, and mostly everyone did. The pond was quite large, a good two hundred feet wide. It graduated from about one foot and never became any deeper than four feet. Cat-o'- nine-tails grew on three sides in the mucky edges; but the center was delightful. This is where I spent most of my summer afternoons. At first I needed a tire inner tube to keep me afloat, but I soon learned to swim and spent more time under water than on top. Mugsy would join me swimming: his little snout pushing forward as he doggie paddled toward me. I'd doggie paddle with him and round and round we'd go. I became friendly with Mr. Carmer's grandchildren, Lynn and Eddie. They were sister and brother, both blond and blue eyed one and two years older than I. Lynn's friend Bessie had two sisters, one my age, the other one year younger. All of them lived in Carmersville year round. Most days we were all in the pond together for a few hours. Even rainy days were fun; the girls invited me to walk with them. In bathing suits and bare feet, we'd walk feeling the rain on our heads and the mud sloshing in between our toes. Sometimes we'd even swim in the rain.

At home in the late afternoon, I'd shower outdoors wondering if the people in the airplanes could see me naked. While Aunt Helen cooked dinner, I would run to the renovated chicken coop anxious to play records on the wind up Victrola. I'd put on *Alice in Wonderland*, or Aunt Helen's Al Jolson records. Aunt Helen had Enrico Caruso's *I Pagliacci*. After she told me the story, I would pretend I was the clown with a broken heart, and passionately sing the Italian words with Caruso. By the end of the song, I sometimes would be down on one knee, clutching my heart and sometimes tears ran down my cheeks. *Put Your Little Foot Right Out* was the record I would dance with and perform for Aunt Helen when she came to call me for dinner. In the evening she'd always wear a clean starched summer housedress. Just being outdoors for one week, her skin was golden brown, which made her blond hair lighter and her blue eyes deeper. Gradually, I too had gotten darker and by the end of each summer, my color was almost chocolate.

We always waited for Ronnie and then the three of us would eat together. Everything Aunt Helen cooked was so good. While we ate, Ronnie would tell us about his day as a caddy. "Some golfers give really big tips," he said proudly, smiling.

After doing the dishes, on most evenings we'd go outside to sit on the swing that held four. We'd glide back and forth. Aunt Helen sat tranquilly with a beer, content to be swinging and conversing until after dark. Ronnie and I sipped Kool Aid and sometimes roasted marshmallows on sticks. Occasionally, Mr. Carmer would stroll up and join us. His slender body, weather beaten face and broken teeth did not detract from his warm and easy manner. He seemed to love everyone, especially children. Joining my aunt for a beer he'd take great interest in hearing what we did, where we went, or what we had for dinner. Aunt Helen always had a "how do you fix it question" for him. He seemed to know how to do everything. He would always start with a chuckle, "Well, you take this here gizmo...." Then he'd tell Ronnie and me a story, real stories, about when he was young. "I'd ride my horse and carriage to lower Manhattan. It was a two day trip in those days and Broadway was just a small road. I still have a horse, not the same horse," he'd chuckle. "Why don't you kids come on down and ride her sometime?" Winking one eye and raising his other brow he'd nod, making the statement both a question and answer. We did go. Tess was a gentle chestnut brown horse. I would sit on her back, pat her neck, and talk into her ear, but Ronnie wasn't afraid to actually ride her up and down the road.

Some nights we would just walk down and sit in Mr. Carmer's apple orchard, talking to him and his wife, Aunt Beulah. She worked in a bakery and always had bags of donuts for us to eat. More often than not, Lynn and Eddie and their parents would walk over from across the road. Bessie and her sisters often showed up also, and before long we'd all be running around, playing tag or hide and seek and lighting punks to keep the mosquitoes away. We often held the slender punks like cigarettes in holders and flicked the gray ash movie star fashion as we pranced haughtily around the orchard.

Once back at Picky Pine, we'd get into our nightclothes and listen to the radio. We especially loved *The Goldbergs*. At the beginning of the program, Aunt Helen and I would say in unison, "Yoo hoo, Mrs. Goldberg!" After it was over, we would make one last trip to lift our nightgowns and sprinkle the grass before going to bed. I'd look up at what seemed like a million stars. It was so peaceful...no yelling, no slamming doors, no hitting, and no nights alone.

At the end of the week, in preparation for the weekend, Aunt Helen would drive about three miles to the nearest grocery store in the town of Farmingdale. When Uncle Bill came home, the weekends were filled with major projects, like digging a well or a cellar. Mr. Carmer, Uncle Andy, Ronnie and Aunt Helen would help while my uncle gave orders. Actually, he seemed to give more orders than he ever did work. He even had me fetching tools. I don't think he liked or disliked me; I was just Ronnie's little sister and the "the tool getter."

On Saturday nights Ronnie and I would hop into the rumble seat and they would drive to the local auction to buy tools that Uncle Bill needed. Aunt Helen always came home with some new gadget for the kitchen. The best part was bringing home submarine sandwiches and ice cream to eat.

On July fifteenth I would be five years old. Mommy was coming to visit for my birthday. I could hardly wait to see her. It was Saturday afternoon. Ronnie wasn't home from the golf course yet, so just the three of us went to pick her up from the Lackawanna train in Farmingdale. As the approaching train's whistle blew, the loud warning bells and blinking lights at the railroad crossings heightened my anticipation. Pulling into the station with a thunderous roar, the train let out clouds of steam and deafening screeches as it came to a halt. Mommy was the first off the train. "Mommy, Mommy!" We ran through the steam to each other. Her hug felt so good.

"How are you, Eva?" Aunt Helen asked as she kissed her cheek. "Eva" again. Why didn't they call her "Tommy" like everyone in the Bronx? Mommy just nodded politely to Uncle Bill when he helped her into the rumble seat. I climbed in beside her and snuggled next to her. She would be here a whole week! This was the best, being at Picky Pine and having Mommy, too. When we turned at the wagon wheels, Ronnie and Mugsy were waiting and excitedly ran beside the car until it came to a stop.

During that week, Mommy and I would take walks, listen to records, or just lie in the sun. At night we'd all hang out by the swing. Aunt Helen and Mommy would drink beer and talk, but Mommy never got drunk. The best part was that Mommy slept with me in the pull-out loveseat like last year.

I had a great birthday. Aunt Helen baked a cake, and Mommy and I decorated it with white icing and I made the number five from cherries. After singing Happy Birthday, everyone applauded. I felt very grown up.

The week was wonderful, but it went too fast. Now we were already taking my mother back to the train. She kept saying, "Let's promise not to cry, because if you cry, you will make me cry. I'll come back to see you in August, Sweetie." I didn't want to see her cry, so I was very quiet during the ride. I knew if I said one word, I would start to cry. When the train pulled away, we waved and waved until I couldn't see her anymore, then I let myself cry. That night I missed her most when I got into bed alone. Mugsy must have missed her too, because he inched up and put his head on my chest. I thought about how happy Mommy was all week. That brought a smile to my lips. I drifted into sleep.

The next week, I fell back into the routine that Aunt Helen and I had established. Everything was back to normal until Uncle Bill brought Aunt Mae back to spend the weekend. After greeting Ronnie, Aunt Helen and me, Aunt Mae and Aunt Helen went for a walk. "Ronnie, play cards with Kathy for a while," Aunt Helen said. As we played cards, I could see my aunts through the porch window. They both looked upset at whatever Aunt Mae was telling Aunt Helen. When they returned, Aunt Helen began to fix dinner.

"Is everything all right?" I asked Aunt Mae. I thought she was probably having more troubles with Uncle Pete, "the goose." She pulled me onto her lap. "You have a little cousin, you know. Aunt Jean had a baby boy. She named him Billy. His birthday is July thirteenth, two days before your birthday. You'll be like a big sister to him." Aunt Mae was holding me so tight I could hardly breathe. "You are so sweet, my little Puddin', I am going to eat you up."

I felt like she was eating me up, and treating me like a baby too. It didn't seem she was going to tell what they were really talking about outside?

"Auntie Mae," I managed to slide off her lap by urgently stating, "I need to go to the bathroom." When I returned she was busy talking to Ronnie so I helped Aunt Helen set the table. Dinner was kind of quiet, even Uncle Bill wasn't bellowing. Whatever it was, they weren't talking about it.

That night while lying in bed, I heard Aunt Helen and Aunt Mae, talking quietly on the porch. "Let's wait until she's asleep," I heard Aunt Helen say. When Aunt Helen tiptoed into the parlor, I pretended I was asleep. I heard fragments of their conversation. "Slashed all her clothes into little pieces with a razor blade…broke the furniture…." I wanted to get closer to the porch, but I was afraid they would hear me, I lay frozen. "Blood all over the place…neighbors called the police…." Then I heard these words, "The police think Joe killed Eva, but they can't find either one of them."

CHAPTER 13

Into the Rabbit Hole

"Joe killed Eva? Killed…who?" It took a few seconds to realize they were talking about my mother, Eva. I barely heard anything after that until they said goodnight and Aunt Helen went to her bunk bed. Aunt Mae was sleeping with me in the pull-out. I didn't want her to know I heard, so when she got into bed I lay very still with my eyes closed. I lay frozen until I heard her whistling air through her nose. Awake, I kept picturing Daddy cutting Mommy, her body full of blood lying dead on the parlor floor. "If I had been home maybe it wouldn't have happened," I whispered to Poochie. Daddy stopped hitting Mommy when I begged him to. But they said they couldn't find Mommy or Daddy. Maybe he carried her body to the trunk of his car and dumped it in the river, like in the movies. Or maybe Daddy was so sorry for hitting her that they kissed, made up and went on vacation together. The next morning, I very carefully climbed over Aunt Mae, who was still making whistling noises. Aunt Helen was in the kitchen getting breakfast ready, Uncle Bill was already working outside, and Ronnie had left for work. "Did Ronnie know?" I wondered. I would ask Ronnie when he came home.

I thought Aunt Helen might say something to me, but she didn't. When we all sat down for breakfast, I wasn't able to eat; even just smelling the bacon upset my stomach. "Aren't you hungry, Kathy?" asked Aunt Helen. Right then I wanted to ask her about Mommy, but I couldn't. Then she would know I was listening, and besides, everyone was looking at me. I just shook my head no. For the most part they were behaving like nothing was wrong, except later when Uncle Bill was shouting orders, Aunt Helen got very cross with him. "Will you stop yelling orders at me!" she said in the angriest voice I ever heard her use. After that Uncle Bill was very nice and kept calling her "Ducky" for the rest of the day.

I didn't feel much like going to the pond that week. I was afraid I would cry in front of my friends, so I spent most days in the little back house listening to my records. Mugsy would occasionally scratch at the door to come in, but his visits were brief; he would scratch again to go out, leaving me alone with my thoughts. "If Mommy were dead, who would take care of me?" Just thinking that she might be gone, made me break into tears. An emptiness ripped at my stomach. I quickly put on Caruso's *I Pagliacci* so if anyone came they would think I was crying about the record. I really didn't feel like playing other songs right then. I sat there thinking, "I would love to live with Aunt Helen but not with Uncle Bill, but that would still be better than living with Aunt Mae. Would Daddy take care of me or would he have to go to jail?" I sang with Caruso in Italian, repeating words I did not understand, but I knew we shared a deep sadness. I cried without the record and then I played *Alice in Wonderland* over and over. I really didn't know if Mommy was alive or dead. I wondered if I heard right, or if I was like *Alice*, only dreaming. I wanted to talk to Ronnie.

At dinner Ronnie flashed his usual smiles, beaming about what a good caddy he was and what great tips he made. They all complimented him and got involved in asking questions about his customers and the golf course. I watched him. He was his usual cheerful self and didn't act like he knew anything. I just couldn't find a way to begin. I wanted to tell him but I was afraid he'd say, "Stop making up stories." When he knew I made up a story, he'd swat me with a rolled newspaper.

On Monday morning Aunt Mae drove back to Newark with Uncle Bill and Uncle Andy. I was glad I was going to have the bed to myself again but I couldn't sleep; I kept thinking about my mother and cried quietly until my eyes burned. I wanted to ask Aunt Helen if I could sleep in the bunk with her. I didn't because I didn't want her to suspect that I'd heard anything. For the next week we stayed to most of our routine, although in the mornings she told me to go play my records instead of doing chores. "I think you're catching something, you're not eating and your eyes are all red," she said as she felt my forehead. Maybe it would have been better to be helping her because I cried a lot in the back house. I wished I had my Frank Sinatra records; his voice was always so soothing to me.

Usually Uncle Bill's return on weekends came fast but this time Friday seemed long in coming. There weren't any telephones in Carmersville, and even if there were, Aunt Mae, Aunt Jean or Granny didn't have a telephone. By late afternoon on Friday, I noticed Aunt Helen looking out the window at the sound of each car. As soon as Uncle Andy's car turned into the driveway, Aunt Helen quickly went out to meet it.

I watched from behind the curtain of the kitchen door. I couldn't hear what they were saying, but just before I ran toward the parlor to pretend I was sitting there all along, I saw Uncle Bill put his arm around her and a smile came to her face. She was humming again as she finished making dinner and asked me to set the table. When we sat down to dinner with Ronnie, I dared to ask. "Will Mommy be coming to visit soon?" After a very long pause Aunt Helen said, "I don't think so, she is staying with Granny in Newark for a few weeks." Relieved, I thought, "Mommy is okay, she isn't dead." I believed what Aunt Helen told me. Then she added, "Before you know it, it will be Labor Day, so you'll be seeing your mother real soon." I wanted to jump up and dance on the table. I think I had a smile on my face for the next few days.

Somehow, through bits and pieces I overheard most of the story. At four in the morning when Daddy came home from closing his bar, Mommy wasn't there. Filled with whiskey, he didn't wait long before he started yelling and throwing whatever he could get his hands on. As he worked himself into a rage, he took a razor from the bathroom and, removing her clothes from the closets and drawers, he slashed them one by one, cutting his hands badly in the process. There was blood all over the apartment. He slashed the sheets, the mattresses and all the upholstery, pulled out the stuffing and flung it, and smashed all the dishes. Then he ran out in a fury to find her. The neighbors heard him yelling, "I'll kill her, I'll kill her."

A short time later, Mommy staggered in and saw the destruction. Terrified, she fled to her friend Eva Prokapchak's apartment, where she stayed until morning. In the meantime the neighbors called the police. Several reported that from their windows they saw both Daddy and Mommy running out of the building. The police assumed the worst. Daddy was arrested for disturbing the peace, assault and battery, and suspicion of murder.

The next day Eva and Mr. Pearls drove my mother to Granny's and then informed the police that she was unharmed. After Daddy paid a fine for disturbing the peace, they let him go.

Some of this was now discussed in front of Ronnie and me. Two weeks later, Aunt Helen told us at dinner that my father drove to Newark to ask my mother to forgive him for wrecking the apartment.

"What exactly happened?" Ronnie asked.

"It seems when he came home at four in the morning and your mother wasn't there, he let his temper get the best of him; broke a lot of the furniture. When your mother saw what he did she was afraid he was out of control so she went to stay with your grandmother."

"She wouldn't have to be afraid of him if she stopped drinking," Ronnie stated.

"He shouldn't hit Mommy, even if she drinks he shouldn't. Right, Aunt Helen?" I argued.

Aunt Helen answered, "Well, she shouldn't drink and he shouldn't hit her, so they are both wrong. Anyway she forgave him and went back to the Bronx to help him fix the apartment before you and Ronnie go home."

Uncle Bill said with distaste, "Forgave him? Your sister Eva should ask him to forgive her." Then he looked at me. "Your Mother is a lucky woman. I wouldn't take her back, carrying on like that, drinking and running around too." Aunt Helen darted a look at him and he didn't say anything else about Mommy. I was angry, feeling I was the only one sticking up for Mommy. I knew Uncle Bill didn't like her. "Well, my mother doesn't like you either," I thought. I wished I could say that and stomp off, but I just sat there. Actually, not too many people liked him; he always talked down to everyone. They came to help or visit because they adored Aunt Helen. Even his sister, Aunt Jessie, didn't like him and she liked everyone. She was so sweet, with gray hair and glasses over her wide gray eyes. She would loudly suck in a breath before she delivered each sentence and when the words came out of her mouth, it always seemed like a complete surprise to her. She and Uncle Andy were very affectionate toward each other and very nice to everyone.

"My Andy," she'd breathe. "My Andy is the most wonderful man. Helen, I don't know how you put up with our Bill," she exclaimed. She visited during the week and avoided coming on the weekend when Uncle Bill was home.

"Ducky, I don't know how you can stand to be around that wind-bag, Jessie," Uncle Bill would say to Aunt Helen. Even though he didn't like too many people, not even his own sister, it made me very angry that he didn't like Mommy.

For the rest of the summer, I visualized Mommy and Daddy happy, shopping, her making breakfast, him going to work, her sitting at his bar again and laughing with the customers, them having dinner together and dancing like they did at Aunt Jean's wedding. The next few weeks were the best of the summer. I didn't even mind the weekends when Uncle Bill came. I joined Lynn and Eddie and the girls for Sunday school. We would all jump into the back of Mr. Carmer's pickup truck and ride to the Protestant church.

"God loves Protestants better," Bessie said.

"No! You can't go to heaven unless you're a Catholic," I said.

"You are so wrong," Bessie stated.

When we went into the plain wooden church, I told them how pretty St. Ann's Catholic Church in the Bronx was with marble altars and beautiful statues of saints.

"We don't believe in saints," Lynn said, dismissing me.

I knew I would not go to heaven if I didn't stay Catholic, but I sure liked the Protestant Sunday school and the way they told us stories. I loved *Joseph's Coat of Many Colors*. Teenagers provided the voices for all of the little cardboard characters as they moved them around a large bulletin board to act out the story. We had such a good time sitting on the floor listening in a circle. Afterward we sang and talked as they served milk with cookies made by the moms. We each were given a cardboard figure, and because I was a guest, they presented me with Joseph. I felt guilty on the way home for thinking being Protestant was a lot more fun than being a Catholic. At St. Ann's, you had to keep quiet for a very long time, kneel on the hard pews until your knees hurt, and listen to the priest speak in Latin, which I didn't understand.

"Isn't Protestant better?" Bessie asked.

"They're both just as good," I shrugged.

We had other differences, like the way we spoke. There were many words we said differently, but one day an argument led to a really big fight. In the Bronx, I would pronounce pajamas, pa-jaah-muz. In South Jersey they would pronounce it per-jam-miz.

After going back and forth with this word, Bessie's sister Lily put her hands on her hips and stamping her foot screamed in my face, "It's not pa-jaah-muz, it's per-jam-miz, say it right."

"I am saying it right, you're saying it wrong," I screamed back at her.

Lily then picked up the toy gun that we had been playing Cowboys and Indians with and walloped me with the butt of it, splitting the skin above my eyebrow open. Blood came gushing out and my screams were so loud that Aunt Jessie said she could hear me all the way at her house down the road. Aunt Helen came rushing over to dab at the blood. It burned when she took me in the house and put iodine on it, then she pinched it together and put on adhesive tape very tightly. Lily had followed us in saying, "I'm really sorry, but she's been acting like such a brat, she made me so angry...I'm really sorry." Aunt Helen scolded Lily. "You go home now, Lily, and don't come back until you know how to behave." Lily started to cry and ran out the door. Aunt Helen said, "Those three sisters have a mean streak in them, you've got to watch your step with them." The next day when I saw Lily at the pond, she said she was sorry and I forgave her, and we were friends again.

As Labor Day drew near, I was sad about leaving Picky Pine but anxious to go home again and see my mother. I also would be starting kindergarten at PS 80. The kids on the Jersey Shore started school a week earlier than in the Bronx. I watched them being picked up by a school bus and waved as they drove off through the trees already turning their autumnal colors. With no one to play with me, the last week there was very quiet. A few ladies, including Aunt Jessie, came to the house to have Aunt Helen cut their hair and give them a "permanent wave" before they went back to the city for the winter. Even though she didn't have her beauty parlor anymore she always did some permanent waves at home. When Aunt Helen used the lotion for the "Marcel

Waves," the whole house smelled of it and burnt hair from those big smoking steel rollers and clips. I would go to the back house and play my records. Mugsy couldn't stand the smell either, so he'd trot over with me. Some afternoons after singing to him, I'd put a blanket on the floor and join him for a nap.

Aunt Helen made some school dresses for me on her Singer sewing machine. "Don't you look purdy," she said, as I modeled one of them for her. I wanted to try on the dresses with my Mary Jane's. Most of the summer, I went barefoot or wore my sandals to town. I could not get my feet into my Mary Jane's. My feet had grown an entire shoe size. I started to cry.

Aunt Helen lifted me on her lap. "It's those country cows, little Puddin'. That country milk from those country cows sure makes feet grow fast."

"But I don't want to have big feet," I wailed.

"Now, now, you're getting to be such a big girl you can't walk around with teeny weeny feet can you? You'd look purdy silly. We'll buy you some new Mary Jane's in Farmingdale."

The shoe store in Farmingdale didn't carry Mary Jane's, so that weekend Aunt Helen made Uncle Bill drive us all the way to Asbury Park. "I don't see why she just can't get her shoes when she goes home," he grumbled.

"Because I want new shoes too, Ducky." Aunt Helen couldn't find any she liked; but I got a brand new shiny pair of Mary Jane's.

The day before Labor Day, with everything packed into the Ford, Ronnie tied Mugsy's leash, and we three were in the rumble seat ready to make our trip back to the Bronx. As we drove away, I took a last look at the umbrella trees and when we turned at the wagon wheels I kept looking back at Picky Pine until I could see nothing but woods.

CHAPTER 14

Home

It was early Sunday evening when we pulled up to our apartment on Mosholu Parkway. Ronnie untied Mugsy and he dashed into the building. We were still climbing out of the rumble seat when my mother came running down the stairs to greet us.

"Mommy, I missed you so much," I squealed as I jumped up into her arms, wrapping my legs around her waist. With me clinging to her, she leaned over to kiss Ronnie. These days Ronnie always got red in the face when anyone kissed him. Ronnie's friend Putchie saw us arrive from his window and came down to see Ronnie.

"Mommy, can I go up to Putchie's house?" Ronnie asked. My mother nodded as Aunt Helen hugged Ronnie goodbye and Uncle Bill saluted and yelled, "See you" from the car.

"How are you, Eva?" Aunt Helen asked.

"Now don't you start yakking, Ducky, we have a long ride back to Newark," Uncle Bill ordered.

Let me just help Eva up with the suitcases," Aunt Helen replied. While walking up the two flights of stairs, I thought the hallways seemed so dark.

"So tell me, how have things been going, Eva?" Aunt Helen asked with concern.

"Okay I guess," my mother said as we entered our foyer, which looked so much smaller to me; everything looked smaller. The kitchen looked smaller and the Mexicans on the border seemed old and worn, but there sat a brand new yellow Formica table and chairs with shiny chrome legs. As Aunt Helen followed my mother through the parlor to put the suitcases in the bedroom, I noticed the new furniture in the parlor. Still wrapped around her waist when we entered the bedroom, I looked around and it seemed pretty much the same, except Mugsy was sitting on a new colorful spread covering Mommy and Daddy's bed.

"Everything looks real nice, Eva," Aunt Helen was saying as I realized that the mirror, my large round mirror on the dressing table...my dress-up mirror was gone! "Mommy, where is my mirror?" I started to cry.

"Sweetie, don't cry, we ordered a new mirror, it isn't ready yet."

"See Puddin', you are getting a brand new mirror," Aunt Helen said giving me a few pats on my behind. "Well Eva, I better go, you know Bill, in another minute he'll be yelling and honking." Aunt Helen reached over and took me from my mother's arms and now I stayed with my legs wrapped around her as we went down to the car. I gave Aunt Helen a big kiss and slid down to the sidewalk in front of the passenger side. Aunt Helen barely closed the door of the Ford before Uncle Bill was driving away. Aunt Helen kept throwing kisses but the only goodbye from my uncle was one honk of the horn as they turned the corner and were gone.

I felt strange with Mommy. I didn't know what to say; she was quiet and didn't offer any conversation. We held hands as we went back upstairs. I asked, "Will it be the same mirror?"

"Almost the same," Mommy said. "It will be here next week."

I was glad when Ronnie came home because he was always talking. Mommy made us veal cutlets, mashed potatoes and peas, one of our favorite dinners. Veal was a real luxury during the war. It used up almost all the meat rations. Mommy began to talk. She told us that she and Daddy were getting along better. He still wouldn't give her more than one dollar a day for food. Looking at me she said, "Sweetie, I would like to buy you a new dress for your first day of school but I just don't want to ask him right now."

Ronnie told Mommy he made a lot of money at his caddy job and offered to give her some of his earnings for my dress. Although Aunt Helen made me a few dresses, I did want a special new store bought dress for school. Ronnie turned red as she gave him a kiss on the cheek and she started to cry. "I'll pay you back," she said. Ronnie rolled his eyes and winked at me.

"By the way, tomorrow Daddy reserved a whole room in a restaurant on City Island and is treating his entire family for a Labor Day feast—he even hired a band. So after dinner let's figure out what we are all wearing."

In the bedroom, I unpacked and chose a white peasant blouse and colorful skirt with ruffles. I was very dark from the summer sun. "I will look so pretty, like Dorothy Lamour." I got ready for bed and lay there watching my mother. She took a soft white dress out of the closet and hung it on the outside of the door. Then she picked up the silver brush and comb from the dressing table and began to set her hair. Looking into the makeshift mirror she took toilet paper and folded it over section by section of her wet hair and turned it under, then carefully rolled the hair as far as she could, twisting the paper ends tight to hold it in place.

"That brush and comb set is so beautiful," I said.

"Your Daddy got it for me."

"The perfume too?" I asked, observing all the matching blue bottles of *Evening in Paris* lined up.

"Yes, he bought me the perfume too."

I felt content. I thought as I snuggled in my own bed with Poochie, "If he didn't love her he wouldn't buy her those special presents." I heard the sound of the spray bottle, and once again smelled the familiar sweet scent that was my mother's.

I woke up once during the night and peeked over to Mommy's bed and was relieved to see her sleeping there and not out for the night. In the morning when I opened my eyes both Mommy and Daddy were in still in bed. I stood looking at Daddy; black hair still slicked down, snoring softly, with a smile peeking from under his mustache. I wished he would always stay smiling and never fight with my mother again. I thought of him smiling at the bar when I found coins in the magic box. I wanted to give him a kiss but was afraid I would wake him. Instead I tiptoed out. Mugsy followed as we passed through the parlor where Ronnie was sleeping on his twin-size roll-away. Sitting on the new chair in the kitchen, I looked out the open window, the elevated train was clacking by, causing a cloud of the pigeons to burst into the air then descend again onto the station's platform. Over the rooftops, I saw the wine garden of Daddy's bar; it was all familiar, but strange. Already hot, the city odors assaulted my nostrils, and I yearned for the smell of grass and honeysuckle. I couldn't wait for everyone to wake up; I wanted to hear my Frank Sinatra records again.

Ronnie was the first one up. We sat in the kitchen eating cereal, and I resumed being the monitor of his sugar use. "Mommy said we don't get enough rations for you to use three spoons of sugar."

"Oh, shut up," he hit me with the newspaper.

"I'm telling Mommy," I yelled.

Mommy came into the kitchen, "Be quiet, you're going to wake your father."

"He used three spoons of sugar. You told me to tell him not to use so much. You tell him, and tell him not to hit me with the newspaper." I was starting to cry.

Daddy came in rubbing his red eyes. "Jesus Christ, what the hell is going on here, can I please get some damn sleep?" he barked looking angrily at Mommy. The three of us got quiet as he turned and went back to the bedroom.

My mother got my clothes and, once dressed, we went across the street to sit on a park bench for a while. Gretchen emerged from the basement with her grandma. Seeing me on the bench, she waved and yelled, "Kathy, I'm so glad you're home, I missed you." They crossed over. "Look how big you got."

"I turned five," I said proudly.

"I turned nine," she beamed.

"I'm twelve," Ronnie mimicked her tone.

Her grandma chatted with Mommy for a few minutes. As they went on their way, Gretchen was waving and saying, "Come down to play."

"She's a nice girl, but she's too old for you to be playing with," Mommy said.

"But we have fun and she is my only good friend," I said as I thought of my country friends, missing them.

"When you start school you'll make lots of new friends with children your own age," Mommy said hugging me.

"I don't know why you like Gretchen, she's fat and ugly," Ronnie said shaking his head.

"She is not."

"Is too."

"Is not."

Mommy snapped. "Stop it, it's time to go back and wake Daddy so we can get going to City Island."

As soon as we opened the door, I saw Daddy at the table, drinking coffee and smoking his Lucky Strikes. Peering from under his red eyes he asked, "Are all of you ready to go?" Mommy said we were, and he went to the bedroom to put on his shirt. I followed to get Poochie and he asked, "How do you like the new furniture?"

"It's very pretty," I said.

"I'm glad you like it. We are going to see grandma and all your cousins, aunts and uncles today."

"Mommy told me," I nodded.

I tried to find something else to say to him, but I didn't know what. Then I burst out and said, "I love to go to City Island." "Good," he smiled with a twinkle in his eye. I hoped he would never be angry again.

We got into Daddy's black Packard, dropped Mugsy at the bar and drove off. When we crossed over the bridge to City Island, the sun reflecting on the Long Island Sound transformed the surface of the water into tiny sparkling crystals. I inhaled the smell of the sea as I watched the seagulls swooping down and then soaring skyward. I felt tears on my cheeks.

"Why are you crying?" asked Ronnie who was sitting with me in the back seat.

"Because it's like being in a movie," I smiled, not being able to stop the tears. Ronnie held my hand and looked out the window too.

At the restaurant the sweet odor of steamed clams and melted butter permeated the large room Daddy rented. I enjoyed dunking the long clams into the butter; My mother kept wiping it off my chin. It was a good thing the waiter gave me a lobster bib or I would have been a mess. The room opened out onto a large wooden deck, and in between kissing relatives, my cousins and I ran in and out all day.

Grandma seemed very old; I hadn't seen her in a long time. She wanted to squeeze my hand. Her thin bony hands made me think of *Hansel and Gretel*. I could tell Daddy liked it when I paid attention to her, so every time I ran past, I put out my hand so she could squeeze it. It became a game and we both would laugh. There were many other relatives, and Mommy took me around to say hello to them. It was hard to hear their names with the band playing. They all kissed her and told her how beautiful she looked. When she laughed her pretty curls bounced. Her soft white dress with little pink flowers seemed to swirl in time with the music. Everyone seemed nice but I had enough kissing and hugging. Besides, I really only knew Daddy's brothers and sisters and my cousins. My cousins were all boys but Ronnie let me hang out with them. I even danced with Louis and bad Albert.

Daddy was having a really good time, clanking glasses, drinking wine, saying *"Salute!"* to everyone as he mingled at different tables. He sat in for the drummer. I thought he was great and was so proud of him when everyone applauded. I think I applauded the loudest. He sat me on his lap and sang right to me, and he even asked me to sing with him. We sang his favorite, *Sentimental Journey*, and everyone applauded some more. Singing with him, I really did feel like Dorothy Lamour with her leading man. I watched him dance with Mommy, his sisters, and his mother. He also danced with me. I put my feet on top of his shoes and we danced the Fox Trot—more applause. Now we were Fred Astaire and Ginger Rogers. That was a happy day!

CHAPTER 15

School Days

On Tuesday, the day after Labor Day, the weather was glorious. The warm Indian summer day made my mother decide to join one of her friends and walk to Fordham Road to shop for my school dress. Kindergarten would start tomorrow. Mrs. Ridberg pushed her infant son in a baby carriage, while her daughter June and I had a great time skipping through the red and golden leaves that had fallen to the ground early this year in Mosholu Park. Occasionally we would take an armful and fling them at each other, watching them drift down. After we crossed the Grand Concourse onto the sidewalk, we had hopping contests all the way—even a few falls and scraped knees didn't stop us. Our mothers chatted together and Mugsy trotted along with us. When we shopped in the stores, he would sit and wait until we would come out again. After several stores, we got to Hearn's where I tried on a pretty purple dress with a ruffled bottom. It reminded me of the kind of dresses Shirley Temple wore in *Curly Top*. Tiny cloth buttons and a belt of the same material fastened in the back made it very form fitting. It was a little more money than Mommy had, but seeing how much I longed to have it, Mrs. Ridberg loaned her the rest.

"I'll pay you back as soon as I can," Mommy told her.

"Don't worry, just treat me to a few beers at the Venetian," she said while rustling my hair. Leaving the store, baby Danny started to shriek and black storm clouds threatened to explode any moment. We all ran for the elevated train and while Mrs. Ridberg tried to calm the screaming baby, two men helped carry the carriage up to the platform. We no sooner got upstairs then the train came, but not before the sky opened up, soaking us all. As we pulled away from the station, I caught a glimpse of Mugsy galloping onto the platform as the subway pulled away. The four subway stops totaled about forty blocks away from where we lived. We had forgotten Mugsy! I started to cry; I thought we would never see him again.

"Please Mommy, we have to find Mugsy," I sobbed in a panic. She kept telling me Mugsy would more than likely find his way home. I was very angry with her for leaving him and kept screaming that we had to go back to get him. I was pounding at the subway car door until the next station. We left Mrs. Ridberg with Danny still screaming and June looked frightened at my outburst. We got off and took the next train back to the Fordham Station, but we didn't see Mugsy anywhere. It was thundering and lightning. I kept calling, "Mugsy, Mugsy!"

Mommy said, "He's probably on his way home already." Mommy was very afraid of lightning and kept ducking into storefronts. We were both soaking wet. I loved Mugsy so much; the thought that I might never see him again made my body rack with uncontrollable sobs. I kept picturing Mugsy looking deserted and worried. I was so upset that I vomited when we got back on the train to go home again. My mother tried to comfort me, and kept telling me he might even beat us home. Upon getting home we didn't find Mugsy, but a good while later he did arrive. I was so relieved when I heard him scratching at our door. I tried to hug and kiss him but he was too excited—all squeals and wiggles. Mommy said laughing, "I think he's trying to bawl us out for leaving him."

This was the same behavior he had whenever we stayed out too long. He had never been a leash dog. He was very smart and independent. When Mugsy had to go out, he would scratch at the apartment door and one of us would open it for him. Coming back, he'd scratch at the outside of our door to get back in. Sometimes he would come right back; other times he would stay out for hours. He would wait at the locked front door for someone to let him in. The other tenants knew that this little black dog with the brown patch over one eye was ours. Then he'd run up and scratch at our apartment door, as usual. If we weren't home, he would leave again to search for us. First, he'd go to my father's bar, then to the Golf bar, third to my mother's friend Eva's, and last to Mrs. Ridberg's. He'd scratch and wait to be let in all of those places, come in, sniff in all the rooms, and then leave without even acknowledging the people who were there. If he didn't find us, he would then wait at our door and really squeal and bark to reprimand us when we got home.

When I finally calmed down, Mommy pressed my new dress and hung it on the bedroom door ready for me to wear to school. I still wasn't feeling very well and after a bath, I went to bed early, content to have Mugsy next to me.

The next morning was to be my very first day of school. I woke up with my two cheeks swollen like a chipmunk. I had the mumps! I couldn't go to school, but insisted I wear the new purple dress to the doctor's office. My mother and the doctor chased me around the table as I shrieked, until he and the nurse finally held me down to give me a large needle in the cheek of my behind. I had been looking forward to school and was disappointed at not being able to start with the rest of the kids. The paper doll book that my mother bought me did not cheer me up. Feeling really sick, I was finally talked into taking off my dress and going to bed.

It was two weeks later when I was finally allowed to go to school. My mother took me to school that day, and then I was on my own. She introduced me to the teacher, Mrs. Archer, and then left me at the door of the classroom. I immediately noticed a wonderful large playhouse in the middle of the room.

Mrs. Archer announced, "Let me introduce Kathy, she couldn't join us sooner because she had the mumps." They said hello to me but everyone stuck to the friends they had already chosen. I felt very left out. I went into the playhouse, which had a little table and chairs in it. When I looked in the mirror before I left my house, I thought I looked so nice in my purple dress and Mary Jane shoes. Now they seemed out of place, I peeked out the playhouse window and saw the other children were dressed in jumpers or skirts with blouses. Only one girl had on a dress and it was wool plaid. Mrs. Archer called to me. "Come, Kathy, I will show you where we keep everything."

She took my hand as she led me to the box with colored chalk, crayons and paper, and pointed out where other things were kept. I chose to draw and drew a picture of Mugsy. When it was rest time, we all had to sit Indian style on the floor and lower our heads down between our knees. It hurt the inside of my legs so bad to stay bent over like this and then an awful thing happened. All the buttons on the back of my dress ripped open. In the silence the pop, pop, pop, was quite loud. Everyone began laughing; I could feel my bottom lip trembling but I made myself hold back the tears. Mrs. Archer got some pins to hold the back of my dress together. Then as I bent down again, rip, rip, rip. The girls giggled and mimicked, "Pop, pop, pop—Rip, rip, rip!"

"Girls, that will be all," Mrs. Archer snapped. Every time she wasn't looking they kept pointing and laughing at my ruined dress. I couldn't wait for the day to be over.

PS 80 was only up the hill and across one street so I came and went by myself. My instructions were to always ask someone to cross me. I saw mothers holding the hands of the children in my class and asked, "Could you please cross me?" Later when I knew my classmates' names, I would call out, "Sam's mother, please cross me," and if I didn't see anyone I knew I would just yell out, "Somebody's mother, please cross me." I pretended to be very adult and independent going by myself, but it was reassuring when one of the mothers would clutch my hand and guide me across the street. I would also use this means to cross back and forth from our apartment house to the park across the street. Decades later when I visited the Bronx, an old neighbor who had been a park bench sitter for years recalled, "I always chuckle when I think of you, so adorable, so self-sufficient, yelling across to the park benches, 'Somebody's mother, please cross me.' I wish I had a dollar for how many times I crossed you myself."

On school nights my mother would comb my hair into two thick neat braids fastened by ribbons so she could stay sleeping in the morning. I was instructed to wake Ronnie and make sure he did not put too much sugar on his Wheaties. He would leave before me, then I would dress myself and say goodbye to Mugsy or sometimes Mugsy would walk with me to school and then go home again. On the way, I would begin unfastening my braids letting my hair loose in my Dorothy Lamour style. Again I thought I looked quite beautiful, but my teacher was not of the same opinion about my hairstyle. All the other girls wore their hair neatly fastened in ribbons or barrettes. She kept writing notes to my mother about my grooming. My mother did give me a few spankings for this and told me to keep my hair in braids, but I just kept loosening them and, somewhere along the way, I got to keep my hair down. Maybe my teacher just thought my mother did not respond or care. Actually, most afternoons when I returned home she wasn't there. I hated that she was drinking again. I could smell beer on her breath, but at least she would now come home to make dinner and she didn't slur her words. For a while she didn't take me with her to the bars so I would come home and play pretend, singing and dancing in front of the large new mirror over the dressing table, or I'd go down to the basement to play with Gretchen. I hadn't made any friends at school yet. There were no play dates made; our household was not very desirable for other children to visit. Gretchen was still the only real friend I had. Even though she stopped hitting me she continued to make me take things from Woolworth's. Unless I did what she said, she threatened to tell about the stealing and our secret games.

One day after school, Gretchen insisted I go with her to see her father because it was his birthday. I was always supposed to stay home and wait for my mother. Her father lived quite a way down on Webster Avenue, a good twelve block walk. Only allowed to cross the streets going to school or to the park, I knew I would get spanked if we were found out. I felt really guilty the whole walk there and back. Including the brief time with her father, we were gone for about two hours. Gretchen didn't want her grandparents to know where she had gone, so neither they nor my mother knew where we were. She said her mother, who only visited Gretchen on occasion, told her that her father was "a no good louse" and she never wanted Gretchen to see him again. Yet, we climbed up four dark flights of stairs to his apartment and she knocked on the door.

A very tall, thin man opened the door and, glaring down, asked, "What are you doing here?" Gretchen squeezed my hand tight.

"I came to see you," she whispered.

"How did you get here?" he growled.

"I walked, Daddy."

"You should not be walking by yourself. Tell your mother to have the guts to bring you, not to send you alone. Go home and don't come here again without her."

"But she didn't send me," Gretchen started to say, but he had already shut the door.

Gretchen cried all the way home. I cried too because I knew it was late and I would be spanked. I also cried for Gretchen because her father was so mean to her. She never even got to give him the present for his birthday. "At least my father was not mean to me," I thought. When we got home my mother and her grandparents were furious. Her grandmother smacked her across the face and my mother started to wham me on my bottom. Gretchen ran over to my mother, "Please don't hit Kathy, it was my entire fault. I made her come with me to see my father." We were told we would not be allowed to play together anymore. We were both crying hard. I didn't have any after school friends and neither did she.

That Halloween I came home to find no one there. I waited awhile for my mother but felt anxious to go out Trick or Treating. I looked at her clothes in the closet and chose one of her dressing gowns. It was a cream colored satin with various shades of scarlet roses and green leaves. I put it on and with my hair flowing and combed over one eye, I thought I looked just like a dark haired Veronica Lake. Carefully putting on my mother's reddest lipstick, I grabbed a shopping bag and off I went to Trick or Treat. There were twin boys in my kindergarten class who lived a few apartment houses away from me. I had a crush on the one named Michael; he played the piano in class. In my living room I would play my Frank Sinatra love songs and pretend I was singing them to him while he played the piano for me. I wanted Michael to see me looking so beautiful. My heart was pounding when I rang his bell, but much to my disappointment only his mother came to the door and gave me a few pennies. Later a couple of nice older kids let me trail along with them, and I collected a lot of loot. I didn't get home until quite late, proudly lugging two large bags full of treats. Mommy was frantically screaming that she had been worried, waiting and looking for me. When she saw her ruined dressing gown, which by now had been dragged for hours over the sidewalks and stairways, she came after me with my father's belt. I could smell beer on her breath as I kept running around the bed. As usual she would miss me and hit her own hand or leg and I would feel badly that she hurt herself, but not bad enough to stay still like Ronnie always did. She did manage to give me a few really hard whacks and I was crying and telling her how sorry I was that I ruined her dressing gown. She took the gown and threw it on the dumbwaiter.

The next day when I saw Gretchen in front of the building, she said, "I found a beautiful dressing gown someone threw out, it's pretty dirty but I bet my grandmother can clean it for dress up." We started to play together again and promised her grandparents and my mother we would not go out of the house, except to the movies.

CHAPTER 16

Katie Did

The City Island party was the last time I remember my mother and my father looking happy together. My mother started drinking heavily again and the fights between the two of them became more frequent and very physical. It seems I stepped between them many more times during this period, but not always before Daddy had already punched her in the eye or had given her a bloody nose. When I would stand in front of her and spread my arms, saying, "Don't you dare hit my mommy again!" Daddy still would get very red in the face, turn away, slam the door and leave. I always thought he would be mad at me the next time he saw me, but he never mentioned it. I don't know exactly what happened that made her start going to the other bars every day and night, but we stopped going into Daddy's bar and went repeatedly to the Golf and Ryan's. Ryan's had a piano and a really nice man called Kokomo Joe. He would spend a lot of time teaching me how to play *Chopsticks* and *Heart of my Heart*. Many of the men would buy Mommy beers, put their arm around her, and laugh and joke with her. I knew Daddy would not like them doing that.

During that time, I remember that my father's mother became ill and he had forbidden my mother to see her. There were many arguments about that. Once he got so mad when she begged him to please let her visit, he threw all the dishes from the table out the window. They crashed, echoing loudly in the alley below. Looking out the parlor window I could see the broken glass scattered over the cement, and saw many of our neighbors looking out their windows as well. Two policemen knocked a short time later and asked me to wait in the bedroom while they stayed to talk to my parents.

Since we weren't going to Daddy's bar, I only saw him asleep in their bed when I woke up in the morning. Mommy was out at night but, again, she always came back before him. When Ronnie was there, he would sleep through the night, but I always tried to stay awake in my bed or on the fire escape and wait until Mommy came home safe. It was on the weekends I saw Daddy when he got up and sat at the kitchen table with those bloodshot eyes, smoking his Lucky Strikes one after another, drinking black coffee, and not really speaking to Mommy or me. If he wanted to tell her something he would say, "Tell your mother she needs to buy razor blades." She would say, "Tell your father I know." I would not say a word for fear I might make him angry with me. When he was ready to leave, he'd throw a dollar bill on the table and slam the door as he went out.

My daily routine was to go to kindergarten, come home, listen to records and play dress up. I still didn't really have any after-school friends. The two girls I was friendly with at school were picked up by their mothers and whisked off to dance or piano lessons. Their mothers also knew each other and no one knew my mother. I often went down to Gretchen's. Although she was somewhat nicer to me, she continued to order me around and insisted we play mom and dad, "doing it," which always made me feel uncomfortable.

The fall flew by, as did Christmas and New Year's. I don't remember much except for highlights. Ronnie actually was not home a lot; either he was sleeping at a friend's or visiting Aunt Mae or Granny in Newark on weekends. He spent his vacations with Aunt Helen and Uncle Bill. In fact, that winter vacation Ronnie went to visit them in Baltimore, where Uncle Bill had been transferred to work as the regional manager of Social Security. Ronnie came back with many small brown 78-speed records that he recorded. I didn't know it was very popular to record these 78's in a booth at the Penny Arcade. I thought that someone believed that because Ronnie was so talented, he was specially chosen to make these recordings. I listened to them in awe of Ronnie having his voice on a real record. I dreamily played them, my favorite being Ronnie singing Al Jolson's *Dixie,* "Rock-a-bye your baby, with a Dixie melody. When you croon, croon a tune, from the heart of Dixie...." As I listened to Ronnie sing, I thought he sang just as well as anyone on the radio, except Frank Sinatra, of course. No one else could sing like Sinatra.

That spring, I recall Ronnie had to go to the hospital for a hernia operation. I had no idea what that was and I was afraid he would die. Hospitals did not allow children to visit, so I pictured him really sick. I was so relieved when Mommy told me she was planning a surprise party for his return. Aunt Mae, Aunt Jean, Granny, and all the aunts and uncles from Daddy's family, our cousins, Eva Prokapchak, and a few other friends were all jammed into our apartment, waiting to surprise him. Granny only spoke in Lithuanian, so I could not understand what she, Aunt Mae and Aunt Jean were saying. Granny kept kissing me and calling me *Mažiukas,* little one. With her dark flowered dress draped over her fat body, thick beige cotton stockings and old lady laced black shoes, she looked very foreign. I kept trying to get away from them, but Aunt Mae kept holding onto me by the hand. We watched out the bedroom window as my mother and Ronnie came down the elevated train stairs. I was so excited as everyone scattered to hide. I stooped behind the parlor door with Mugsy nervously wagging his tail beside me. It was very crowded and as we heard the door open, everyone yelled "SURPRISE!"—then clustered around Ronnie. I could hear Granny saying *"Mažiukas, Mažiukas"* to Ronnie. "Granny!" Ronnie burst out, pleased. Mugsy rushed forward and was yelping but I was squashed in the middle, trying to push through the barrier of grownups, sweating in my pink organdy dress and unable to see Ronnie.

"I want my brother, I want to see Ronnie! Ronnie! Ronnie! I want to see you!" I screamed out with tears running down my cheeks. I was so thrilled when he broke through to me and said, "Where is my little Katie Did?" He reached for my hand and held onto it as he made his rounds to kiss everyone hello. I was so happy that he was well and home. He had never called me Katie Did before, but he did from that day on. I was so proud to be his little "Katie Did," it made me feel very special. For years to come when I listened to the crickets in Picky Pine make their katie did sounds, I thought of Ronnie. Mommy seemed really glad to see Daddy's family again. They all hugged and kissed each other a lot but my mother kept crying. I asked her why she was crying.

"I'm so happy Ronnie's home," she said as she kissed his cheek, "and I'm very glad to see everyone again," she smiled through her tears. My father only took a few minutes off from working at the bar. He brought a large platter of fancy little triangular sandwiches he'd made; he even made bologna ones for Ronnie. He shook Ronnie's hand, said hello to everyone, then he left. We all had the sandwiches and soda and a piece of the big white butter cream cake with yellow flowers that had WELCOME HOME RONNIE written in blue letters. When Ronnie cut the cake he gave the only three flowers to Albert, Louis and me.

Several hours later, Granny and my aunts left to make their long trip back to Newark. Ronnie hugged them all, but my grandmother kept coming back for another kiss from him, which he was only too glad to give. We all watched from the window and waved until they ascended the elevated stairs to the train.

Louis and Albert stayed a while and the four of us played Parcheesi together. It was the first time Ronnie let me play that game with them. When they left with their mother, Aunt Ola, Ronnie and I waved from the window as they also disappeared up onto the elevated train platform. That was the last time I remember a gathering in our apartment.

A few weeks before school broke for summer vacation, I remember having to bring a note to my teacher to excuse me for a day. Mommy, Daddy, Ronnie and I had to go to the courthouse on the Grand Concourse. Mommy looked so nice in a beige suit and Daddy had on a suit as well. I had no idea why we were there but it seemed like a very long time sitting on a long dark wooden bench while my mother and father were on the other side of the door, which was half glass, marked "Family Court." That door opened and out trotted a woman with a blue suit, gray hair and glasses. She motioned for us to slide apart and sat between Ronnie and me. Then she took my hand in her sweaty palm and asked, "Katherine (I hated to be called that, it made me feel like the person was angry at me), would you like to live with your mother or your father?" I wanted to say my mother but I was afraid Daddy would find out and get really mad at me. So I said, "I want to live with both of them," as I tried to pull my hand from hers.

She held tight and insisted, "No, you must choose one or the other, Katherine," she said staring into my eyes, "your mother or your father?"

I did not answer. I was afraid of her and I wished she would let go of my hand, but instead she tightened her grip again and raised her eyebrows in question. She just kept staring at me and waiting. I still didn't answer. Finally, she turned to look at Ronnie with the same question on her face.

Ronnie seemed upset when he answered, "I want to live with my grandmother in Newark."

She was shaking her head and telling us we didn't understand. "You only have two choices; you must pick either your mother or your father."

I was very scared. I thought she was going to make the choice for us if we didn't answer, so I whispered, "I don't want to be without my mother."

We sat in silence for a few minutes, then sobs sprung from my throat. She nodded and patted my hand, got up and walked across the hall back into the room.

Ronnie put his arm around me. "Don't worry, Katie Did," everything will be all right. Mommy said they wouldn't separate us."

"But where are we going to live? Do I have to live with Granny, too?" I asked Ronnie. I didn't want to live with my grandmother, I couldn't even understand her. I didn't tell Ronnie because I knew how much he loved her. Aunt Mae was always saying to Ronnie, "Granny loves you so much, she is more like your mother than your real mother. After all, she really brought you up."

That day we all went home together. My father drove us in his car, but no one spoke, he just dropped us in front of the house. Over the next few days I kept asking Mommy what was going to happen to all of us. She said it would be all right, but she would get so upset, I stopped asking. I also wondered where Mugsy would live. I told him we would never leave him, I remembered the movie *Lassie*, and how sad and lonely Lassie was when he was separated from his family.

We went back to the courthouse one more time before we went to Picky Pine for the summer. This time Aunt Mae, Aunt Helen, and Aunt Bridget (Daddy's sister) were at the courthouse. Everyone took turns going into the room while we others waited quietly in the marble hallway on the brown bench. When it was our turn, Ronnie and I went into the room together while everyone stayed outside. The same gray haired woman in the same navy suit was seated at a large brown wooden table. Next to her was a very large gray haired man who looked like Santa without the beard. He leaned forward, stared at us and asked in a whisper, "If you had to choose, who would you feel more comfortable living with?" He looked at me and then at Ronnie. "Would you want to be with your mother or your father?" he whispered again. I thought I'd better say what I wanted now. I was afraid he would decide for me, so I whispered back, "My Mommy." Ronnie answered in his regular voice, "My grandmother." The man nodded, thanked us, and then told us to please go outside again. Aunt Helen, Aunt Mae, Aunt Bridget and my mother and father went in next. They were in there a long time. Finally, Aunt Helen came out with a smile and said, "I have good news, the judge and your father decided to give your mother another chance to show she is a 'fit mother.' She promised not to drink and your father promised not to hit her anymore. So you can all stay together." I yelled "Hooray" very loudly. A passing man put his fingers over his lips and told me to shush. Ronnie winked at me and said, "I told you everything would be all right."

Aunt Bridget came out next. She gave Ronnie and me a big hug and kiss. "I'm very happy for you both, God bless all of you, you will be in my prayers," she said in a very kind voice. Needing to get back to her family, she walked swiftly down the long corridor, waving to us until she turned down the marble stairwell.

Then Daddy drove us home, but no one said very much, except for talk about what they were going to make for dinner. Aunt Helen said she would make a stew. Aunt Mae was going to bake a cake. They were both staying over because in two days Ronnie was graduating from PS 80. Daddy didn't sleep at home so there would be room for them. I thought we might have another party for Ronnie after his graduation, but instead Aunt Mae, Aunt Helen, Mommy and I went to Schweller's for a celebration dinner. We had just been seated at a U shaped booth in the back when Aunt Helen stood up and waved to my father who had come across the street for a few minutes. "Congratulations, Ronnie," he said. He shook Ronnie's hand and presented him with a box wrapped in silver foil. "Wow!" Ronnie exclaimed when he opened the box. It was a Parker fountain pen with his initials on it.

"That's to use at Dewitt Clinton High School in the fall. Have a good summer." "Be a good girl," he said to me as he patted my head. I nodded and didn't know what to say. He winked at my aunts and turned to leave.

"Bye, Daddy," I yelled and waved as he went through the door.

He waved without turning back and said, "Bye, bye. Tommy, you be a good girl, too." Everyone looked at Mommy. She nodded, looking grim.

"Eva, don't get upset, let's just order," Aunt Helen suggested.

"I see the princess has her family with her tonight," said Sam giving me a wink. "This is Sam, my favorite waiter, he always takes good care of me." I introduced my aunts. My mother knew him and he had seen Ronnie a few times. "Ronnie just graduated," I proudly announced. Sam shook his hand and then took our orders. I had my usual chopped chicken liver and hot turkey sandwich. Ronnie ordered prime rib of beef. It was much more fun to be eating at Schweller's with everyone instead of by myself. After dinner, Sam brought Ronnie a white carnation and a big piece of Nesselrode pie with five forks. "The pie is on me," he smiled. While swinging his pen, Sam led us in singing "Congratulations to you" to the tune of "Happy Birthday." Ronnie beamed.

The next morning, Uncle Bill picked up Aunt Helen, Ronnie, Mugsy and me. We were off once more in the rumble seat. Aunt Mae would take the train back to Newark later. I managed to hold back my tears as I kept waving to my mother until we turned the corner. "Well, Katie Did, we are off to Picky Pine," Ronnie smiled as he put his arm around me and started singing, "Rock-a-bye your baby with a Dixie melody...." Then the tears came running down my cheeks. I wiped them with the new hankie Mommy gave me. Mugsy wagged his tail and his ears blew in the wind as we picked up speed.

CHAPTER 17

Lariats

Picky Pine welcomed us with the blue and white hydrangeas in full bloom. As we drove by the white wagon wheels and umbrella trees, the sweet little white cottage, with its dark green awnings shielding the sun on the intensely hot June day, promised a glorious summer. Ronnie unfastened Mugsy, who leaped out of the rumble seat, running into the grass to relieve himself. A calm came over me as we entered the small house that was my summer mansion. I unpacked my clothes and took Poochie out of the suitcase to position him on the maple pull-out loveseat where we would sleep. Aunt Helen made dinner and afterward we listened in the stillness of the country to a few radio programs. One was *The Shadow*. Sleep came easily; the darkness was peaceful and soothing, as were the sounds of the katie dids.

The next several weeks flew by, yet each day seemed deliciously endless. Being almost six, I had a little more freedom. I'd walk alone to the very end of the road and visit Uncle Bill's sister Jessie and her husband Uncle Andy. Aunt Jessie liked my visits. We'd sit on rocking chairs in her screened in porch, drinking lemonade and eating cookies she had always just baked. Rocking back and forth she'd talk to me as long as I would listen about her family; deep sighs of fondness preceded every family member she spoke of. The very manner of speech that annoyed my Uncle Bill fascinated me. Aunt Jessie and Uncle Andy did not have children; however, they loved their nieces and nephews as though they were their own. Halfway between Aunt Helen's house and Aunt Jessie's was Uncle George Carmer's large piece of property with the pond and apple orchard. The orchard was still where all the kids hung out, including his grandchildren, locals, and other visiting city kids like me. We numbered about eight or ten, depending upon who was on vacation at the time. That year, Uncle George also built a little wooden refreshment stand. It was a good place to be sheltered from the hot sun or rain and housed a single cooler, which contained bottles of soda and lemonade. The drinks were ours for the taking. It became like a tiny clubhouse where we'd all gather and talk. Mostly it was frequented by his grandchildren, Lynne and Eddie, Bessie and her sisters and me. We'd hang out there after swimming in the pond until dinnertime, sometimes playing the card game War with a double deck.

After dinner, most of us would go back to the apple orchard to sit, play tag or hide and seek, or just listen to more of Uncle George's wonderful stories. His warm and friendly wife with blue gray hair and buck teeth, Aunt Beulah, still brought home left-over donuts from her job at the bakery. We'd happily bite into the sugar covered or jelly donuts, our smiles framed with smears of red jelly or white powdered sugar. While wiping our sticky fingers on our clothes, we'd sit wide-eyed while Uncle George would tell us more of his real life tales about how he discovered and settled in Carmersville or how he bulldozed the earth to make the pond we swam in. They were always intriguing stories and we'd do a lot of oohing and aahing. Aunt Beulah would give out lit punks to ward off the mosquitoes.

Aunt Jean and Aunt Mae came that July, bringing with them my soon to be one year old cousin Billy. It was fun to play with this little blond baby, even though he did seem to cry an awful lot. When he sucked his thumb, he would insert it in his mouth holding one hand over the other. They all swooned over him and thought it was the cutest thing they had ever seen. "Blowing his bugle," they called it. His first birthday was July thirteenth, two days before my sixth, so we had a joint party on his birthday. I felt neglected because they made a big fuss over him, even Aunt Helen. My mother had not made it down to Picky Pine, but she sent a gift of two pretty sundresses with Aunt Mae.

Except for my birthday, I had a really good summer, picking huckleberries, swimming in the pond with my friends and Mugsy, eating Aunt Helen's great meals, running barefooted with the kids, or playing my records on the old Victrola in the back house. Ronnie still worked as a caddy at the golf course so he was gone until dinner.

In early August, Ronnie and I were told we had to go back to the Bronx because the family court people wanted to see us again. We were both going to return to Picky Pine afterward, but only Ronnie went back. Mommy and Daddy decided to keep me in the Bronx because it was too long a trip to expect someone to pick us up by car. Ronnie was old enough to take the train himself, plus he wanted to go back to his caddy job.

The city was hot and lonely in August. I missed my summer friends, Aunt Helen, Uncle George, and especially Ronnie, very much. At least Mugsy was home with me. Gretchen was away so my time was spent between going to the movies and Daddy's bar. The summer movies were mostly about the war or detective stories, *Sam Spade* and the *Thin Man*, only shown in black and white. I walked up the block to the Tuxedo Movie Theatre while Mommy hung out at Daddy's bar. Somehow Daddy no longer seemed to mind her drinking there and kept an eye on her. She was afraid of the court people so she did what he wanted. As always, he'd tell her when she couldn't have any more beer and when to take me home. At the bar, I still listened to all of my favorite Frank Sinatra records on the jukebox. I also liked to dance to the Andrews Sisters' songs, especially *Rum and Coca-Cola*.

A really big event occurred that summer—VJ Day on August 15, 1945. The war with Japan was officially over and I was in the Bronx to celebrate. The war was over! The day was glorious with the sun shining down on exuberant crowds. The Army greens, Marine blues and Navy whites, intermingled with the red, white and blue that many of the celebrants wore, made Jerome Avenue in the Bronx very colorful. Masses of people were hugging and kissing, kissing and smiling, smiling and crying with joy. In the middle of Jerome Avenue, a local band played Glen Miller tunes. Adding to the cacophony of sounds, radios boomed from the open doors of local businesses, car horns honked, whistles blew, and the ra-ta-ta of noisemakers filled the air. People were dancing the jitterbug, throwing confetti, waving flags, and swirling lariats in the breeze. It seemed like New Year's Eve—but better.

I wore my red and blue plaid, short sleeved dress that day, one that Mommy had sent to Picky Pine for my birthday. I was always very fussy about what I wore. I still remember being three and refusing to go out in a yellow pinafore because my nipples were showing. My mother said, "You are going to wear that dress or not go out at all." I stubbornly chose to sit on a chair in the hot parlor all day, rather than be seen on the street so exposed. To this day, I still will not wear yellow. So there I was, a fashion conscious six year old in my red and blue dress, squeezed in the middle of the crowds on the street right outside of my father's bar, watching the red, white and blue lariats lassoing in the breeze. I loved lariats; their colorful crepe paper swirling in a ring as you held it by the string, swinging your arm in large circles. I decided to get some money to buy one of my own.

Pushing through the crowd, saying "excuse me" a lot, I went into Daddy's bar, which was mobbed. My father and uncles were trying to keep up with the drink orders. It was hot in there and smelled of whiskey, beer, and cigarette smoke. As I inched my way through to my mother's barstool where she sat with her beer and a cigarette, the roughness of suits and uniforms rubbed against my bare arms and face.

"Mommy, Mommy! I need to buy a lariat." I never said I wanted, I always said I needed. "Mommy! Mommy! Mommy!" I yanked on her dress. With her hair long again and her soft white flowered red dress, she looked like a movie star. "Mommy, I need to buy a lariat." Holding my hand still, her head thrown back as she laughed at something the man on the next barstool said, she finally looked down, patted my hand and gave me a quarter. "Bring back the change, Sweetie," she cooed.

I clutched the quarter in my fist and pushed out of the bar and around the corner to Mrs. Schmidt's tiny candy store. I could see the lariats through the sliding glass doors on the lower shelves. All the red, white and blue were gone. I waited anxiously for Mrs. Schmidt to come and open the doors so I could get my lariat. "What can I do for you, young lady?"

"May I please have a lariat?"

"A lariat, sure, and what color would you like?"

I had already decided on pink but the word would not come out of my mouth and I heard myself say green. Green was my favorite color but I thought pink would be more festive and closer to red. "How much are they?" I asked.

"A nickel," she said, taking out the green.

"I think I'll have a pink and a yellow, too." I thought pink, green and yellow were as close as I could get to red, white and blue. She handed me yellow and pink. Now I was holding three lariats...the colors looked so pretty together. It was the end of the war! I was so excited. I could already imagine the circles of different colors in the air. Having no pockets in my dress, I ran back to the bar to give my mother the change. Squeezing through the crowd, I could hardly wait to get outside again and swirl my lariats. Finally reaching my mother, I squealed. "Mommy, Mommy, I got pink, green and yellow." Guzzling her beer and still laughing, she stopped short and looked at the dime I just handed her.

"I didn't tell you to buy three. As soon as we get home you are going to get it with the strap."

I went outside with my lariats, but the threat of the spanking definitely put a damper on my mood. I started to swirl my lariats, but only having two arms and hands I could only manage two at a time. I swirled the pink and green. I thought, "Maybe if I only bought two, Mommy wouldn't be so angry at me." I wished Ronnie were there to celebrate with me.

A boy about my age was standing next to me smiling and looking up at my swirling lariats. I gave him my yellow one, it looked nice against his blue suit, and I could only swirl two anyway. His mother and father both thanked me. His name was David, David Goldberg. David and I both swirled and swirled the lariats until our arms felt like they would fall off. His parents occasionally came to our rescue as our lariats collided and tangled together. During the time we spent together I pretended I was his sister. I thought to myself, I am Kathy Goldberg. The four of us stayed together for hours until his parents announced they had to leave for supper. "Thank you," David said as he handed me back the yellow lariat. "You can keep it," I said. He burst into smiles and then held both his parents' hands as he skipped off waving to me and they disappeared into the crowd

I realized I was very hungry. Mommy and Daddy sent me across the street to eat at Schweller's, where I ordered my usual on my father's bill. I always sat in the corner booth so I could look out at the whole restaurant and be with my waiter Sam. Today I had to wait a little while since Schweller's was busier than usual, filled with families eating out to celebrate. Although Sam was always cheerful, today he was especially happy and still found time to tell me jokes, even as busy as he was. He always served my food with a royal bow. Today he called me his "special little princess," and I felt like one when I left.

After dinner, I went back across the street to my father's bar. Daddy gave me a lot of nickels, so while waiting for Mommy I played Frank Sinatra songs on the jukebox. Sinatra and I sang *Blue Skies* together, blocking out the loudness of the bar. He sang it much better than Bing Crosby. "Blue skies, smiling at me, nothing but blue skies do I see...."

It was late into the night before we left for home. By now my mother could hardly walk straight. Mugsy was waiting at the door jumping and frantically barking to "bawl us out" for being gone so long. After we both petted him, I then braced myself for the battle, my mother running after me with the strap, me jumping over her big bed, my mother tripping and accidentally hitting herself in between hitting me. But she must have forgotten all about the spanking I was supposed to get, because she said, "Sweetie, get yourself ready for bed." I was Sweetie again! Upon getting into bed she began kissing me. Reeking of the familiar sour smell of beer, she held onto my junior bed rail for support. For once the beer was my ally.

The war was over. Tonight air raid sirens would not awaken me or make Mugsy bark and wail. No more crouching behind the couch to hide from the Japanese until the all-clear siren sounded. I could hardly wait for the summer to end and Ronnie to come home. I missed him. "Now we will live happily ever after," I told Poochie and Mugsy as we cuddled together and fell asleep.

CHAPTER 18

Goodbye

We didn't live happily ever after. My father was always angry and my mother often had bruises. I don't remember very much of the rest of 1945, I guess I wanted to shut it all out. Ronnie was a freshman at Dewitt Clinton High School. I was almost seven when I was in the second grade at P.S. 80 with Mrs. Hawkney, a strict and nasty teacher. This gray-haired witch managed to call each one in the class at least once to stand in front of the blackboard. I can't recall exactly why I was summoned up, but I do know I went up twice. Twice! She would have us stand straight with head erect and our back to the blackboard. With her bony hand she clutched our chin and thrust our heads up and backward so it hit hard and loudly against the blackboard. This hurt and was humiliating, because in addition the class laughed at whoever was getting punished. I also remember a substitute teacher, named Mrs. Tom, sharply screeching, "Katherine, come up here." When I arrived in front of the class, she snapped, "Put out both hands, palms down." She then slammed the ruler over my knuckles several times. I later learned my crime had been pulling up my knee socks instead of giving her lesson my undivided attention.

That Christmas is a blur. I'm sure we must have had a live tree. My mother always decorated it meticulously for hours. She'd apply hundreds of strands of tinsel, which she called rain, so that the large multicolored lights shimmered softly through the coat of silver. The smell of the fresh evergreen filled the air. She'd play Bing Crosby's *White Christmas* over and over, carefully moving the arm of our phonograph so she wouldn't scratch the record. My mother and I would sit for hours comforted by the music and the glow of our spruce Christmas tree.

In February of 1946, I began Sunday school, taught by the nuns at Saint Ann's Church on Gunhill Road in preparation to receive my First Holy Communion in May. Although it was called Sunday school, we went several days after school as well as after the 9:00 o'clock mass on Sunday morning. Mass was long and church was always crowded. There was lots of sitting, standing and kneeling while the priest spoke in Latin. The Gospel and the sermon were the only English spoken and both were very boring. Afterward we marched through a courtyard to classrooms. I was glad I went to PS 80 instead of parochial school; I found the nuns and the priests very threatening, even worse than Mrs. Hawkney. We learned about God. He watched over us, was always with us, and knew everything. Gretchen still had me taking items from the Five-and-Ten, so I was filled with the dread of God's disapproval, especially since I was aware I would have to confess these sins to the priest when I had my first confession.

My movie going was now mostly limited to Saturday and Sunday afternoons because of the busy week. There were not as many big Technicolor musicals as there used to be. I missed them. Instead, there were many black and white movies with detective and murder stories, but I still enjoyed them, often sitting on the edge of my seat in anticipation. I was disappointed to see Ginger Rogers in a movie called *I'll Be Seeing You*—without dancing! It was about her falling in love with a shell-shocked soldier. It also was not the same seeing Shirley Temple as her niece, all grown up. But the song *I'll Be Seeing You* stayed with me—it was a haunting tune. One day while at the Golf bar, I was so happy to find it in the jukebox sung by Frank Sinatra! I played it over and over and learned all the lyrics. The Tuxedo also showed a lot of the *Tarzan* pictures with Johnny Weissmuller as Tarzan, Maureen O'Sullivan as Jane, and Chita the monkey as himself. At home I would fantasize that the natives captured me and just before they were ready to torture me, Tarzan came to my rescue. The newsreels showed the atom bomb exploding into a giant mushroom in Japan; it was terrifying. I had dreams of the Bronx being bombed and all of us dying by burning to death. I don't know which frightened me more, learning about the bomb or the eternal fires of hell.

After school I went with my mother to the Golf and other bars. She started going to them again even though Daddy had ordered her not to. I imagine this is one of the causes of Daddy's anger getting worse and why he was hitting her a lot more.

One morning I sat down in our small white and yellow kitchen after being drawn out of my sleep by the smell of frying bacon. Daddy was sitting at his end of the table, crouched over a cup of black coffee, wearing a sleeveless tee shirt. His bloodshot eyes darted angrily at Mommy as she quietly moved from the stove, to the fridge, to the cabinets. Not wanting to look directly at either one of them, I kept my eyes fixed on the Mexican border in the middle of the wall.

No one said "Good morning" to me. I wasn't even sure they knew I was there, until Mommy put a bowl of oatmeal on the table in front of me. She forgot the spoon, so I just sat there, pretending it was too hot and kept blowing lightly on it. She went back to the stove, putting the eggs and strips of bacon on a plate. I heard the toast pop up behind me, then the scratching of the knife as my mother buttered it. She then put the two plates in front of Daddy. He looked at them and suddenly his chair screeched against the floor as he slid backward on it. Standing, he grabbed the knife and thrust it down into his toast, while his left hand swept the dish of bacon and eggs off the table, sending it flying upward and crashing down loudly onto the linoleum floor. It all happened so fast I didn't even realize that I had jumped out of my chair and hid behind the kitchen doorframe until Daddy stormed past me. My mother just stood by the window as the elevated train drowned out the sounds of his slamming the door and the drawers in the bedroom.

A few minutes later Daddy charged out of the apartment, shutting the door with such force that Mommy and I both jumped. Leaving the food and broken dishes on the floor, Mommy slumped down onto a chair and buried her head in her arms. I knew she was sobbing by the way her body was shaking. Going over to her, I gently rubbed circles on her back. Looking up I saw egg yolk slowly oozing down from the Mexican sombreros.

About a week later, my mother came to get me at school. Mrs. Hawkney joined us in the school corridor while Mommy told her we were moving that very day, therefore, I would not be in her class or going to PS 80 anymore. I was in shock. Where were we going? My mother was mentioning Ronnie's name (our last names were different). Mrs. Hawkney began cooing affectionately, telling Mommy what a great kid he was, and how much she had liked him. I wondered if she had known he was my brother, perhaps I would have been exempt from the blackboard head knocks. She ran her hand over my head and told me what a lovely child I was and how much she would miss me. I didn't believe her for one minute, but part of me didn't want to say goodbye and leave her class.

Mommy said we needed to hurry and we walked swiftly out the door and the two blocks to our apartment house.

"Where are we going, Mommy?"

"We're going to Granny's house," she answered, offering nothing more.

"Did the court tell you that Ronnie and I had to go live with Granny?" I asked in a panic.

"No, this is what I decided to do," she said.

"For how long?' I gulped trying to keep up with her pace.

"We'll see," she said. I hated that "We'll see" answer. Although it was cold out, I found myself sweating and suddenly feeling sick and almost too afraid to ask, "Are you coming with us?"

"Yes, we are all going," she answered.

I was relieved but felt myself feeling physically worse and worse. "I don't feel well, Mommy," I said, now sobbing.

She stopped for a moment, looked down at me and then continued at a hurried pace, "You'll be all right, Sweetie," she said.

Parked in front of our building was a dilapidated old truck with my cousins' Tootsie's and Stella's husbands inside. Because they were grownups, I called them Uncle. Uncle Stew was in the driver's seat. Stella's husband, Uncle Kangro, was loading our dresser into the already filled truck. Ronnie and Mugsy came down the stairs and got into the back of the old dirty truck where Mommy already had lifted me. Gretchen came out to the sidewalk with her grandmother and grandfather. Mommy hugged both of Gretchen's grandparents and let me lean over to kiss Gretchen goodbye. We were both crying. I wanted to get out of the truck, but Mommy said we had to go quickly in case Daddy came because he would stop us. My mother stayed in the front seat with Uncle Stew and Uncle Kangro joined us on the floor in the back.

"Does Daddy know we are going?" I asked. Mommy just shook her head and told me to sit on the floor of the truck and pulled Poochie from a shopping bag and handed him to me. "Do you have my records and all my things?" I shouted in a panic as the truck lurched forward. She nodded and put up her hand in a keep quiet signal. I clutched Poochie tightly as the truck moved noisily to the corner of Mosholu Parkway, leaving our apartment house behind. I thought of the kitchen wallpaper with the Mexicans in big sombreros. I wondered about all my other treasured belongings. Did we have the *Alice in Wonderland* and the Frank Sinatra records? I knew it was not the time to ask Mommy right now. She was craning her head out the window and taking long drags on her Pall Mall as she looked to the left down Jerome Avenue toward Daddy's bar. I, too, looked toward the Venetian. Part of me wanted to see Daddy running after us and part of me was terrified he would. I could also see Schweller's sign across the street. Schweller's. "Sam won't know where I went," I thought anxiously.

We then made a left on Jerome Avenue until I could no longer see Daddy's bar or Schweller's. I turned to Ronnie; he was looking to the right. From Jerome Avenue you could see Dewitt Clinton High School on the Concourse. I noticed silent tears rolling down Ronnie's cheeks. I think this may have been the first time I ever saw him cry. He was also very quiet. When I reached for his hand, his tears rolled freely as he tried to stifle his sobs. Now we were both crying. Mugsy barked as we drove off. The fumes from the truck were making me feel even sicker, as was Mommy's and Uncle Stew's smoking in the front. My mother was silent except for the occasional exhale on her Pall Malls.

Mugsy paced back and forth for a while and finally lay down with his snout resting on a box. He didn't look like he felt very well either. Ronnie kept holding my hand but he stayed very quiet. This was it; we were really going to live with Granny in Newark, leaving behind my friend Gretchen and my Daddy. We were in for a long and bumpy ride.

My mother at 9 years old (1920)

My mother (front) at 16 years old with
her sisters Jean and Mae (1927)

My father and his mother

My father behind his bar at the Venetian (early 1940's)

Uncle Tony (left) with my father holding
Tiny who was Mugsy's mother

My bother Ronnie in Newark with his cat

My great grandmother, mother and grandmother with Ronnie

Me at 18 months old

My mother holding me at Picky Pine

Picky Pine

Aunt Helen

Part II

CHAPTER 19

Newark, New Jersey

Rush hour and lack of highways, except for the Pulaski Skyway, made our trip on that cold February night seem as if it would never end. But after about three hours of knocking around in the back of the old truck, we finally exited in Newark onto Market Street in the Ironbound section, where it was desolate except for several factories. As we drove past them, my mother pointed out the Ballantine Brewery. I certainly was very familiar with Ballantine Beer—and most other brands for that matter.

On Market Street after we passed Riverbank Park, directly across from the Passaic River, we turned onto Jackson Street. The four story wooden apartment house where my grandmother lived was the first building after the Esso gas station on the corner of Market and Jackson Streets. Across Market Street, the Jackson Street Bridge loomed, separating Newark from Harrison. Attached to my grandmother's house was another identical building where black families lived, then an empty lot before a railroad trestle that crossed overhead on every street. Penn Station, Newark, less than ten blocks away, separated downtown Newark from the four-square mile Ironbound section, nicknamed "Down Neck" for the curve of the Passaic River.

It was dark out and everything looked dreary, not at all like Mosholu Parkway. Diagonally across from my grandmother's house, two huge billboards sat on a broken foundation of what used to be a building. Directly across the street was an empty lot, next to which was a commercial Portuguese bread bakery. The sweet smell of fresh bread baking stood in contrast to the moldy porches of the dilapidated wooden apartment houses behind the empty lot. Except for the color of the traffic lights, everything was dark brown.

When we got down from the truck, our limbs were stiff from the long ride. Mugsy desperately ran to a tree and lifted his leg, then leaped up the four stoop stairs to follow us inside to my grandmother's first floor apartment. With a babushka on her head, Granny clutched her thick sweater to shield herself from the cold and greeted us with a puckered kiss saying "Mažiukas" to Ronnie and me. She seemed so very foreign. During our previous visits, I could hardly wait to go home. I didn't want to live here and did not want to live with her.

We entered into the first hallway door that led to her parlor. The other door at the end of the hallway that opened into Granny's kitchen was the more commonly used entrance. Uncle Kangro and Stew brought our belongings into the parlor, kissed us all goodbye and left right away. Inside, Granny's house seemed even stranger by night than I remembered. Mugsy, having sniffed around the rooms, finally jumped onto the parlor's green studio couch, curled up into a ball and nestled against one of the three back cushions. "This will be Ronnie's bed," said Granny in Lithuanian, with my mother translating for me. The railroad rooms were all very small.

I followed Granny and Mommy into the bedroom. Against the back wall was a very high black iron bed with a cabinet hanging on the wall centered above the tubular headboard. The door of the cabinet had a crucifix in stained glass, inside were little shelves on which sat a little glass dish and a tiny bottle of oil. They were used, I learned, to give the sacrament of Extreme Unction to the dying. Mommy told me that she and Granny would share this bed and she would sleep on the side closest to my bed that was parallel to theirs. Mine was a very narrow twin against the wall nearest the parlor. High above my bed was one of the large interior windows that brought in air from the parlor. Two very large brown wooden dressers on high legs were the only other pieces of furniture in the room. One was placed against the far wall at the foot of the iron bed and the other on the back wall next to my grandmother's side of the bed. An old steamer trunk covered with several long scarves was against the wall under another high interior window between the bedroom and kitchen. Granny's shrines to various saints were on top of the chests of drawers in the bedroom. The flickering of the vigil lights made the atmosphere eerie. My mother interpreted while Granny identified the saints on the dressers: Saint Teresa (known as "The Little Flower"), Saint Anthony, Saint Agnes, the Blessed Virgin Mary, and the Sacred Heart of Jesus Christ. Sepia photos of family members, most of whom were deceased, hung in dark oval frames on the wall. It was all disturbing to me. I didn't want to be here and sleep in this room.

I clutched my little bear Poochie as they beckoned me to the kitchen. Ronnie was sitting in the rocking chair wedged between the kitchen table and a little table that supported a small RCA Radio. He was listening to Martin Block's *The Make Believe Ballroom Time,* singing along with the theme song. Whenever Ronnie was upset, he put the radio on loud and sang every song. A blast of heat hit me as I entered the kitchen. It was very hot because the large black iron coal stove was the only source of heat for all three rooms. The heat traveled through those large, high interior windows, though the parlor always remained quite cold.

Granny said we could eat if we were hungry and put a large pot of mashed potatoes on the table. I asked to go to the bathroom first. It was a small cubicle positioned between the stove and the kitchen sink in the rear corner of the kitchen. The walls were dark yellow and sweating from the cold outside. There was just a toilet bowl and a chain hanging from the tank above it for flushing, which I could not reach. I could no longer hold back the tears. Mommy came in to flush and assured me she would lengthen the chain for me the very next day. She hugged me and said, "Everything will be all right. We have to "bide our time, don't cry, Sweetie." "Bide our time" was another one of my mother's frequent expressions. I tried to stifle my sobs as Granny brought a little stool so I could reach the kitchen sink and handed me brown Octagon soap.

"We use Sweetheart Soap in the Bronx," I said to Granny.

Granny said something I couldn't understand, and Mommy translated. "The water is nice and warm because Granny just heated the water tank," as she pointed to a cylinder next to the coal stove.

"We will buy some Sweetheart Soap tomorrow. Sweetheart Soap for my Sweetie."

I sat at the white porcelain table on one of the three dark wooden spindled chairs and stared at the enamel pot of potatoes. Ronnie had already put a few heaping spoonfuls on his plate and was humming and eating while he rocked back and forth in the chair. Mommy asked Ronnie to lower the radio a little. I realized that Ronnie could understand Granny's language. So for the rest of dinner, if you call potatoes dinner, they all spoke Lithuanian.

My mother kept talking and talking and smoking cigarette after cigarette. Granny would comment occasionally but mostly listened. I had asked what else we were having and Mommy said, "Just eat your potatoes." Actually they were very good, but this didn't seem like a dinner to me. I thought of Schweller's and eating my chopped chicken liver and hot turkey sandwiches with gravy, then crossing back across the street to Daddy's bar to play the jukebox. I wondered if Daddy knew we were gone yet. Part of me hoped he would come and take us all home; the other part of me was afraid of what he might do if he came here.

Afterward Granny cut some pound cake and put up a kettle to boil water for tea. She served Ronnie and me tea in glasses with handles that were usually used to drink root beer soda in. She took out cans of beer from the refrigerator for her and Mommy. Mommy and Granny talked and drank. By their tone and expressions, I could tell the conversation was very serious. Every once in a while Granny would look at me, smile and say, "*Mažiukas*."

When Ronnie got up, I followed him to the parlor, where he began unpacking some of the boxes. My mother brought one of our dressers from the Bronx, which had our clothes in it; I found my pajamas and stepped into the bedroom to change. Ronnie had placed the Victrola on top of the dresser and plugged it in. He began to take the records out of a box and I was relieved to see my *Alice in Wonderland* and Frank Sinatra records. From the two large piles it appeared we had brought them all.

The parlor had two windows that faced the street, slightly above street level. I sucked in my breath and was startled to hear a tap on the window and see a teenage black boy looking into our parlor. Ronnie smiled and waved, then pulled down the shades. "I know him, that's

Leroy, he lives right next door." Mugsy looked up but then curled even more tightly against the pillow of the studio couch. It was pretty chilly in the parlor, and I dug in the drawer for my robe. Next to one of the windows was another rocking chair covered with doilies and scarves, behind it a drape hung over a section of recessed wall, creating a makeshift closet. Across the room, next to the other window sat an upholstered flowered armchair also covered with doilies and scarves. With a large high black oval table in the middle, there was only a small amount of room to move around in. The highly waxed worn flowered linoleum floor was adorned with four oval rugs. I later learned that they were made of braided old stockings and sewn together by my grandmother.

Ronnie put on Tchaikovsky's *Nutcracker Suite*. Mommy called me into the kitchen to wash up for bed. On the kitchen floor was a tin oval tub into which Granny was pouring hot water from the kettle. I refused to get undressed in front of Granny and did not want to get into that tub. Mommy said I could go to bed without bathing. So she just wiped my face with a washcloth and told me to stand on the stool by the sink and brush my teeth.

Granny motioned for me to come into the bedroom; she pulled back the patchwork covers on my little bed. "*Mažiukas*" she said as she puckered her lips and kissed me. She smelled of talcum powder and old people. A bobby pin in her straw-like blond hair scratched against my cheek, and her pop pearl necklace hit against my teeth. I forced a smile as she walked away. I thought again how foreign she seemed in her old lady dark print dress, thick stockings and black laced shoes.

I yearned for my own bed and the windows that looked out on Mosholu Parkway. How could I ever have another bubble bath and eat Spanish olives in that portable tin tub? I hugged Poochie closer and lay there listening to the *Nutcracker Suite*. *The Dance of the Sugarplum Fairies* filled the rooms. I let the music in and my chest swelled with feeling at its beauty. I started to cry. Ronnie heard me and came to ask what was wrong. I said I was crying because the music was the sweetest I ever heard. I let it shut out the Lithuanian talk, and closed my eyes to escape the saints that appeared to move, letting the music lull me to sleep.

CHAPTER 20

Down Neck

It took me a few minutes to realize where I was when I woke up in Granny's dark bedroom. The large interior windows did not let in much light from either the parlor or the kitchen. The vigil lights had burned out leaving behind the smell of wax. The statues of the saints seemed less frightening.

I sat up and could see Mommy still asleep in Granny's high bed. I heard my grandmother in the kitchen, singing a song in Lithuanian. I had to go to the bathroom but did not want to see Granny without my mother present. I peeked into the parlor. The studio couch was empty, and I wondered where Ronnie was. I saw my *Alice in Wonderland* record on top of the dresser and wished, like Alice, that this were all a bad dream. I turned on the Victrola and took the record out of the jacket. Very carefully, I lowered the needle onto the record, then sat on the rocking chair by the window staring at the billboards across the street as Ginger Rogers began narrating the strange and wonderful tale. Granny heard the record and came in to say something that seemed disapproving. My mother woke up and came to my rescue. I wasn't sure what I was being rescued from. While they conversed, I ran to the bathroom.

Sitting on the toilet seat with my knees touching the damp wall, a screeching sound assaulted my ears. These sounds would be a constant since the family next door had a wood cutting business in their back yard. As I sat there, I also heard the railroad train go by with the steam engine letting off hoots. When I came out of the bathroom, my mother and grandmother were both in the kitchen. Granny was on the rocking chair, her leg on a footstool, applying a gooey looking purple suave onto open sores on her leg. I looked in horror at Mommy. She explained that my grandmother did this daily to care for her ulcerated legs and, in addition, had to wear the elastic stockings that I saw her pulling on.

Mommy told me Granny didn't want me to play records early in the morning. "We'll get dressed, Sweetie, and walk around so you can see where everything is. We'll also stop to see Aunt Helen." I really liked Aunt Helen and I was excited to see her. Uncle Bill had been transferred from the Social Security Office in Maryland back to Newark. They now lived on Downing Street in Aunt Mae's old apartment, which was less than two blocks away. My Aunt Jean's husband had died when my cousin Billy was only a few months old. He was shaving in the bathroom and just fell down and died of a heart attack when he was only twenty-nine. Aunt Mae then moved in with Aunt Jean in Kearney to help with the bills and the care of little Billy.

Granny was slicing up a pound cake and serving us coffee in the same handled glasses that we used for tea the night before. She kissed me on the head and said "*Mažiukas.*" I was going to tell her that I didn't drink coffee, but she was being so nice to me I didn't want to hurt her feelings, so I tasted it. She had fixed it with lots of milk and sugar and it tasted really good. Granny pointed at the cake and said, "*Valgyti, valgyti Mažiukas.*" I ate the cake and drank the coffee. Daytime made things seem a little more cheerful in her house.

It was February, so I bundled up with a sweater and my navy pea jacket. Granny gave me a babushka for my head. When we stepped out onto the cement stoop we could see that the Jackson Street Bridge was open, causing the traffic to jam up on both Jackson and Market Streets. The street did not look much nicer during the daytime. Behind the two large billboards, the two shabby five story brown wooden tenements looked even more worn with daylight. At least Granny's house was painted dark green.

Across the street, the glass window of the bakery had IBERIA written in large green letters. The delicious smell of Portuguese bread baking drifted up our noses. My mother said we would buy some on our way back.

As we descended the four cement steps and turned to the left, we passed the black family's house. From the rickety slat sidewalk, we could see them cutting wood in the empty back lot and hear the screeching of the electric saw. We walked under the railroad tunnel, which seemed to be where everyone on foot or in cars flung their trash. I did not like this neighborhood at all. Clover Street, however, which was the next left, was much more appealing. There were little one and two family houses, nicely painted in colors other than brown.

We continued down Jackson Street toward Ferry Street. My mother pointed out Downing Street, where Aunt Helen lived. Ferry Street was the main street filled with stores. Right on the corner of Jackson Street and Ferry Street was the Pic Movie Theatre. On the weekends this little movie house showed old films—dinosaur movies, horror films like *The Wolf Man* and *Frankenstein,* and many of the old cowboy favorites with *Tom Mix, Gene Autry,* or *Roy Rogers.* During the week, old popular movies would be shown. The best part was that the admission for children under twelve was only twelve cents. We clutched at our scarves as the wind whipped around the corner. "Can we go to the movies now, Mommy?" I asked as I looked up at the poster that displayed dinosaurs.

"That movie is playing this weekend," Mommy said. "I will take you on Saturday. Let's walk and look in the store windows." She knew I liked window shopping. We passed a hat shop and I stopped to admire a bonnet that was just being put in the window as an Easter display.

We walked several blocks and turned left onto Jefferson Street. "All the streets were named after United States presidents," My mother said in a tour guide voice. One block further, we came to Saint James, a large gothic Catholic Church designed after Saint Patrick's Cathedral in Manhattan. Attached to it was Saint James School. Mommy told me this is where Ronnie went to school before he moved to the Bronx and this is where I would be going as well.

"Where is Ronnie?" I asked.

"Ronnie went to visit one of his friends," she said.

I realized I didn't know anyone in Newark, except Mommy, Granny, Ronnie and Aunt Helen. I missed Gretchen. "I don't have any friends," I cried.

Then Mommy said in a sad voice, "I don't have any friends either, Sweetie. But don't worry; you'll make friends as soon as you start school. I have to look for a job," she said. I never thought of my mother as working.

"What kind of work will you do, Mommy?"

"We'll see," she answered. "While we're here, why don't we go inside and register you for school?" We went inside to an office where a nun sat at a desk. I was always afraid of the nuns at St. Ann's Sunday school in the Bronx. This nun looked even scarier in her black habit, with her face framed by a rippled white rectangle squashing the eyeglasses that sat on her nose. She seemed very bossy and asked me in a stern voice to sit quietly while my mother filled out the paper work. Then she was very annoyed at Mommy for not having certain documents. My mother tried to explain that this visit had not been planned, but the nun cut her off and said, "If you bring them tomorrow, Katherine may start school on Monday. I will allow her to go into the second grade, but if she cannot keep up, she will go back to the first," she stated as though I was not even there. My mother said she would stop by tomorrow, thanked her and we left.

"Why do I have to go to that school?" I fretted. "The Sisters of Charity are good teachers and you will get a good education. Principals always act strict, but the nuns that will teach you are much nicer." I hoped she was right, but I wasn't too convinced.

We walked down Elm Street; it was tree-lined with private houses. My mother showed me where Granny used to live when Ronnie was little and lived with her. This was much prettier than Jackson Street. I wished she still lived here. "Why did she move?" I asked. Mommy said someone tried to break into the apartment and she was afraid to live there any longer.

We walked from Elm to Lafayette and then down Polk to Ferry Street again. There, with a big marquee, was another movie theater called the Rivoli. I was very excited. Two movie theaters! We looked at the posters of the movies that were coming soon. Playing now was *A Duel in the Sun* with Jennifer Jones. "Oh! I want to see that movie, I saw the coming attractions in the Bronx."

My mother inquired at the box office. The Rivoli's admission was twenty-five cents for children. It opened at noon on Saturday and Sunday and played a feature, a B movie and a short. The programs played Wednesday through Saturday and Sunday through Tuesday.

"Just like the Tuxedo, that means I can go Saturday and Sunday and see a different movie," I said. Mommy replied that, if I wanted to, we could see *A Duel in the Sun* on Saturday rather than go to the Pic.

We were frozen. On the very next corner heading toward home was Jane Logan's Luncheonette. Mommy took me to the counter where we both ordered a hot chocolate and a Charlotte Russe, a round pound cake enveloped in white cardboard with whipped cream on top. I felt warmer and very happy about the movie theatres. I knew I would be spending a lot of time in them.

On the way home, we stopped at Aunt Helen's apartment on Downing Street. It was a third floor walk-up with three tiny rooms. The kitchen, bedroom and parlor were cheerful and furnished very nicely. Aunt Helen gave me a big hug. I only saw her once since last summer at the family court. Aunt Helen beamed, "Look at you Puddin', how big you've gotten. I'm so glad we'll be living close to each other. You can come visit me whenever you like." I knew I would be spending a lot of time with Aunt Helen, too.

CHAPTER 21

New School: New Friends

St. James occupied all four sides of an entire block, which included its church, school and hospital. The large gothic church with a majestic steeple had its main entrance on Lafayette Street, but the school itself sat in an L shape on Madison and Elm Streets. St. James Hospital completed the fourth block. The main entrance of the school, a three story brownstone building, was on Elm Street. Because the most frequently used entrance was on Madison Street, Madison was closed to traffic during school hours for recess, gym and lunchtime. It was through this entrance that I would come and go for the next seven years.

My mother had gotten a job very quickly as a waitress and could not bring me the first day, so my grandmother walked me to school. Since she didn't speak English, I had to ask where the second grade was located. The second grade classroom was actually the first room to the right with its windows facing onto Madison. Sister Maria Williams greeted me at the door and asked that I stay at the front of the room so she could introduce me. As I stood there feeling very uncomfortable and a little frightened, the students gave me curious looks as they straggled into class. "This is Katherine Persico, she will be joining our class," sister announced once everyone was seated. "Please welcome her." A flurry of greetings filled the room; however, I did not feel very welcomed. It was February, more than half way through the school year, and all thirty six desks in the classroom were filled. Sister sat me with another girl, also named Catherine. Sister Maria seemed young compared to other nuns I had seen; she was nice but strict. Sister got into the habit of calling Catherine and me by our first and last names. It always sounded so formal and startled us, because she only called students by their first and last names when she was going to punish them. Neither of us was comfortable in our seat, but Catherine was also upset because the desk had been exclusively her space. My chubby body gave her even less room. Those little wooden desks with an inkwell at top right, attached to the small bench-like seats, were quite cramped. It was also difficult to fit both our belongings in the storage shelf underneath her side of the desk. Sitting on the left, I had to awkwardly extend my right arm diagonally across the desk in order to dunk my nib stick pen into the inkwell. Looking straight at her paper, Catherine would keep her elbow bent and her arm taut to retain her territory. Very often I felt her haughtily jerk her leg away when mine accidentally touched hers under the desk.

Physically, Catherine was the opposite of me. She was slender and delicate with long curly blond hair and eyeglasses. Matching barrettes placed neatly on each side kept any strands from falling into her face. We had to wear dark green gabardine uniforms with a SJS (St. James School) embroidered in yellow on our left shoulders. Hers always appeared brand new and her short sleeved Peter Pan collared beige blouse was starched and crisp. In contrast, my long, thick dark braids always seemed to be half undone. My mother could only afford to buy one uniform, so cleaning was not possible except on long school holidays. Granny, however, always ironed my two alternate blouses nicely.

The worst part of this second grade was that the students were already writing script. In the Bronx at PS 80, we had not yet begun to do so. I feared being put back into the first grade. Besides, my classmates talked about the first grade nun; they said Sister Mary Joseph was very fresh and even crazy, hitting most of the students last year. Apparently, she also threw an alarm clock at a boy causing him to be rushed to the hospital for stitches. After that incident his parents took him out of St. James. Sister Maria did not hit us, but she would throw us an angry darting stare, making us immediately stop whatever we were doing.

I quickly noticed that when Sister Maria had us write on the blackboard, alternate assignments were given. Therefore, I could look down to the blackboard on either side of the person next to me and copy whatever they wrote in script. Most of the time I did not even know what words I had written, but bluffing got me through. To catch up, I spent a lot of time struggling to learn script by myself at home. My penmanship, however, was not very good.

My mother's waitress job was at Child's Restaurant located on Broad Street in downtown Newark. Working the morning shift, she would leave at 5:30 a.m. to begin at 6:30 a.m. Though she only worked until 2:00 p.m., she rarely came home before ten or eleven at night and had gotten into the habit of going straight to Beb's, a bar right around the corner from Child's, where she'd spend time with her new friends. One of them would have to help her into a taxicab since she was too drunk to take a bus home. I looked forward to Tuesdays, her only day off, when she would make us a really nice dinner. My favorite was still her great meat loaf, but all of her cooking was wonderful. She'd make breaded veal cutlets, liver and onions, and veal chops with green peppers with the kidney attached. One dish, which she called "mush-mosh," was made with elbow macaroni, shredded pan-fried chopped meat, onions, peppers and tomatoes. Ronnie and I loved it, so she would make a large pot full. The next day we would make sandwiches for lunch and have the leftovers again for dinner. On Monday nights she brought home dessert for the Tuesday dinner from Cushman's Bakery. Our favorites were their seven layer chocolate cake and coconut custard pie. Sometimes they were a little messed up from traveling with her to Beb's bar and then again in a cab.

Ronnie was attending East Side High School and I rarely saw him. Sometimes he didn't even come home for dinner; other times he would just come in to eat and run out again to his friend's house or the playground. Most times for dinner Granny would make something, like potatoes, potato pancakes with sour cream, blinis, or chicken soup, often mumbling how awful it was that our mother was not home cooking for us. Ronnie loved whatever Granny made. If he wasn't home, I sometimes opened a can of Chef Boyardee macaroni or ravioli. Kraft Macaroni and Cheese was one of my favorites. Ronnie loved it also, so we'd sometimes have that when he was home, but he would add a can of Del Monte tomato sauce to his Kraft dinner and laugh at me when I held my nose in disgust. Granny thought canned and boxed food was awful stuff to eat. Very often I yearned for Schweller's chopped chicken liver and hot turkey.

On the few nights Ronnie was home, he would stay in the cold parlor doing his homework and listening to his records. After dinner, Granny and I sat in the kitchen, she on her rocking chair praying with many different kinds of rosary beads. She had a whole collection of them in different colors and would sit there for hours praying to different saints. In Lithuanian, her whispered prayers sounded like she was constantly calling a cat. In the meantime, I'd do my homework across the kitchen table from her, next to the coal stove. I'd continue doing homework as I listened to the nighttime radio stories from 8:00 to 10:00 p.m. I loved the stories and would sit wide-eyed drinking hot tea that Granny kept pouring. There were great shows like *Fibber McGee and Molly, The Life of Riley, Inner Sanctum, The Thin Man* and many more.

Most nights I would go to bed before my mother got home; however, I'd sometimes be startled out of my sleep by her crashing into the walls of the outside hallway, fumbling with her keys and stumbling into the kitchen. Granny would reprimand her in Lithuanian. *"Nu, jau ateina, alaus prisilakusi!"* I was beginning to recognize certain phrases and knew it translated to something like, "Oh, now here she comes, full of beer!" Granny also told her that she should be ashamed of herself and that God was going to be very angry at her. It frightened me to see her so drunk. I would stay in my bed peeking from under the covers. My mother would cry, they would wind up arguing and Granny would keep muttering, the same phrases over and over. I hated those confrontations. Afterward, I'd manage to pull the covers over my head and snuggle with Poochie and Mugsy until I finally fell back to sleep.

In the morning, I'd get up early to spend a few minutes with my mother before she left for work. She was always cheerful and, of course, sober. The mornings were chilly before Granny fed the stove more coal. I'd sit at the kitchen table, huddled in my pink chenille robe, sipping the coffee she had fixed for me. My mother sat on Granny's rocking chair and in the silence of the morning I could hear her taking long drags on her Pall Mall cigarette while she fixed her hair and put on her make up. I'd watch fascinated as she carefully drew on her eyebrows with a velvet black pencil. Last she would apply her bright red lipstick, smacking her lips together and then blotting them with a napkin. Sometimes I saw her looking at her scarred chin. I know after the accident she didn't think she was pretty anymore, but I thought she was still beautiful. She didn't smile much anymore either. The only time she seemed really happy was when she was drinking; she'd throw her head back and laugh. Each time we said goodbye, I'd wish we could spend the whole day together. She would always say, "Be a good girl, Sweetie," and then bend over, pucker and throw a kiss about an inch from my lips so as not to mess her fresh lipstick. Mugsy would slip out with her to relieve himself and wait until Mommy's bus came. He got into the habit of walking us to wherever we were going.

Up early, I'd get dressed since I'd gotten into the routine of going to seven o'clock mass at St. James Church every morning. I was studying to receive my First Holy Communion in May and felt very close to God and the saints. I prayed every morning to all of them to help my mother stop drinking. When we lived in the Bronx, I recalled my mother and her friend Eva taking me to a shrine that had been set up on Villa Avenue in honor of the Blessed Virgin Mary. A little girl said a vision of the Blessed Mother appeared to her. I would carefully watch all the statues in church, certain that one would give me a sign that they heard my prayers. I told God what a good girl I would be if he would only answer my prayers. I thought He couldn't refuse my request since it wasn't a favor I was asking for myself.

Several of us kids went to mass daily. One was Arlene who lived around the corner from me on Market Street. She lived with her grandmother and mother in one of those apartments with the bathroom on the back porch. We began walking back and forth to school together and became friends. When we walked to mass, Mugsy often followed us. Most days Mugsy would only walk as far as the empty lot on Downing Street. While we cut diagonally across, he'd stay to play with the many large and small dogs that gathered there, but not before looking up at me. I'd say, "Okay, Mugsy, go play," and he'd run off wagging his tail.

After mass, Arlene and I would exit on the side of the church into a courtyard, which was a shortcut to the cafeteria located in back of the school. The cafeteria was closed in the morning but we'd sit at one of the tables and eat a buttered roll or sweet bun and drink our jars of tea that we'd brought from home. Arlene was a friend of Elaine who was one grade ahead of us. We three would chat and started hanging out together. Elaine lived on Clover Street, the block with really nice houses, which was only down the block and around the corner from Granny's. Elaine and her family lived in their very own house with two floors, a yard and garages. Mommy was right—I did meet new friends. I liked Arlene, but I liked Elaine even more. She was smart, pretty, sweet and had a really nice family. Her father was a plumber of Portuguese descent and her mother was an Italian housewife who cooked the greatest meals. Elaine also had two older sisters and one of the few television sets in the neighborhood. Her house was very pretty, with flowered bedspreads and lace curtains. Elaine shared a bedroom with one of her sisters. In it they had a dressing table with a large mirror and a pink ruffled skirt on the bottom. It looked just like one Betty Grable had in a movie. I thought Elaine had everything anyone could ever want.

After nine o'clock Sunday mass, which was the mandatory children's mass, Elaine's mother would invite me over. We'd watch *The Ted Mack Amateur Hour* and nibble on rolls while the delicious smell from the simmering pot of the Sunday Italian gravy drifted through the entire house. Her homemade macaroni with meat sauce, meatballs, sausage and *braciole* (rolled beef stuffed with parsley and garlic) was even better than the one Daddy's mother used to make.

I thought of Daddy and missed going to his bar. I had gotten a few short letters from him after I sent him samples of my script and arithmetic. He wrote he was very proud of me and sent me five dollars, which could buy a new dress or pair of shoes, but I often chose to donate most of it to the missions in the classroom collection at school. He wrote that he would come to see me when I made my First Communion in May and take me to the Bronx. I wrote and asked him if he would take me to Schweller's again.

At about noon on Sunday, Elaine's entire family would noisily eat dinner together. In between the chatter and laughter a frequent loud Italian exclamation like *"Marrone!"* would float into the living room where Arlene, Elaine and I were sitting, eating our macaroni at the coffee table and watching TV. This was such a treat; everything was so delicious. I always said yes when Annie (that's what her mother wanted to be called) offered me more. At 2:00 p.m., I would go to watch movies at the Rivoli. I usually went alone since Elaine and her family went to visit her grandmother on Market Street and Arlene went home to spend the day with her mother.

At the Rivoli, I stayed for the entire feature presentation, the B movie and the short, sometimes even staying to see the feature for a second time. Walking home from the movies on Sundays at 6:00 or 7:00 p.m. was kind of scary. Maybe it was because few people were out and everything seemed so dark and still. It felt as if something was going to happen any minute. The newsreels were filled with stories of the atom bomb and Hiroshima; those terrifying images stayed with me. There were also huge storage cylinders of oil on Market Street that I feared might explode. Many times I had a feeling of impending doom and would break into a run until I got home safely. Often no one was home, but I'd usually find Mugsy waiting in the hallway outside the kitchen door. The minute I'd open the street door he'd start to squeal loudly and jump up at the kitchen door until I opened it.

Granny frequently went to the bar with her cronies or sometimes to a Novena (nine days of prayer to a particular saint) at one of the churches. Holy Name was the Lithuanian church, St. Casimir the Polish, and Saint Joseph the Spanish. With about ten churches Down Neck, there always seemed to be a Novena going on in one of them and she went to them all. At other times, Granny would be home with three or four of her buddies drinking in the kitchen, with the smell of beer and whiskey permeating the house. Most of her friends seemed very old fashioned, some with gold teeth and some with no teeth. One old man, whom they called "Poop Poop," kept winking at everyone as they sang Russian and Lithuanian songs. He always managed to pinch my cheek as I hurried by him. Mugsy and I would hang out in the cold parlor. I'd sit on the rocking chair by the window with a blanket thrown over me while I let my records drown out the loud singing or the thoughts of bombs. Mugsy would curl into a pillow on the studio couch, glad to be home.

CHAPTER 22

Mirror, Mirror

Daddy did come in May for my First Communion day, but did not make it to the nine o'clock mass. I wished he could have seen me receive communion for the first time. I felt so holy walking down the church aisle, cleansed of all sin and guilt. The day before I had made my first confession to the priest and all the stealing and lying in the Bronx were now forgiven. The choir sang; they sounded like angels and I felt close to heaven. My mother took off that Sunday. Ronnie, Granny, Aunt Helen, Aunt Mae, and Aunt Jean with my little cousin Billy were also at church.

At home afterward, I opened my gifts. Mommy bought me my first wristwatch. My father arrived about noon and as he walked through the kitchen door, everyone greeted him at once. Mugsy went crazy squirming and yapping, he was so excited to see him. Daddy seemed to feel the same way about seeing Mugsy, stooping down he kept petting him and laughing through his hellos to everyone as Mugsy kept licking his face. Then Daddy kissed me on the cheek and although he had his arm around my shoulder while he continued his greetings, I think the only person that he really saw was Mommy. She looked lovely in her beige linen dress. At church she wore a large matching beige straw hat. He spoke softly to her and it looked to me like he loved her. My mother had told me he had written to her several times asking all of us to come back to live with him in the Bronx. "That's what your father thinks. It will be a cold day in hell before I'd do that," she'd slur on occasion. I wondered if she might change her mind now that she saw how nice he was acting. My father gave me a two sided silver medal enclosed in an octagonal shaped crystal. One side had the Blessed Virgin Mary and the other the Sacred Heart of Jesus. He fastened the silver chain around my neck and it hung sparkling brightly on my communion dress. I really loved it.

Granny put out a ham she had cooked and we all made sandwiches with fresh rolls from the Portuguese bakery. Daddy always dressed in a suit and tie but everyone still told him how great he looked in his new tan suit and brown-striped tie. Even though it had only been a few months since I'd seen him, I remembered him taller. When he said goodbye to everyone and tried to hug Mommy, I noticed she kind of pulled back. They all came out front to admire his new black Cadillac. He opened the car door for me, then Daddy and I started out for the Bronx.

I felt very strange with him. This probably was the first time we were spending time alone together other than me sitting across from him at the kitchen table in the Bronx when he was red eyed and drinking his black coffee silently. I didn't know what to say, so we rode for a while without saying anything. It was a long car ride in 1946 from Newark to the Bronx. I sat there smoothing the ruffles of my white nylon dress over and over. Finally he said, "That is a very pretty communion dress you have on."

"Thank you," I answered, feeling my face getting red. I can't remember what else he said in the car or what else I said. We must have talked to each other, but I just can't remember the conversation.

When we got to Mosholu Parkway and went up to my old apartment, I remember walking into the foyer and looking in awe at a stunning new gold leaf mirror and shelf. I thought it was one of the most beautiful pieces I had ever seen, even before Daddy proudly pointed out this new purchase. I had loved living here, loved being across from the park, loved the little Mexican hats on the kitchen border, and loved eating at Schweller's. I wished that I could live here again and that the new mirror would be mine. I walked up to it and saw myself in my pretty white dress with my new crystal medal. I imagined that I saw Daddy walk up behind me, put his hands on my shoulders and say, "You are my beautiful little girl. I'm so proud to have you as my daughter, and I love you with all my heart and have missed you so very much. I wish we could be together again."

But Daddy didn't say that. He had gone into the bedroom and was calling me to see how he had redecorated it. The bedroom looked larger with only the master bed covered in a lovely new cream chenille bedspread. My junior bed was gone and I wondered what Daddy had done with it. A large vase with scarlet silk flowers sat on a new blond wood dresser. I went over to touch the delicate cream silk shantung curtains that were tucked back with fringed sashes. Looking out of the window, I longed to once more play in the park across the street. "I wish your mother could see how nice the apartment looks," Daddy said.

"I'll tell her, Daddy," I said, looking up with a smile. Daddy seemed lost in thought and looked a little sad. He nodded and said we ought to get going if we were going to fit in seeing my aunts and uncles. I can't remember the rest of the day. I must have seen his sisters, my Aunt Bridget, Ola, and the other Mae and my Uncles Johnny, Terry and Tony, but I can't remember. I just remember that wondrous gold framed mirror in the foyer, wanting it to be mine, wanting to live with it. I can't even remember the ride home. How I wish I could remember more. Little did I know this would be the only day I would ever spend alone with my father.

I remember that when I got home, my mother had been drinking heavily. It must have been late because Granny and Ronnie were already in bed. I stared describing the beautiful new mirror to her. "Go, live with your father and his new mirror if that's what you want, go on and see if I care," she said with tears rolling down her cheeks.

"Mommy, I don't want to live with Daddy, I just wanted to tell you about new mirror he bought," I started to cry myself.

"Go ahead, go and live with him, live with your father," she kept saying.

"I want to live with you, Mommy," I was now sobbing. I couldn't bear the thought that she didn't think I loved her. I knew I could never say anything good about my father again or she would think I loved him more than her. I wanted to say, "I had an awful day and I hated being with him," but that would have been a lie and the words wouldn't come out of my mouth.

There was a wedding going on in the corner beer hall. Polka music boomed into our kitchen from their windows that opened into our backyard. It was hot for May and the smell of beer filled the air. I felt like I was going to be sick to my stomach and ran into the bedroom to change into my nightgown. I took off my communion dress and threw it on the floor of the closet, but the next day when Granny asked me what my dress was doing on the floor, I told her it must have fallen off the hanger. This was my first lie since confession. I would tell the priest in the confessional next week.

I went to bed without saying good night to my mother; a short time later I heard her get into bed with Granny and soon I could hear her snoring. I lay there in a half sleep, the vigil lights flickering in front of the saints, creating moving shadows on the walls. A vision of Daddy's new mirror came into my head. I saw myself with large white wings in my First Holy Communion dress and veil. Weightlessly, I floated up and entered into the mirror, spread my wings and flew into a deep blue sky with puffs of soft white clouds. I heard angels singing and looking down, I could see Mommy and Daddy in the foyer on the other side of the mirror smiling and waving to me. I'm not sure how much was my imagination…or was it a dream?

CHAPTER 23

The Letters

The Tuesday after my First Holy Communion day, I was sitting in the parlor by the window listening to my *Alice in Wonderland* record while doing my homework, when Granny came in to hand me a letter. I saw Daddy's name and return address on the Holland Linen envelope and got really excited because it was the first letter that was ever addressed just to me. I wrote him a couple of letters over the last few months and he usually wrote something back in Mommy's letters. She would read that part to me. All his letters to her seemed to make her very angry so I felt uncomfortable when she read my part, even though they mostly said, "Say hello to Kathy and tell her I miss her," or "Give her this five dollars." I carefully opened the small envelope with matching paper.

> *Dear Darling Daughter,*
>
> *Received both your letters today and was very happy to hear from you also that you are all feeling well. I am coming to see you Sunday, so you will get the letter after I come out there, but I am writing just in case something turns up and I am not able to make it.*

Glad to see you are getting along fine in school. I checked the examples and they are all correct—good for you. I have been feeling alright, but may have to go away soon for a little while. If I do I will send you the address where I am.

I miss you and love you very much, and want you always to be a very good girl to your grandma and everybody. Now that the weather is getting warmer I will be able to spend more time with you. I will come out early and we will go out together. Give my best regards to mother and everybody—and remember I will always love you.

With love and kisses,
Dad

P.S. Here are some stamps so you can write to me. Thanks very much for the crucifix and the prayer card, I shall always carry it with me and pray that you all will always be healthy and happy.

He had never mentioned this letter to me on my First Communion day, nor had he mentioned possibly moving. I pressed it to my heart and kept repeating "My Darling Daughter." I hadn't felt like his darling daughter on Sunday…but here he wrote, "I miss you and love you very much." That is just what I wanted him to say. I could not stop smiling for a long time. I thought of the white jewelry box Aunt Mae had given me for my First Communion. I went to get it from the little dresser behind my bed. When you opened it, a ballerina in a pink tutu twirled to the melody of *Begin the Beguine*. I had decided I would keep all of Daddy's letters in this box. It had a key and I would lock it so my mother wouldn't read them and get angry with me. He said he would come out often. I was already thinking of some of the things we could do together, maybe go to a movie or drive to Olympic Park, an amusement park with rides and games. I pictured us laughing together on one of my favorite rides, the whip. The lyrics of *I'll be Seeing You* swirled around in my head, "I'll be seeing you in all the old familiar places…."

But Daddy never came to Newark again. The next letter I received said he was selling the business and moving to Miami Beach to open another bar and grill.

"When I get settled it would be wonderful for you to come and spend time with me during your summer vacation," he wrote.

But that visit did not happen either. When I mentioned going to Florida to Mommy, she said, "Go ahead and stay with your father, see if I care!" She got so upset that I didn't talk about it anymore. I secretly wished I could go to Florida and see palm trees that I had seen in movies. I also thought it might be great to stay with Daddy for a week or two. I decided to lose some weight so I would look really good in a bathing suit. However, when school was out, arrangements were made for me to go back to Aunt Helen's in Picky Pine for the entire summer. Although I loved Picky Pine, I was still thinking about Florida and Daddy. Maybe next year, I hoped.

During the summer in Picky Pine, both my mother and father wrote me letters. Since my father's letters went to my house in Newark and Mommy had to forward them to me, I was careful of what I wrote to him.

I wasn't supposed to know that Mommy was coming for my birthday, but Aunt Jean told me that she was going to surprise me. But she never made it. We didn't have any telephones. It was a very hot that day and I refused to go swimming at the pond because I thought she might arrive any minute. By the end of the day when I realized she wasn't coming, I ran to the back storehouse to cry. I didn't want Aunt Helen to see me crying because then she would be angry with my mother. I wound up the RCA and put on Enrico Caruso singing *Pagliacci.* Somehow it felt better to cry with him singing with such sadness, it felt like someone else understood. So I played it over and over in the heat until I fell asleep on the floor. When Aunt Jean came to wake me I was soaked with sweat. She kept stroking my head and told me she felt awful because she told me Mommy was going to surprise me, and if I hadn't known, I wouldn't be so upset. Aunt Jean said she had presents my mother sent for me. I was very angry with my mother since this was the second July she missed my birthday. "I'll open them tomorrow." With my eyes all swollen from crying, I ran back to the house and was glad that I didn't see Aunt Helen or anybody else on the way. They were all sitting on the glider swing, talking and drinking, so I just went inside and got into bed.

The next day, once again Billy and I had to celebrate our birthdays together with one cake. I suppose he got most of the attention and many more presents because he was five years younger than me. I really didn't even feel like it was my party at all. The dress my mother got me was too tight. A week later, I got this letter from her.

> *Dear Kathy,*
>
> *How are you, Sweetie? I hope you're not getting too fat. I bought you a big coloring book and crayons and I thought I would bring it out to you. I was so disappointed Tuesday.*

(It was my birthday; I was the one who was very disappointed. She doesn't even write she is sorry.)

> *Did Aunt Jean tell you I was going to surprise you? Someone was supposed to drive me out but they weren't feeling well. Did you write to your father? Let me know if you got an answer.*

(Maybe she gave him Aunt Helen's address!)

> *I didn't see anything nice yet to replace your birthday present, but as soon as I do I'll get it. Well, Sweetie, that's about all for now. I miss you. It seems so long that you're away. Be good.*
>
> > *Love & kisses,*
> > *Regards to all,*
> > *Mommy*
>
> *P.S. Here is ten dollars. Give it to Aunt Helen for your board.*

I was startled. I didn't know Aunt Helen charged her board. I thought she just loved having me here. Ten dollars a week was a lot of money. My mother only made nineteen dollars a week before tips. I felt very sorry for my mother because she was always struggling to pay all the bills and I was angry with Aunt Helen. I wondered if she charged Aunt Jean board for my little cousin Billy. The next weekend Aunt Jean brought me another letter from Daddy that Mommy asked her to take to me.

Hello Darling,

Received your birthday card, gift and letter. (Aunt Helen helped me pick out a tie and a book mark.*) Thanks for both. I was very happy to hear from you. I am glad you are happy and well and had a nice birthday party at Picky Pine. I had not found any-thing to do yet and if in another month can't find any work I will have to come back to New York.*

("It would be easier to see him if he came back to New York," I thought.)

How is everybody at home? I hope all are well. I am feeling much better than before, although the doc-tor said I must take it easy. We have had a lot of rainy weather. It has been raining on and off everyday for a month although it doesn't last long.

(I didn't know he was sick, except I now remem-bered Aunt Mae telling Mommy that he ought to do something about his terrible cough, so I guessed that was what he was writing about and that he is getting better.)

I miss you very much and think of you all the time. I can't wait until the day I see you again, which I hope will be soon. Glad to hear you like the presents. I am sorry it could not have been better and more. (He sent me two Miami Beach tee shirts, an assort-ment of tropical jellies and ten dollars.*) Little did I think when I came here that I would lose my money and have to start all over again, but I am hoping for the best.*

("How did he lose his money?" I wondered. Aunt Mae always told me Daddy had a lot of money.)

> *Give my regards to all and*
> *with all my love to you,*
> *Dad*

I wrote and thanked Daddy and told him I loved the jellies, but I really didn't, and that the tee shirts fit perfectly, but they were both too small. I kept them in my drawer because he sent them to me and in case I lost more weight.

Then I received another letter from my mother.

Dear Kathy,

> *I received your letter and was very happy to hear you had a lovely party. Sorry I couldn't be there. They didn't have the dress in a bigger size so I am still looking for something. I hope you liked your father's birthday presents and birthday cards. Sorry it was late, since I had to send it down with Aunt Jean.*
>
> *I didn't go to work today. I had a toothache. I'm glad you liked all your other presents and the money of course. Granny said she missed you; it's quiet around the house, I can't say just when I will be down. Don't forget to write to your father and thank him for the presents and you shame him like Aunt Mae said and tell him you need a lot of things that I can't buy and that I gave up my vacation because I couldn't afford to take one. Well, Sweetie, I guess this is all for now. I've got to leave some room for kisses. Be good. I miss you very much.*

> *Love,*
> *Mommy*

My cousin Billy was a real two year old pain, but I tried to be a good cousin. When he wasn't whining, I would read to him and teach him things, like tying his shoelaces, but he was more of a nuisance than fun. Aunt Jean was his real mother but Aunt Mae acted more like his mom. She was always hugging and kissing him. I thought he was very spoiled. His tantrums became worse when Aunt Jean and Aunt Mae were both here together. I did not think his "blowing his bugle" was cute. I thought it was disgusting; his thumb was always wet and smelled of bad breath.

In spite of Billy and my disappointing birthday, I had some really good times playing with my summer friends. None of them liked Billy either and we would scare him with ghost stories. On the hot days, I would go swimming in the cool spring water pond with my friends and Mugsy. Mugsy loved the water. He would swim for hours, barking and barking, running out, shaking off and then running back in. We would doggie paddle next to each other, have a race and I swear he would always win. I was so glad I didn't have to take Billy; he was too young to be with us in the water alone. But I would have to take him with me at night when we'd walk down the dirt road and sit in Uncle George's apple orchard listening to his stories. It was dark in the orchard with only the sounds of the crickets and Whippoorwills. This was a perfect place to scare Billy. My friends and I would light punks to keep the mosquitoes away. We would wait until Uncle George finished his stories and headed for his house. Then we'd run after Billy telling him the punk was the *"Man with the Red Eye"* who was going to "get him." He would scream and cry and run to me for help and I would pretend to save him. Then we would walk home while he held onto my hand tightly.

Most mornings were cool while I did my chores with Aunt Helen. Now that I knew Mommy paid Aunt Helen, I felt like I shouldn't have to do so much work. It was still my job to make all the beds, sweep, shake out all the rugs, dry all the dishes, and iron. Billy was too young to do anything. But I did like to do things with Aunt Helen. On the weekend when Uncle Bill came, I loved going to the auction on Saturday nights. Several Sundays during the summer we went to the Atlantic Highlands. Uncle Bill's brother Don and his wife Ceil shared a house there with another of his sisters, Edna. We would spend the whole day at the beach. Edna had two boys, Bobby was my age and Michael was two years older. They were a lot of fun to be with. After the beach, we would play cards in the tiny bungalow they rented, while the adults drank beer and whiskey and sang. Uncle Bill sang in harmony with his brother Don and Edna's husband, Pat. They sang songs like *Down by the Old Mill Stream, When Irish Eyes are Smiling,* and *Turra, Lurra, Lurra.* They sang really well—like the barbershop quartets in the movies.

Uncle Don owned a nightclub in Elizabeth, New Jersey called the Bandbox. He knew how much I loved Frank Sinatra and he relished telling me the story about how Frank Sinatra sang at his club and he fired him because he did not like his singing. "Yes, that is my claim to fame, I fired Frank Sinatra," he'd roar and they would all laugh. I couldn't believe he didn't like Frank Sinatra's singing. I thought, "I bet he would like Frank Sinatra singing in his club now that he is a big star." Uncle Bill loved it when Don told this story; he was always in a good mood in the Highlands. We would drive home very late at night and I usually fell asleep under a blanket protected from the cool night wind in the rumble seat.

That summer Aunt Helen and I had a new routine we did together. On Sunday mornings, I would sit on her cozy bed while she read at least three newspapers. She would tell me about all the news and about the sales in the stores. However, now that I made my First Communion, I felt very guilty about missing mass on Sundays. The church was in Farmingdale, which was a half hour drive. There was no way for me to get there. So once in a while, I went to the Protestant church with my friends. I always had a good time and loved the Bible stories. At night when I said my prayers, I apologized to God and promised when summer was over, I would go to mass every day to make up for missing Sundays.

CHAPTER 24

Third Grade Trauma

After a summer in the country, Newark looked very shabby to me, especially our block. The weeds had grown tall under the large brownstone railroad trestle and along the sidewalks and once again gave off an unpleasant odor. School began the day after Labor Day. I looked forward to beginning the third grade with Sister Margaret Helen, who seemed like a really nice nun. I was also anxious to start choir practice with Sister Maria Williams, who had been my second grade teacher.

It was great to see Arlene and Elaine again. Walking to school together, we told each other about our summer. Elaine and her two sisters always went down to the Jersey Shore to Seaside Heights, where her parents rented a house by the ocean for a month. Arlene went to visit her grandmother's sister in Pittsburgh for the whole summer. Elaine and Arlene were one class ahead of me. Before I left second grade I had become friends with one of my classmates, Lucille. It made it so much more comfortable to start the third grade having a class friend. Sister Margaret seated us alphabetically by last name, so Lucille Tarno's began with a T and she sat directly behind me.

After auditioning for the choir at the end of the second grade, I was thrilled to be selected to join them in the third grade. Sister

Maria, who directed the choir, scheduled choir practice three times a week during school hours and on Thursdays after school for two hours. Many of the kids in the choir complained, but I loved singing the hymns we rehearsed for Sunday mass; we also began preparing for the Christmas midnight mass. The choir was divided into high soprano, middle soprano (that is what I was) and alto, and most hymns were sung in those three parts. I thought angels couldn't have sounded as sweet as we did.

On other afternoons, Arlene and I, along with several other kids, would hang out at Elaine's. She had a large cement courtyard between the back of her house and the garages, where we'd play until dinner-time. Kick the Can and Giant Steps were two of our favorites; other times we'd jump rope or play Hopscotch. Nights I spent doing home-work while listening to the radio programs. One of my favorites at the time was *The Shadow*. On Saturdays and Sundays, I would go to the movies all day. On Sunday after singing at the nine o'clock mass, I'd rush home to listen to *The Frank Sinatra Hour* between eleven and twelve o'clock. Granny was usually still at church. There were many Catholic churches serving different nationalities in the multi-ethnic Ironbound section, each only a few blocks from one another. Granny began attending the eight o'clock mass at her Lithuanian church and then she'd move on to the Polish or the Russian church, meeting some friends in each until the twelve o'clock mass. Then she and her friends would go to the corner bar where they'd use the "ladies" entrance to drink together for a few hours. Ronnie was usually out playing ball with his friends and Mommy was waiting tables at Child's Restaurant. With the whole house to myself, I would sing along with Frank Sinatra at the top of my lungs, swinging back and forth in Granny's chair next to the kitchen radio with Mugsy as my only audience.

On Sunday afternoon after having a plate of macaroni at Elaine's, I'd head out to the Rivoli Theatre to see whatever feature movie was playing. One favorite movie was *Two Sailors and a Girl* with June Allyson (whom I adored), playing opposite Van Johnson. It had many musical numbers and I sang *Oh, You Beautiful Doll* for weeks after-ward. Jimmy Durante was also in it. He made me laugh so much! By the time I would arrive home at about nine, Granny's friends were just about leaving after having spent a few more hours in our kitchen drinking and singing.

Daddy's letters kept arriving about once a month, and in them he usually sent me a five or ten dollar bill. Although my mother was always broke working as a waitress at Child's, she refused to take any money that came from Daddy. One thing that made me popular was that I always had more money than the other kids. At St. James all the classes would collect money each day for the missions. I always gave enough money so that my third grade class would win by having the largest amount of all eight grades. I also thought the nuns would like me better for giving so much money to the missions.

One Tuesday at about eleven o'clock in the morning, Sister Margaret Helen called me to the front of the class. "Katherine (I cringed at the way she said Katherine), go home and tell your mother to come see me, and don't come back to school until she does," she snapped, peering down at me, her face flushed red against the white accordion frame of her black habit. I was so afraid because I didn't know what I had done. Since Tuesday was Mommy's only day off, she would be sleeping. She slept all day until I came home from school. Then she'd cook the best supper, our once a week feast. She was always very irritated if anyone woke her. I felt my chin trembling as I ran the whole eight blocks home. It was Indian summer and quite warm, I felt my blouse wet under my uniform, and with chest heaving, I quietly put my key into the kitchen door. Granny was out, so I tiptoed into the bedroom. Mommy was snoring lightly in Granny's big iron bed. I watched her for a few minutes and finally got the courage to tap her on the shoulder as I whispered, "Mommy, Mommy," until she finally opened her eyes. She looked at me blankly for a few seconds as she sat up, "What is it, what's the matter, Sweetie?"

I heard "Sweetie" and could no longer control my tears. I barely got out the words. "Mommy, Sister Margaret Helen said you have to come to school right away or I can't ever go back." My mother sat up.

"What did you do?" she asked worried.

"I don't know, I don't know why she is so angry at me," I sobbed.

While Mommy got up and dressed, I wiped the sweat off my face with a wet washcloth. She lit up a Pall Mall, took a long drag and fixed my messy braids. Then she took me by the hand and we walked silently to school. When we arrived it was after lunch. My mother knocked on the classroom door, pressing her face against the half window: Sister gave her the wait a minute signal with her index finger. We waited in the dimly lit stairwell until she came out. I was very scared; I had no idea what she was going to tell Mommy.

"Thank you for coming, Mrs. Persico. Let me get right to the point, I believe *Katherine* is stealing money." She made my name sound like a dirty word.

I wondered what she was talking about. "Did one of the kids have money stolen?" I thought. I was shocked to think she suspected me.

Mommy crossed her arms and asked, "What makes you think that, Sister?" Sister looked down at me and said accusingly, "She always has so much money and gives large sums to the missions."

I started to protest and tell her my father had sent me the money, but Mommy said, "Kathy, I will handle this." In her slow quiet voice she used when she was angry she asked, "Couldn't you have just asked Kathy where she got the money, why did you send for me?"

Sister said, "I thought she might not tell me the truth."

I was so hurt to think Sister thought I would also tell lies. I felt my chin trembling again but I held back crying.

"Then you could have sent a note home to me," Mommy continued in the same tone.

"I wasn't sure she would give you the note," Sister stated.

Mommy put her arm around my shoulder saying, "*Sister* (now Sister sounded like a dirty word), Kathy is a wonderful girl who does NOT lie and certainly does not steal."

"Oh boy, if she ever knew about Woolworth's!" I cringed at the thought.

"I am very upset with the way that you have handled this. For your information, Kathy's father sends her five and ten dollars at a time."

Sister was quiet for a few minutes and then looked down at me with her face even redder than before, "Katherine, I am so sorry."

I just kept looking at the black slate floor. I wished I could kick her.

"You may go back to class now, Katherine," she said, patting me on the shoulder.

"No! I think Kathy is very upset and needs the rest of the day off. She will be here tomorrow." With that my mother took me by the hand and we descended the staircase. I wanted to look back but I didn't want Sister to see the big smile that was now on my face.

"Let's go to the butcher…what would you like for dinner, veal cutlets or meat loaf?"

It took me a few minutes choosing between my two favorites. "Meat loaf," I blurted out as I skipped down the street still holding Mommy's hand, a big smile still on my face. The day actually turned out pretty well. Not only didn't I have to go back to class, but I also got to spend the rest of the day with my mother. I decided that on the following day, when Sister took up the collection for the missions, I would only give one nickel like most of the other kids did, and that is all I gave from then on.

Recipe for my Mother's Meat Loaf

1 1/2 Pounds of chopped beef
1 large green pepper grated
1 Large onion grated
2 eggs
1 cup of raw Oat Meal softened with hot water (wait until it cools before mixing it in)
1/3 cup of ketchup
1 teaspoons of mustard

Salt and pepper to taste
Mix all ingredients in well then keep smacking it hard to make it firm.
Shape into an oval and make about an inch dent down the middle
Put in heated oven at 350 degrees. Baste frequently over the dent with
    its' own juice.
Add very slight amounts of water to pan while basting.
Bake 1 to 1 ½ hours-till brown
Yum!

CHAPTER 25

Happy Holidays

For once we were going to have a real family Thanksgiving dinner. Aunt Mae cooked dinner at the apartment in Kearny that she shared with Aunt Jean and her son Billy. We all crowded around the fold-up table, which took up the entire parlor. It was covered with a bright yellow linen tablecloth embroidered with fall leaves and the matching napkins. The china trimmed in gold had been Aunt Mae's wedding gift. There were nine of us, including Ronnie, Granny, Aunt Helen, and Uncle Bill. Mommy had to work at Child's so she came halfway through dinner. Aunt Mae was a really good cook and I ate and ate. The turkey and turnips were delicious; but my favorite was the stuffing, which they called "*košě*" in Lithuanian. I had three helpings with thick brown gravy and lots of black pepper. She also baked pumpkin, apple and raisin pies with her special homemade crust. I liked them all, so I had some of each.

After dinner I played with Billy. I was his older cousin and he looked up to me. We would mostly play with his tinker toy construction set. I built him a Ferris wheel that actually turned round; he was so happy and I was very proud. The day was wonderful, except for Uncle Bill saying things to my mother like, "Eva, It would be nice if you spent more time with your children instead of at the bars." Aunt Helen gave him a poke with her elbow and Mommy got very quiet. I hated him when he said things like that to her.

Christmas Eve was amazing. After months of rehearsal, our choir sang the hymns at midnight mass. I was thrilled singing each one of them. My favorite, *Angels We Have Heard on High,* was sung in three parts. A small group of high sopranos sang *Glorias* very softly in the background, getting louder and louder, until we used full voices at the end. I felt tears run down my cheeks from the joy of singing and the beauty of the music.

After midnight mass I went to Elaine's house, where her mother had prepared a Christmas Eve feast. We were all hungry because we had fasted all day in order to receive communion at mass. Actually, we were not supposed to eat meat until Christmas day, but Elaine's mom served baked ziti with meatballs and sausage, a big ham and a roast beef. She was not very strict about religion. I really wanted to eat all of it but I kept to the fast and had some sardines on bread that tasted awful.

I walked home, which was just around the corner, while Elaine's father watched me until I arrived at my house. It was cold and I saw my breath giving off smoke as I hurried down the empty street. Granny was sleeping, so I quietly tiptoed through the bedroom to the parlor where Ronnie usually slept, but he was already at Aunt Mae's. I plugged in our Christmas tree. Mommy had decorated it on her day off. It looked just like it used to in the Bronx. The large colored lights and glass balls were covered with rows and rows of garland at the end of the branches over which she draped, one by one, strings of silver tinsel. The tinsel was thickly hung giving the lights a soft glowing effect. I thought my mother's tree was better than anyone else's, even Aunt Mae's, which was pretty nice, with bubble lights and lanterns. Around the bottom was a white sheet, our wooden stable placed in the middle, with Mary, Joseph, the shepherds, the three kings and little animals surrounding the baby Jesus. Attached by a wire, a delicate white angel hovered over all of it. On each side of the tree, high piles of presents were all wrapped in pretty paper. I turned the volume very low and played the *Carol of the Bells* over and over as I sat on the rocking chair by the window, cuddled under a blanket in the cold parlor. Mugsy trotted from the bedroom and curled himself up on the studio couch. You could barely hear an occasional car pass in the stillness of the night as snow started to fall. It really felt like Christmas. I listened to my record several times and then heard the outside hall door open. Mommy was home! I turned the key and opened the parlor door for her to enter instead of going through to the kitchen door.

"Merry Christmas, Mommy!" I was very excited to open my presents, even though it was three o'clock in the morning.

Mommy said, "Merry Christmas, Sweetie. Give me a few minutes to dry off and put on my nightgown and robe." Two records later she returned with a beer and a cigarette, steadying herself in the door frame.

The presents my mother usually bought me were all necessities, like socks, scarves, gloves, panties, blouses, skirts, writing paper, books, and soap. Basically, Christmas was when my winter wardrobe was restocked. Some items I had pointed out in store windows, others she picked out herself. My big present that year was a new navy pea jacket that I had been wanting very much. As a special surprise, she also gave me a pink angora stocking hat. As I opened each and every present, I'd thank her with a hug and kiss and exclaim "Wow!" or "Oh boy, just what I wanted!" or "How beautiful!" This pleased my mother and she would wipe away happy tears from her cheeks. I gave her the biggest hug and thank you when I opened Frank Sinatra's recording of *I'll Be Seeing You.*

After I finished opening my gifts, I gave my mother two presents that I bought for her, an *Evening in Paris* perfume set and a pair of nylon stockings. I had shopped by myself for both. When I went into the general store to buy the stockings, I asked for socks. The saleswoman asked what color and I said "pink," thinking of Mommy's flesh color. She then brought out pink ankle socks. I finally made her understand I wanted nylons in a natural tone. Mommy was so pleased with my gifts that she cried more happy tears and hugged me several times. The only gifts left under the tree were the ones that I bought. Ronnie had taken all the other gifts to Aunt Mae's to open later.

I bought Granny a little statue of Our Lady of Fatima and Ronnie a pair of blue and yellow argyle socks. With my craft set, I made all my aunts two potholders to match their kitchens, and I bought two little cars for Billy. I had sent my father three handkerchiefs with the letter J monogrammed on them. He sent me a red coat double belted in the back. Now I had a coat for Sundays and the pea jacket for everyday. Mommy and I didn't get to bed until four thirty. I had to get up at seven thirty to sing at the nine o'clock mass. Christmas was the only day Child's was closed, so my mother could sleep late. I got up for church without effort and sang the hymns again with all my heart.

That afternoon we all had Christmas dinner at Aunt Jean and Aunt Mae's. Aunt Mae cooked just about the same things she made on Thanksgiving except she made a cherry pie instead of apple. We all sang, "Can you bake a cherry pie, Billy Boy, Billy Boy, can you bake a cherry pie, charming Billy?" Little Billy laughed and laughed and sang it over and over. As usual, Uncle Bill and my mother didn't talk to each other all day. We opened more gifts; each one of my aunts gave me a pretty sweater and Ronnie bought me a miniature Spanish señorita doll, dressed in red satin with a black mantilla. Billy had gotten a starter Lionel train set so after dinner we both played with it for a long time.

I loved Aunt Mae and Aunt Jean's apartment. It was modern with new furniture Aunt Jean bought when she was married. When Aunt Mae moved in she brought some really nice pieces with her, like a mirrored curio cabinet with little figurines on the shelves. The two swirling crystal lamps on the woodcut end tables on each side of a brocade couch made the parlor look like a movie set. Aunt Mae and Aunt Jean slept together in one bedroom so Billy could have the other one to himself. His room had yellow walls with blue furniture. There was a nice tile bathroom with a tub and Aunt Mae said I could come over anytime to take a bubble bath. With that, Billy said he wanted, "Bubbles, bubbles." We decided to take a bath right then, so we shared the tub together and played in the bubbles with his water toys, splashing and laughing together. It was a really great Christmas.

CHAPTER 26

The Easter Bonnet

Sister Margaret was always very nice to me after my mother came to school that Tuesday, but I still never gave more than a nickel to the missions. It was a fun school year for me. Our choir was now rehearsing hymns for Holy Week and Easter. During Lent, the forty days before Easter, all good Catholics fasted, and in addition I personally gave up candy and cake. This sacrifice made me feel good; I loved God deeply. It was a great comfort going to mass every day before school. I felt protected and loved. I even went to mass on Saturdays during Lent. A few weeks before Easter, our class went to see the Passion Play, presented annually in Jersey City. I was glued to the stage performance; it was the first time I had ever seen live actors. It was horrifying and sad to see Jesus die on the cross while his mother Mary looked on. I cried all the way home.

At home, I reenacted the scene. I'd pin a veil on my head and pretend I was Mary. I was fully involved in the passion of Jesus during Holy Week, from his condemnation and suffering through his crucifixion and resurrection on Easter morning. I cried again when the priest went through the Stations of the Cross on Good Friday. I prayed to St. Monica to help Mommy stop drinking. I chose St. Monica because she had a deep faith and prayed for seventeen years for her son to return to the church. He did and became St. Augustine.

Easter was not only a holy day, but also a day for new clothes. For weeks we'd shop for a spring coat, dress, shoes, pocketbook, and gloves. Most important of all was the Easter bonnet. On my way to school each day, I passed Anna's Millinery Shop on Ferry Street. In the window was the most perfect bonnet I had ever seen. It was straw with a tiny sprig of pink and white flowers tucked into the navy blue ribbon that wrapped around the wide brim. Each day I longed for it more. "It would look great with the navy coat," I told Mommy. I never thought for one moment that it would be possible to have that bonnet. Every hat at Anna's was very expensive and we bought most of our things at the more affordable Lerner's or Ohrbach's.

One day while walking with Elaine and Arlene, I noticed that the hat was no longer in Anna's window. It was very difficult to hold back my tears. A few days before Easter, Mommy presented me with a box from Anna's. She had bought the hat! On her nineteen dollars a week salary, she had paid seven dollars for it. She cried as I took it out of the box and said, "Sweetie, I know how much you wanted it, so I had to get it for you." Thrilled, I hugged and hugged her again, but a piece of me felt very guilty and undeserving. I had just confessed to the priest that I often was angry and talked back to her. I vowed I would not do that anymore. I tried the hat on in front of the bedroom mirror; it was perfect and I could hardly wait until Easter Sunday to wear it.

Easter morning I got up at four to dress myself and get ready to sing at the five o'clock sunrise mass. In the mirror through the glow of the vigil light, I could see myself in my entire Easter outfit. The new hat, with my two shiny braids hanging down on each of my shoulders, made everything look even more special. I thought I looked very much like Margaret O'Brien, who played Judy Garland's younger sister in *Meet Me in St. Louis*. Usually I walked the eight blocks to Saint James but it was dark so I waited across the street for the bus. It started to drizzle before it came. Getting off the bus I made a dash for the church, getting slightly wet.

Upstairs in the choir loft, I sang the Easter hymns with all my heart. Downstairs the altar was adorned in white satin surrounded by dozens of lilies. As I walked down the aisle to receive communion, I saw people looking at me. I felt so stylish in my new outfit.

When I got home, my mother was still sleeping and Granny had already gone to church. I went to look into the bedroom mirror again, but this time broke into sobs. Devastated, I saw the straw brim of my new hat drooping on all sides.

"What is it, what's wrong?" Mommy said, waking.

"My hat…the rain…the rain ruined my beautiful hat," I cried.

Mommy saw the hat and yelled, "Why didn't you take your umbrella?"

I just kept crying and tried to explain that it wasn't raining when I left, but my mother didn't hear me, she was saying, "I should be crying after all the money I wasted on that hat." She was so angry. "You are punished, go sit on a chair in the living room for the next two hours while I get some sleep."

I sat on the rocking chair looking out the window at the rain, trying to fix the brim of the hat, but it was no use, it was completely ruined. I listened to my *Alice in Wonderland* record as Ginger Rogers said, "Down, down, down, down…falling, falling, falling, falling…."

When my mother woke up again, she came in, lit a cigarette and said, "I'm sorry about the hat, Sweetie, I guess it wasn't meant to be." She always said that after something bad happened. I was so glad she wasn't mad at me anymore, but I still felt very guilty about the hat. "Happy Easter," she said as she handed me a large Easter basket filled with candy: chocolate and coconut eggs, jelly beans, yellow marshmallow chicks, and in the middle, my favorite—a big dark chocolate bunny wrapped in gold and purple foil. "Thank you Mommy, Happy Easter," I said and threw my arms around her neck. I went to my drawer in the bedroom to get the card and two eggs I made for her. First, I had dyed them, one pink, one green, then I wrote MOMMY on each one using silver glitter that I carefully sprinkled over the letters written with Elmer's glue on the end of a toothpick.

When my grandmother came home from church, she baked a big ham. In the afternoon, Aunt Mae and Aunt Jean came over with Billy. Ronnie had gone to Picky Pine to spend Easter vacation with Aunt Helen and Uncle Bill. As we talked and laughed, we ate Granny's delicious ham with horseradish and mustard, coleslaw and boiled potatoes on the side. My sodden Eastern bonnet hadn't ruined the day after all. I was so proud when my mother showed everyone the eggs I had made for her. "Thanks again, Sweetie, they are so beautiful," she smiled, wiping away a tear. She always cried a little when she was happy.

CHAPTER 27

Still Adjusting

One Sunday morning just after we had moved in with my grandmother, I woke up to the smell of something cooking. When I asked Granny what she was making, she said in Lithuanian, "*Viščiukas*." I started to cry because Granny always referred to a woman's private parts as *viščiukas*. I learned later that *viščiukas* was the diminutive for chicken and meant "little chicken." The prelude to Granny's chicken dinners was always the pungent odor of singed flesh as my grandmother held the fresh bird over the flames of the coal stove to burn off its pin feathers. The aromas that soon followed were much more pleasing.

I was getting used to Granny's ways and was beginning to learn Lithuanian. It helped me feel more comfortable with her. I kind of liked being called "*Mažiukas*." She washed and ironed all my clothes and often cooked dinner for Ronnie and me. Granny was a good cook and made things my mother never made, like blinis and what she called "*košė*," a potato pie that she would slowly cook in the coal oven all day until the crust was a flaky, dark brown and the inside was soft and delicious. Pig's knuckles or kielbasa with cabbage was a frequent Saturday night treat. I began to look forward to some of her dishes. One thing I could not stand was the soup she made on Fridays with fish heads; just the smell of it made me gag.

On Sundays, I still hated coming home from the movies when her friends were still there, drinking and singing. They'd stay until at least nine o'clock, sometimes later. I'd close the door to the parlor, barely able to hear my records. Often Mugsy would scratch at the door, go out, and not return until they had gone.

On most days, Mugsy walked me to school, which was eight blocks away. Descending the cement steps of our stoop, we turned left on Jackson Street, and then passed under the brownstone railroad trestle, hearing the familiar sound of the 8:30 a.m. Jersey Central Railroad train toot its horn. Mugsy's four-leaf clover good luck charm would jingle against the buckle of his collar, sounding like a tinkling triangle, while he trotted happily beside me. Crossing Jackson to the other side, we'd turn right on Downing Street, passing the four story wooden house where Aunt Helen and Granny's sister, whom I called Aunt Elizabeth, lived. Sometimes Aunt Elizabeth would wave to us from her second floor window. Mugsy's ears would perk up when he heard the sweet old lady, in her flowered babushka, give him her daily greeting in Russian. Often in good weather, she would sit on a chair on the sidewalk outside of her first floor apartment. Mugsy would then cut across the vacant lot. When I was in first and second grade, Mugsy always walked me all the way to school, but now that I was in third grade, sometimes he would look up at me as if asking permission to stay in the lot where many dogs were usually romping around together.

"Go ahead, Mugsy," I'd say, and off he'd race, his pretzel tail wagging, to join the frolicking. He especially loved to play with the little gray Bull Terrier, Harry, and the German Shepherd, Heinz.

"See you later," I'd wave, as I continued up the street then turned right on Ferry. Sometimes I walked on one side of Ferry Street and sometimes on the other; both had store windows to look into, with clothes, shoes, or even furniture. I loved the florist shop; its garden of different colored flowers and working fountains looked like a peaceful country scene.

Just as you turned the corner onto Jefferson Street, there was a storefront where gypsies lived. Granny warned me that they might put a curse on me. Terrified, I'd run past so fast that by the time I got to St. James School on the next block, I was out of breath.

At three o'clock, Mugsy would be waiting for me directly outside the school's two large oak doors. After licks from him and pets from me, we would start our walk home.

One day when we got to the lot, right in the middle of crossing it diagonally, a mean snarl startled both of us. A large, mangy red dog charged at Mugsy. With teeth bared, he grabbed Mugsy by the scruff of his neck and threw him in the air. Mugsy's loud yelp was accompanied by my screams. Mugsy, a medium-sized dog, seemed very tiny compared to this large, vicious creature. Although stunned, Mugsy lunged back at the enemy. I feared Mugsy would be torn apart. The dog again grabbed Mugsy by the neck. I didn't know what to do, I wanted to hit him but I was afraid he would bite me. I threw my books at this wild beast, screaming and stamping my feet. "Get away you! You get away," I kept screaming. The books seemed to have no effect at all. Harry, Heinz and a few other dogs started to bark and run toward us, but before they could reach Mugsy, a large gush of water hit the monster red dog right in the face. Thankfully, the attack finally stopped. There stood the old Russian lady with a large empty pot in her hands, shouting at the dog in Russian. He backed off and ran away. I picked up Mugsy and held him close, my heart feeling as if it would burst out of my chest. The lady stroked his fur while Mugsy licked her hand. I took my hankie from my coat pocket, dabbing at his wet neck. I was so relieved that there was no blood on it; he seemed fine. Harry, the little bull terrier, was squealing and jumping up on my leg. As soon as I put Mugsy down, Harry, Heinz and two other dogs circled him, all five tails wagging.

Just then Aunt Elizabeth came over, put her arm around my shoulder, and asked if I would like to come up for a cup of tea. I said yes, and tried to call to Mugsy to come up with me, but he seemed to want to play with his dog friends. Aunt Elizabeth assured me I could watch Mugsy from her window. The Russian lady, Aunt Elizabeth, and I walked together to the building. After my aunt and the woman said something to each other in Russian, the old lady patted me on the head. I turned to make sure the red dog had not returned. He hadn't.

We had tea and homemade cookies. In her southern drawl, Aunt Elizabeth called me "daarrlin'." She told me stories about West Virginia and showed me pictures of her three sons, who were all in the Navy. I liked talking to her. That was the beginning of many nice tea parties we would have together. When I went downstairs, the Russian lady's pot was filled with water again as she washed her windows with a brush on a long stick. Mugsy ran from the lot to join me and we turned down Jackson Street toward home.

CHAPTER 28

Sleep Tight...Don't Let the Bedbugs Bite

At first I thought they were mosquito bites causing the large welts on my neck and arms. "It's hives," Granny said, "May is too early for mosquitoes." Night after night, I woke up digging my nails into myself until I drew blood. During the day the welts would flare up and I'd scratch and scratch. One night, after a bite on my neck woke me, I lifted my head from the pillow. Through the flicker of the vigil lights, I thought I saw something moving. Picking up my pillow, I screamed and leapt out of my bed. A tiny bug scurried to take cover. Mugsy jumped up and started barking. My screams and his barks awakened Mommy and Granny. I ran into the parlor, only to see one of these little bugs running down the front of my baby doll pajamas. I screamed even louder. Mommy ran to me as I smacked at my chest, smashing the bug and I watched in horror as blood squirted out onto my favorite pink baby dolls. I was shaking and my body was sticky with sweat. My mother hugged me and said soothingly, "I think we have bed bugs."

"See, it isn't hives," I sneered at Granny bursting into sobs. Granny was standing in the doorway to the parlor. Her short blond hair stuck out on both sides. She slept in her cotton undershirt, a cluster of religious medals pinned to it. The shirt was tucked under her large sagging breasts hanging over long pink bloomers, which came almost to her knees.

"Go back to bed. In the morning I'll take your mattress outside and wipe it down with kerosene," Mommy translated.

"I will absolutely never sleep in that bed again," I yelled as I stormed into the kitchen; the clock said four o'clock. Taking a washcloth, I wiped myself down with cool water. My mother dabbed at the large welts on my neck and arm with Calamine lotion, "I must get some sleep, Sweetie, I have to get up for work at five-thirty." Braiding my hair back, she yawned, "Don't worry, Sweetie, Granny will get rid of the bed bugs." Then she joined Granny, who had already gone back to bed.

When I calmed down, I went into the parlor and lay on top of Ronnie's studio couch. Ronnie was lucky; he often got to go to Picky Pine with Aunt Helen or he'd sleep at Aunt Mae and Aunt Jean's apartment in Kearny. Mugsy jumped up and curled into the back of my legs. Just as I felt myself drifting into a sleep, I felt another bite, this time on my cheek. I screamed and shot out of the bed so fast Mugsy yelped because I had rolled on him. He jumped off the couch, but seemed to be okay. This time only my mother came running in, but I could hear Granny saying, "Jesus, Jesus," from her bed.

"I hate this house," I screamed at Mommy. I wanted to say I hated Granny and all her old things. It was her fault we had bedbugs. I hated living on Jackson Street. I wanted to go back to my home in the Bronx or have a house like Aunt Helen or an apartment like Aunt Mae and Jean, but I only thought it because I knew Mommy would get upset if I said it out loud. I knew my mother didn't make much money and this was the only place we could afford to live in right now. "Bide your time," Mommy always said whenever I complained about living here.

"It bit my cheek, my cheeeeek," I groaned as I felt the welt getting larger.

"Sweetie, I'm sorry but I have to get some sleep," she sighed and kissed me. "Go put some Calamine on it. Granny will take care of the bed bugs first thing tomorrow." After I put on the Calamine, I sat in the plain wooden chair in the kitchen for a while. I was angry with Mommy for leaving Daddy and bringing us here to live. She should have planned it better, not just run away that day without any warning to Ronnie and me. We never even had time to take any of our nice things. I thought of our big console radio in our Bronx parlor. I wondered if Daddy ever even listened to it. I began getting angry with Daddy, too. I hoped he really missed us and was sorry that he was so mean to Mommy and made her run away. Maybe if he told Mommy he was really sorry, she would go back to him. I felt my eyes getting heavy. I wanted to lie down so badly. I lifted up the tablecloth, pulled it over me and lay on the cool enamel kitchen table. I didn't get much sleep, but at least no bed bugs attacked me.

The next day at school, while sitting at my desk, I felt a bite on my leg. When I looked down at my green knee socks, I saw a large welt near the elastic and a bug running down my sock. I screamed and jumped out of my chair, right in the middle of the Catechism lesson. Sister Margaret snapped sternly, "Katherine, what IS the matter with you?" The entire class was looking at me. I don't know how I thought of the lie so fast, but I said, "The pin that keeps my hanky fastened to my blouse pocket, opened and stuck me. May I be excused to go to the lavatory?" I asked.

"Fix yourself and come right back," Sister barked. In the bathroom there was a girl from the seventh grade. I waited until she finished washing her hands and left, before I unlaced my brown and white oxfords and pulled off my sock. I didn't see the bug, but I had a whole group of swollen bites on my calf. I shook out my sock and rushed back to class. I didn't hear a word of the lesson because I kept trying to control myself from scratching the itch on my leg. I was also worried that the bug would show up somewhere else on my body when I heard Sister Margaret asking, "So, Katherine, what are the seven cardinal sins?"

My mind went blank, and then I answered. "Thou shall not kill, thou shall not steal, thou shall...."

"Katherine, you are reciting the commandments. I asked for the seven cardinal sins," she snapped her hands crossed in front of her habit. She waited, her foot tapping. "I guess I don't know," I could feel my cheeks getting hot as I heard a few snickers from the class.

"Well, I guess you'll have to stay after school and write them on the blackboard fifty times and then, I hope, you will know them."

I didn't get home until after four thirty. Granny was out in the backyard, a babushka tied over her hair, wiping down my mattress and the mattress from the studio couch, with rags drenched with kerosene. Everyone's sheets, pillowcases and blankets hung on the clothesline, so I guessed there were bugs in their bed too. She washed all of them by hand and looked so tired. The front of her flowered cotton housedress was soaking wet.

"Hi, Granny, can I help you?" I asked in my sweetest voice.

Shaking her head, she gave me a go do what you have to do wave. I went over and kissed her on the cheek. The fumes from the kerosene pinched my nose and burned my eyes. I felt bad about my thoughts the night before. Granny said, "Vargsyte" in Lithuanian (Poor little one), and something else that I didn't understand, but I think it was assuring me everything would be all right. I looked up and saw Mrs. Yurich waving at us from her third floor window. She was the grandmother of one of the girls that went to St. James. Everyone was going to know we had bedbugs. Just then I noticed our neighbors' teenage boys looking over the fence at Granny. I ran into the house. I could not bear people knowing, they would think we were dirty. If any of my friends found out, I would die. This was the worst thing that ever happened to me.

After sulking in the parlor for a while, I decided I'd better do my homework. I was sitting in the rocking chair next to the window when, after about an hour, I jumped up feeling a familiar bite on my left thigh. I saw the bug darting away under the cushion. I ran to the backyard. "Granny!" I exclaimed, and motioned for her to come inside so that no one would hear. She came in the hallway. "Granny, they are in the rocking chair, too," I blurted out, sobs starting to tighten in my throat. I couldn't believe this nightmare, they were everywhere. I wanted to run away from home. I followed Granny into the parlor where she lifted up the rocking chair. With sweat pouring down her forehead, she carried it out to the backyard. I knew I should have helped her but I wouldn't go near it, I just stood at the kitchen window watching her shake out each layer of scarves.

Later we discovered the bugs were in the drapes, closets, and in their bed also. It was an invasion of bugs, like a horrible dream. I don't know how she did it, but finally after a week of kerosene and washing everything, the house was finally rid of those bedbugs. Every night for a few weeks, before I would lie down in my bed, I'd examine it from head to foot. I'd even lie there a while staying very still as though I were sleeping, then suddenly jump up and lift my pillow to see if any of them were hiding under it. I was terrified they would come back.

I told Elaine I had a lot of homework that week and kept away from my friends fearing that a bug would show itself. I missed everyone so much and spent most of the daylight hours in our backyard, terrified to go in the house. Over the weekend, I stayed in the movies even longer, watching the feature, *Abbott and Costello Meet Frankenstein* twice—it was so funny, it cheered me up.

Elaine, Arlene, and a few of the other kids in the neighborhood had decided to put on a performance of *Cinderella* in Elaine's garage. They began to rehearse and saved one of the stepsister's parts for me. Of course, Elaine was the director and cast herself as Cinderella. Being involved with rehearsals helped me to forget about the bedbugs. Elaine's mother and sisters made our costumes. In three weeks we were ready to perform for the neighbors and all the kids' parents. My mother couldn't come because she had to waitress on Saturdays and Granny didn't come because of her poor English. Ronnie had already left for Picky Pine since his high school got out earlier than St. James. I put my whole heart into my part and was sorry that no one from my family could see me perform.

We charged a nickel for admission and made enough money for the entire cast to go to see the new musical *Words and Music*. Watching Vera-Ellen and Gene Kelly dramatically dance to Richard Roger's *Slaughter on Tenth Avenue* was astounding. It was a love triangle that ended with them both shot and dying in each others arms. Buying the record was a definite must. While I watched Vera-Ellen, I secretly pretended to be her. I knew that if I said it out loud, Elaine would want to be her and I'd have to choose somebody else. Then we all went back to Elaine's and her father brought home two large pizzas from Cortese Restaurant. Part of me wanted to stay in the city for the summer; I loved being with my friends. But the other part of me wanted to go to Picky Pine and get away from Granny's house. Aunt Helen kept Picky Pine sparkling clean and the only bites I would get there would be from mosquitoes. When Aunt Helen kissed me goodnight, she always said, "Sleep tight and don't let the bedbugs bite." I used to think it was very cute rhyme. But now that I knew exactly what it meant, it certainly didn't sound so cute to me anymore.

CHAPTER 29

Changes

Uncle Bill had already picked up Aunt Jean and little Billy at their apartment in Kearny. I hoped to say goodbye to my mother, who would be home any minute, but Uncle Bill was shouting, "Get in and let's get going. The Friday shore traffic is awful." I climbed up into the rumble seat with Mugsy, and waved to my grandmother as we drove away.

"We both love Picky Pine, don't we, Mugsy?"

Through the car window I could see little Billy sucking his thumb and clinging to Aunt Jean. He was still such a baby at four. Thinking back five years ago when I was four, I remembered going to the movies, restaurants and stores alone, and traipsing around by myself on Halloween. "Wow!" I thought. "Was I really that young when I spent so much time alone?"

As we passed Newark Airport, I burst out singing *Don't Fence Me In*. I felt the blood rush to my face as a man in the car next to us chimed in while waving his hand like he was conducting an orchestra. "Let me ride through the wide open country that I love, don't fence me in…." I hadn't realized we had stopped dead and everyone could hear me. I kind of slumped down into the rumble seat while Mugsy barked at the man. Then traffic moved and he waved and drove off.

The sky started to get dark. I was afraid it was going to thunder and lightning. There was always a big plastic cover tucked under the seat. Aunt Helen sent for it from a catalogue that showed a picture of two people sitting in a rumble seat being protected from the rain. I hoped it wouldn't storm; it got so hot under that plastic. Although I was afraid of the lightning, I remembered that Aunt Helen always told me the safest place to be was in a car because the rubber tires grounded the electricity. I thought of my mother, who was terrified during storms. In the Bronx, she huddled in the foyer closet until they stopped. At my grandmother's apartment, our bedroom was the middle room without windows so she felt more protected. As we drove along, the storm passed over; the sun was setting and it started to get a little cool. I reached for the blanket stored next to the plastic. The next thing I knew we were pulling into Aunt Helen's driveway. It was almost dark, the lightning bugs twinkled and the sweet smell of honeysuckle seeped into my nose.

Ronnie came out of the house to greet us. He looked so handsome tanned, and his hair was blonder from the sun. Aunt Jean and Aunt Helen kissed and hugged Billy, who started screaming because he was afraid of the lightning bugs. Uncle Bill was taunting him, "Mah, Mah, Mah." That made him cry even more. Aunt Helen snapped, "Bill, stop that." She only called him Bill, not Ducky, when she was angry. I could see Aunt Jean was annoyed but she never said anything to Uncle Bill. I think she was afraid of him, too.

"How is my Katie Did?" Ronnie was saying as he helped me down from the rumble seat. Mugsy had already jumped down and was watering the nearest tree. I caught a firefly and held it in my fist. "See Billy, they won't hurt you." He just jammed his thumb in his mouth and ran behind Aunt Jean. Aunt Helen said, "Why don't we eat first and then you can all unpack and settle in." Aunt Jean came and joined us half way through, because she put Billy in for a nap.

There was big news. Uncle Bill and Aunt Helen were telling Aunt Jean and me that they bought Mrs. Arnold's house. It was the large property next to Picky Pine and was the only two story house in all of Carmersville. I saw Mrs. Arnold once; she was very old and I was a little afraid of her. The house had worn brown shingles and looked like a haunted house from the movies—not like Picky Pine, all white with green awnings and flowers all around it. Uncle Bill was saying that they were going to fix up Mrs. Arnold's house and move in there, and then rent out Picky Pine in the summer. The other small house in the back of Picky Pine, that had originally been renovated from a chicken coop into one large space, had now been divided into two little bedrooms, a tiny living room and kitchen. The remainder of the work on that little house would be done this summer and Uncle Bill thought they might even be able to rent it out by August.

"What happened to the wind-up Victrola?" I anxiously blurted out. "Right now it's stored in the tool shed," Ronnie assured me. "I've been playing the Al Jolson records there." I could see from the way Uncle Bill looked at me that he did not like the interruption, so I just listened. I was not happy about moving to that big brown house; I loved Picky Pine.

After the dishes, Aunt Helen helped me put away my clothes. We opened the maple love seat in the living room into a bed and put on the sheets and pillows. Everything smelled so fresh and clean. "Is my little Puddin' tired?" Aunt Helen asked as I stretched out in the comfy bed. I nodded again as she kissed me once more on the forehead. "Goodnight," I murmured. Thank goodness she did not say, "Sleep tight and don't let the bedbugs bite."

I said a short prayer asking God to keep my mother safe and to make sure she came to Picky Pine for my birthday. I could hear them talking over the sounds of the crickets. I looked over at Ronnie; he winked at me again and said, "Get a good night's sleep, Katie Did." I nodded and smiled. The radio program *The Shadow* was just beginning, one of my favorites. The last thing I remember was hearing Lamont Cranston saying, "Who knows what evil lurks in the hearts of men? The shadow knows."

CHAPTER 30

The Summer of 1948

Hello, My Darling,

Why haven't I heard from you? I thought you would write me long before this—how have you been feeling—have you lost any weight? I have been sick for the last 3 weeks but am now feeling much better. Business here has been very bad—your mother never wrote me letting me know if you're coming to stay here with me for a while after school closes. I have missed you very much and am sorry I have not been able to make a trip back there to see you. Your Aunt Jean was supposed to take the trip also with little Billy. Wouldn't you like to come for a while? I want you to write and let me know, so I can make arrangements for your trip.

How has everybody been at home? I hope everyone has been OK and all are feeling well. Here the weather has been wonderful and the beach is only 3 blocks from here, but I don't get a chance to go there at all. I'm sure if you came for a trip you would enjoy it here. Tell your mother I had expected an answer to my letter. I wrote her—the least she can do is answer what I asked of her. Give everyone my best regards and answer real soon.

Love and kisses,
Daddy

P.S. Sorry you did not get the money I sent you last time in time for what you wanted it for. I had mailed it in time. I am sending you $5.00 to buy your-self something.

My mother had forwarded the letter to me here at Picky Pine. I didn't know Daddy wanted me to come this summer. I was very upset that she hadn't told me. Just when did she get his letter? I then remembered one night, quite a while ago, when she had been drinking, she did say, "Your father wants you to come for a visit sometime, go ahead and go if you want." I could tell by her tone that she really didn't want me to, but she never mentioned it was for this summer. I also never knew that Aunt Jean had planned to go to Florida. If Aunt Jean went, I would feel more comfortable visiting. The last time I saw my father was on my First Communion day when we drove to the Bronx. I felt so bad about Daddy expecting an answer and wanted to write to him right away.

Dear Daddy,

I just got your letter. Mommy forwarded it to me. I guess Aunt Jean is not going to Florida with Billy, because we are both here with Aunt Helen at Picky Pine for the summer. I really didn't even know she might be going, and I didn't know you wrote to Mommy about my coming to spend some time with you this summer. I will write to Mommy and tell her to answer your letter. I won't see her again until my birthday.

I am sorry you were sick and happy that you feel better now. Thank you for the $5.00. When Aunt Helen and Uncle Bill go to the auction, I will buy *some new shorts. Today is the 4th of July and we are going to Asbury Park to see the fireworks. I wish you could come with us.*

I love you and miss you,
Kathy

I needed to ask Aunt Helen to help me pick out something for Daddy's birthday at the auction so it would get to him in time. Since Aunt Jean left last Monday, little Billy followed me around all week; I became his second mother, which made me feel very grown up. Saturday evening when we drove to the auction, I sat in the rumble seat; Billy sat up front with Aunt Helen and Uncle Bill. The auction was only a few miles away off Highway 34 on a large lot in the woods. Trucks, wagons, and tents sold a large variety of merchandise. As soon as we arrived, Billy slid off Aunt Helen's lap, reaching out to clutch onto my outstretched hand. Aunt Helen was pretty strict with him because he was so spoiled and a real crybaby, and he was very afraid of Uncle Bill who still bellowed, "Mah...Mah...Mah!" which made him hide behind me with his thumb thrust into his mouth. I felt sorry for him because I understood that he desperately missed his mother and Aunt Mae.

First we went to sit among many rows of folding chairs that were in front of a small platform with a podium where an auctioneer stood with a gavel. He took bids on various items like beach umbrellas, lawn mowers, small kitchen appliances and many other things. It was exciting to sit with Aunt Helen while she bid on things. That night she bought a hair dryer with an entire set of different sized metal curlers. She often permed or set the local ladies' hair at the house. We passed different food stands that filled the air with tempting smells as Aunt Helen walked us over to the wagon that sold jewelry. I picked out a pair of black cuff links with a gold letter J for Daddy's name, Joe. I paid two fifty for them. Aunt Helen said they were small and easy to mail; we would wrap them and drive to the Post Office first thing on Monday morning. I still had enough money to buy a red pair of shorts I found. Being a little chubby it was great to find a pair with an elastic waist. Aunt Helen told Billy and me that she would spend five dollars for each of us for our birthdays, so if we saw something we wanted, she'd buy it tonight. We looked around. I saw a few things; one was a pretty white peasant dress with different colors of bric-a-brac around the ruffles of the skirt. Billy saw an army pup tent but it was ten dollars. Aunt Helen said, "No, I said I will only spend five dollars for each of you." Billy started to cry and then sob so loud that people were looking at us. Good thing Uncle Bill had gone to the tool tent. Although he was acting so spoiled shouting, "I want it…I want it…please, please," I felt very sorry for him because wanted it so badly.

I said, "Aunt Helen, let's buy it, you can use my five dollars, it will be half mine and half his."

"Are you sure, Puddin'?" she asked, her blue eyes looking straight into mine with one eyebrow raised. I thought again about the pretty peasant dress, but nodded yes.

The next day after breakfast, Aunt Helen helped us put up the pup tent. Billy was so excited and could hardly wait. I was glad we got it for him. We held up the poles while she hammered the pegs into the ground. Billy and I played house in it for a while. When it started to rain, we sat in the tent eating bowls of huckleberries and I read him *Goldilocks and the Three Bears*. He loved it when I read to him, and I liked it too. I read it three times and would act out all the parts for him.

This summer was different. There were always workmen around fixing the big new house. Because the house only had a pump outside and in the kitchen, Uncle Andy and Mr. Carmer came over on weekends to help Uncle Bill dig the new well. I did my chores every day, went picking berries often, and met with the kids at the pond with Mugsy most hot afternoons. Thank goodness Billy was too young to come with me. I needed a break, because he was always clinging to me. Sometimes Aunt Helen walked him down. They'd only stay a short time; he still needed to nap every day and always left tired and cranky.

Ronnie still worked as a caddy at the golf course. He left early in the morning before we got up and didn't come back until after dinner. The golf course was about a mile away, right in back of a mansion belonging to Arthur Brisbane, the editor of the *New York Times*. Uncle Bill knew the caretaker, so one day we went through the mansion on a tour. It was three stories high with a game room that had a full size bowling alley. I could barely take in the beauty of all the rooms. I felt I was walking through a movie set. The caretaker gave me a very small china doll that he took from a floor to ceiling display case with at least a hundred dolls. She was dressed in a long blue dress, so I named her Alice Blue Gown.

On cloudy or rainy days, I liked to read my library books. The library in Newark let us borrow twelve books over the summer. One day when Billy was out playing with his pail and shovel, I went into the tent to read a story in *Grimm's Fairy Tales*. Billy started screaming. "That's my tent—you can't go in there without me…you get out, get out, get, get out NOW!"

"Billy, Aunt Helen bought this tent for both of us," I reminded him. He didn't seem to understand or care. He kept at it until I felt like smacking him.

"Get out, you get out, out of my tent!" he screeched.

I was so angry, I went over and yanked out the pegs on one end and took down one pole shouting, "This is half mine, so I am taking my half down." Of course the entire tent collapsed. He screamed like someone was killing him. Aunt Helen came rushing out of the house with her teeth clenched, ran over and pulled us both by the hair. She was furious, "Don't you two make such a commotion! What will the neighbors think?" I never saw her so angry. I started to cry and tried to explain how selfish Billy was being and that it was my tent too. She wasn't listening. She took down the other half and marched off to store it in the tool shed. I stuck my tongue out at Billy and stomped off to the house to retreat into the bedroom.

That night we were all very quiet at dinner. Ronnie came in as we were having dessert. "Hi, everybody…what's wrong?" Aunt Helen told him what a commotion we had both made over the tent. When she wasn't looking Ronnie winked at me. Suddenly, I felt he understood how unfair Aunt Helen had been to me.

We didn't dare ask Aunt Helen to put back the tent until Billy's birthday party. Of course, it was also my party. Because I never had mine separate anymore, I resented Billy getting most of the attention. The good news was that my mother did make it down for my birthday that year. We went to pick her up in Farmingdale Station on Friday morning. Billy was thrilled to see the train pulling in. "Choooo-Choooo," he roared over and over clapping his hands. When my mother stepped off the train, she looked so pretty in her red dress with a black and white polka dot sash around the flare skirt. She had a few days of vacation from Child's Restaurant and would stay until the next Thursday. After hugging each other, I hopped into the rumble seat while she went up front with Aunt Helen and put Billy on her lap. Billy was squirming and kicking, he wanted to come in the back with me; he didn't see my mother often and didn't want her holding him. I worried he would make a mess of her dress. He finally calmed down and put his thumb in his mouth. I could hardly wait to get home so we could talk. I wanted to ask her about going to visit my father, but I knew it had to be the right time. I didn't want her to get angry with me, but I didn't want my father to be angry with me either, or to think I didn't want to see him.

When the car turned into the driveway, Mugsy, squealing and wagging his pretzel tail, galloped to Mommy. "I'm happy to see you too, Mugsy," she laughed. Aunt Jean and Aunt Mae would be driving down tonight with Uncle Bill to stay for the weekend.

The next few days were fabulous, I didn't even mind our joint birthday celebration. Mommy bought me more shorts and three pretty blouses and a new two piece bathing suit in a gold color. Everything fit except one pair of shorts was too tight. Aunt Jean and Aunt Mae each gave me a card with five dollars so I could buy what I wanted. Granny sent me a pretty little white pocket book. When you unsnapped the front it had a little mirror...I loved it. Inside she put one dollar. "I have eleven dollars, so now I can buy the white dress at the auction," I beamed. Aunt Helen said we would go to the auction the following Saturday. That evening when Ronnie came home he gave me a card with another five dollars. Now I had sixteen dollars!

Two days later, on my actual birthday, Aunt Helen baked a small cake and afterward, Mommy, Billy and Aunt Helen sang Happy Birthday to me, but we had to light the candles again so Billy could blow them out. My mother had saved one present to give me. It was a tiny silver locket on a chain.

During my mother's visit, I didn't go down to the pond. We just hung out together. On two days we picked berries alone, up on the hill near the gravel pit where it was sunny and peaceful. When we leaned over the bushes to fill our pots with huckleberries, Mommy would hum and take long, slow puffs on her Pall Malls. While we were alone, I wanted to ask her about my father's letter, but I knew whenever I spoke of him it changed her mood and she became very irritable, so I kept putting it off.

For lunch Aunt Helen would put liverwurst, ham, lettuce, tomato, mayonnaise and mustard for us to make our own sandwiches on fresh rolls, rye bread or Wonder Bread. I had reminded Aunt Helen to buy one of my mother's favorites, canned Spam. Mugsy always got two pieces of liverwurst, but Aunt Helen would not let us give him more than that since she always fed him leftovers.

In the evenings, my mother sat with Aunt Helen on the swing, rocking back and forth, both of them drinking cold bottles of beer while Billy and I had cherry Kool Aid. Some nights when Uncle George Carmer came, he made us laugh at his humorous tales. I loved to hear my mother laugh. She never drank too much when she was with Aunt Helen. She wound up staying until Friday morning, a day longer than she planned. Even though she didn't have to go back to work until Sunday, she told me she would rather not be here Friday night when Uncle Bill returned.

When the train pulled away, Mommy was still waving from the window. I held back my tears; I wouldn't see her again until after Labor Day. With his thumb in his mouth and his hand gripping mine, Billy watched the train until it was out of sight. I think he was happy to see my mother go because now he had me all to himself again.

That afternoon when we got home the flag was up on the mailbox. I got a birthday card from Daddy. He sent me ten dollars and he wrote, *"One for each year, and one for good luck. I can hardly believe you are nine years old already."* He asked me to send him my picture. I was so glad my father didn't write anything in my card about coming to Florida. I never got the courage to ask my mother if she wrote to him or to tell her that I thought she should have told me about him asking if I could visit this summer. I wrote a little note.

Dear Daddy,

Thank you for the $10.00. I got some nice presents. Billy and I had a joint party because his birthday is two days before mine. He was four years old. I wish you could have been here. I thought of you on your birthday. I hope you liked your gift and had a very nice birthday.

Aunt Helen and Uncle Bill bought another house. We will be moving into it in a few weeks, but

we will have the same address. I will write you a longer letter soon, but I wanted to write this note to thank you for the card and the money.
I love you.

Hugs and kisses,
Kathy

At the beginning of August, we moved into Mrs. Arnold's old house. Inside, the walls were painted in light colors of yellow and green but the outside still looked like a haunted house from the movies with dark brown, worn out old shingles. A large truck arrived with Aunt Mae's furniture that she had kept in storage since her divorce. Since she now lived with Aunt Jean and Billy she didn't think she would ever use it again. Aunt Helen spent a few days arranging everything in the new house and then let me come in to see.

Everyone became accustomed to using the side door that opened into a small dining room where a stairway led to the upstairs bedrooms. "That is a Duncan Phyfe folding table," Aunt Helen pointed out as we walked straight ahead into a big kitchen. In back of the kitchen, another doorway led into a tiny room. Here Mrs. Arnold had left an old green cylinder washing machine on four legs that had a clothes wringer attached to one side of it. The parlor, which was to the left of the side entrance door, now had an expensive floral carpet and some of Aunt Mae's wedding furniture. I loved the two crystal lamps that were on the circular end tables. "Those table tops are marble from Italy," Aunt Helen beamed. "Ronnie will sleep down here on a fold-up bed, or if it's hot, he can roll his bed out to the screened in porch." That is where the real front door to the house opened into the parlor.

Upstairs, a long narrow room with a pitched ceiling served as the bedrooms. The first thing you came upon was a large white dressing table with a mirror. The first part of the room had a full bed on one side and a twin bed on the other. The twin bed would be mine; Billy would get the big bed so that when his mother or Aunt Mae came, they could sleep with him. Aunt Helen's and Uncle Bill's twin beds were at the very end of the long room, which was partitioned off by a high wardrobe and a dressing screen. In the corner was a small door that led to an attic.

In the next few weeks, Uncle Bill kept pulling things out of the attic which Mrs. Arnold's family left behind when she died. There were some nice paintings in what appeared to be expensive frames, but Uncle Bill tore off the back or cut through the paintings, hoping to find hidden money. He also took apart dressers and bookcases. He said that it was rumored that Mrs. Arnold had a lot of money and he was sure she had some hidden. He never did find any money. Then he made a huge bonfire and burned everything.

On August sixteenth, Ronnie came home in tears. I had only seen him cry one time before when we left the Bronx. Both Aunt Helen and I ran to him. "Ronnie, what's wrong?" we both asked.

"The Babe is dead."

"What Babe?" I asked.

"Babe Ruth died today," he barely could speak and ran up to the house.

We followed behind him. When we entered, we could hear his sobs upstairs. I started to go up but Aunt Helen shook her head, "He'll be all right, just let him cry it out."

That night we all listened to the radio. The solemn voice of a news commenter announced, "Today, August 16, 1948, Babe Ruth has died of cancer, he was only fifty-three years old." The program then proceeded to tell us more details about his life with the Red Sox and the Yankees. Ronnie was very quiet. Actually, we all were. I felt badly for my brother. I knew that Babe Ruth was his baseball hero. After a few days, he seemed better. I was so relieved since I hated to see him without his usual smiling face.

By the third week in August, a family came to rent the little house. They were going to stay until Labor Day. Aunt Helen seemed really happy about everything, but I wasn't; this big house wasn't as cozy as our sweet little Picky Pine. At night when we went upstairs to sleep, Aunt Helen put a metal pail in a corner to use in case we had to go to the bathroom. When I peed in it, I was embarrassed by the loud noise, but Billy giggled and tried to make different noises while he peed by waving around his little penis. I'd wait until it got light in the morning and dash to the outhouse. One nice thing about the house was that while I was lying in bed, I could see right out the window that went from the floor to the start of the pitched ceiling. I loved to look at the moon and stars and listen to the crickets chirping. I discovered that when I wiggled my big toe it cracked and sounded just like a cricket was in the house. Some nights, when Uncle Bill was ready to go to sleep, I would wiggle it. He would get up yelling, "Where the hell is that damn cricket?"

I'd pretend I was sleeping and, of course, I'd stop wiggling my toe when he came toward the cricket sound. Sometimes I did it two or three times. I loved upsetting him. When it was quiet, I looked out at the moon. I could hear Bing Crosby crooning *Moon Over Miami* in my head. I thought of Daddy and wondered how it would be if I did visit. Would we be shy with each other? Would we laugh together and run to the beach?

I heard little Billy sigh and I looked over at him asleep on the big bed across from me, peacefully sucking his thumb, looking like a blond angel. Even though he was a real pain, he was my new little pal. I chose other songs to play in my head, *Daddy's Little Girl, Peg of My Heart, You Always Hurt the One You Love,* and *I'll be Seeing You,* until I myself fell into a sound sleep.

CHAPTER 31

Upsetting News

During August, Aunt Helen took Billy and me to Belmar Beach many times so we would be out of the way while the men worked on digging the well and building a bathroom. I'd rush into the ocean and pull myself out on the ropes supported by buoys until I reached the last row of floating metal barrels bobbing up and down beyond the reach of the breaking waves. I loved hearing the sound of the waves crashing onto the beach. Aunt Helen and Billy would wave to me from the blanket, where Billy played with his pail and shovel. Not many people were out that far, so I'd belt out my favorite songs in the same gentle rhythm as barrels did their dance, the hot sun caressing my face and shoulders. Mostly I sang Frank Sinatra's *I'll be Seeing You,* over and over. Sometimes I thought of Daddy and Mommy or I would fantasize a future lost lover. It was so peaceful. I'd stay out almost the entire time, coming in water-logged and famished. I thought the warm soggy sandwiches with an occasional crunch of sand were absolutely delicious. Once I ate, Aunt Helen would not let me go back into the water. She insisted I would get cramps and drown, so I would build a sand castle with Billy. Then I'd rinse myself off at the shore and snuggle on my stomach on my beach towel, often slipping into a summer doze—with beach chatter, waves and an occasional airplane seeping into my daydream. Later we'd walk on the boardwalk to the Dairy Queen. A vanilla Blizzard was my standard; it was so thick, cold and refreshing. Most of the time, I'd drift into another nap in the rumble seat during the half hour ride home.

The peace of the day stayed with me as the outdoor shower washed the sand from my body, cooling my hot skin. Wrapped in a towel, I'd run into the new house and leap upstairs. Examining my naked body in the dressing room mirror, I saw how white my budding breasts looked compared to my chocolate-sunned skin. Putting on fresh clean shorts and a blouse, I scampered downstairs toward the tantalizing smells of dinner and helped Aunt Helen set the table. The sunset through the window lit the dining room orange. It was so perfect during the week when only Aunt Helen, little Billy and I—and sometimes Ronnie— had dinner together.

Aunt Jean came most weekends to see Billy. She was much younger than my mother, Aunt Helen and Aunt Mae and she talked to me about a lot of things. She told me how Billy grew in her stomach and how a baby came out, which sounded a little scary and painful. It was from her I learned that the "Aunt Martha" my aunts and mother always referred to as "an expected visitor"…the "Aunt Martha" that kept us from going to the beach or doing some other activity…the "Aunt Martha" that never actually appeared at our house, was their name for the menstrual cycle. My mother never really talked about any of it. What I knew, I knew from my friends, especially my new friend Sissy who lived across the street from me in Newark and was four years older than I.

I was flattered when Aunt Jean asked if I'd watch Billy on Saturdays during the coming school year while she worked at her waitress job at Hayne & Company. She'd pay me; I said yes. He had come to be like my very own little brother. When he wasn't having a tantrum, he was fun to play with and read to. But he did do things that upset everyone. The worst was one morning during breakfast when he told all of us the color of our pubic hair. He had gone around in the early morning peeking under all our sheets while we were still asleep. My face reddened with embarrassment since I was just starting to get a few hairs and he said this in front of Uncle Bill and Ronnie. They thought it was very funny but I thought it was disgusting. After that I vowed never to wear a nightgown again, only pajamas, and to tuck the sheet tightly around my body.

The summer was coming to an end. Uncle Bill took his vacation the last two weeks before Labor Day. Dinners weren't as much fun with him there; mostly just he and Aunt Helen talked. I missed my mother, I missed going to the movies and to church. Going to the Protestant church with my country friends wasn't the same. Uncle Bill heard me mention missing church to Aunt Helen. He said he would take Aunt Jean and me if we wanted to go. Everyone was very surprised that he offered. I was flattered because it seemed as if he liked me a little better lately. So for the last three Sundays he took us to church and waited outside in the car reading the *Asbury Park Press*. At night we'd all listen to programs on the radio in the living room together. *Amos and Andy* was very funny and Uncle Bill liked *Break the Bank,* a game show with Bert Parks.

The local kids started school a week before Labor Day, so for the last week, I had no one my age to hang out with. I had read my twelve library books and there was just so much time I could spend with little Billy. Aunt Helen and Uncle Bill thought it would be a good idea if I helped him with the extension of the cellar he was digging under the house. I would load the dirt that he dug out into a pail, lug it up the steep cellar stairs, and dump it into a wheelbarrow. When the wheelbarrow was full, Uncle Bill would wheel it over to an area of the land that needed filling. Pail after pail I filled and climbed up the stairs. It was very tiring and I was sorry I had agreed to help, but now he expected me to do it—and day after day I did, getting very dirty and sweaty. It was difficult to scrub the dirt from under my nails, and I ruined two blouses and my red shorts. However, the big reward was that Uncle Bill bragged to Mr. Carmer and the workmen that he and I were digging the cellar. "Little Puddin' here is helping me dig the cellar." I welcomed his approval.

Aunt Mae had come to visit for Labor Day weekend. That Saturday night while I lay upstairs in bed, I overheard her tell Aunt Helen that my father had sent papers for my mother to sign so he could get a divorce. My stomach turned over. Though I knew she was very angry with him, I somehow still thought maybe, just maybe, they would get back together.

I now wondered if a divorce is what Daddy wrote to Mommy about and that's why she didn't answer his letter that asked about my visiting him in Florida this summer. The more I thought about it, the more I thought I was right, because in his last letter to me he didn't write about my going to visit him in Florida anymore. I went to unlock my white jewelry box I kept on the dressing table. As I opened it, the little ballerina in her pink tutu spun round against the bright pink velvet lining. Reaching for his last letter (I kept them all in order) I slipped it out of the envelope. My eyes scanned the writing until I saw *"How are you!"* I tried to imagine his voice, but I couldn't; it had been two years since I had seen him. I smelled the paper; it smelled slightly musty. All the letters smelled the same. "Is it the smell of Florida?" I wondered. *"How are you!"* I read again. He had an exclamation point instead of a question mark. Why? I reread the entire letter again.

My Darling,

> *I am sorry I didn't write sooner. I have had too much to do here and have been very tired. I thought by now I would have been able to sell this place and take a trip there to see you, but now business is very bad and I have to wait until it picks up.*
>
> *How are you! Are you being a good girl? Did you lose any weight? I have lost 25 lbs. I work very hard and long hours and it's very hot in the kitchen. We have had rain every day, it doesn't rain too long, the nights are nice and cool for sleeping.*
>
> *Have a little dog now, I call her Trouble. She is very cute and smart. She shakes hands with me and barks when I tell her to speak to me. I lost her a week ago and I called the radio station here and they kept broadcasting for her, the whole neighborhood was looking for her. I got her back the next day. Now you know why I call her Trouble. I'm sending you a picture of her, and also the front and side room of my place. Do you like it? How are you feeling! I hope you*

*are alright. Give my regards to all. I hope everybody
is well.*

> *Write me soon.*

> *With love and kisses,*
> *Daddy*

I couldn't find anything in the letter that might be a clue to the divorce. Except why did he wonder if I was feeling alright? *"I hope you are alright."* I wondered, "Did he think I knew about the divorce and was upset about it?"

Suddenly I felt sorry for my mother. She always said she'd never go back to him, but I'd bet she's upset too. Somehow I knew she wanted him to still want her and liked to punish him for having been so mean to her.

I heard Aunt Helen say it was for the best. "Eva had enough of Joe beating her up. Maybe now she can put all this behind her and find a nice man to marry." Marry! A stepfather—it was a frightening thought. I was glad I was going home the day after Labor Day; I wanted to talk to my mother. Maybe she changed her mind. Maybe she would go back to him now that he was asking for a divorce. I thought about the apartment in the Bronx, that beautiful mirror in the foyer. Then I remembered that my father lived in Florida now. His daughter, my half sister Louise, had moved into our old apartment with her husband Frank and a baby daughter, Helen. My heart started beating so fast and I was breaking into a sweat. The divorce seemed like a bad dream.

I pretended to be asleep when I heard Aunt Mae and Aunt Jean coming upstairs and getting into bed with Billy. They both murmured lovie-dovie words to him as he lay there sleeping contently with his thumb in his mouth. Then Aunt Helen and Uncle Bill came up and climbed into their squeaky twin beds. A while later, I heard Uncle Bill loudly relieve himself into the metal pail. I also had to go to the bathroom, but I was too embarrassed to go into that pail, and was too afraid to go outside in the dark by myself. Feeling miserable, I thought all night about Mommy, Daddy and me. I didn't realize that I had bitten my nails down to the nubs until I tasted blood and felt my thumb throbbing. The sky started to get light and a rooster crowed.

Next thing I knew, Uncle Bill was sitting on my bed in his boxer shorts shaking me lightly. "Puddin', are you going to sleep all day? It's eleven o'clock, don't you want to go to mass?"

Waking to him sitting there made me very uncomfortable. I nodded and slipped quickly out of the bottom of the bed making a dash down the stairs and to the outhouse. The thought of the divorce made my stomach hurt. I was feeling really tired and miserable, making me feel even worse were the flies buzzing around my behind. I ran out quickly but halfway to the house I realized I had forgotten to throw sand from the pail down into the hole like Aunt Helen taught me, but I didn't go back because I had to dress fast to make the twelve o'clock mass. I'd pray to God and St. Monica to make everything turn out all right.

CHAPTER 32

Back to Newark

The day after Labor Day we were on our way back to Newark with Mugsy and me in the rumble seat. Aunt Jean and Billy had taken the train and Ronnie was staying a few more days to caddy and go back with Uncle Andy. It was hot and humid, the traffic was heavy and the ride home seemed longer than going down to Picky Pine. When the car finally passed by Newark airport, everything looked dingy. The smoky air from the factories seeped into my nose and burned my eyes. Turning onto Market Street, I thought that most of the brown wooden houses seemed even browner and more ramshackle than when we left. Jackson Street looked shabby again with overgrown weeds along the sidewalk. Granny's building was uninviting, wedged between the Esso gas station and the wooden house next door, where several black children played on the front stoop, while the noise of the chain saw screeched from their backyard. Adding to it all were the trucks braking at the foot of the open Jackson Street Bridge. All of it assaulted my ears and eyes. Mugsy barked and leapt out of the rumble seat as we pulled up to Granny's.

Aunt Helen and Uncle Bill helped me take my belongings out from the floor of the rumble seat. Then Aunt Helen gave me a big hug and said they'd better be getting home. Uncle Bill grunted good-bye or maybe he was grunting hello at Granny, who had come out to greet me. She was very glad to see us. Mugsy squealed and wagged his tail and seemed happy to see her, too. When we walked into Granny's apartment, it seemed smaller and darker. Mugsy didn't notice or care. Wiggling with excitement, he ran right into the parlor and jumped onto the studio couch.

It was five o'clock and my mother wasn't home from work yet. I could hardly wait to see her. Granny made me some blinis. They were nothing like Aunt Helen's dinners, but they were good and I was hungry, so I ate five of them while Granny said her rosaries, whispering and swaying back and forth on her rocking chair. The house was hot and smelled of melted wax. It did not feel good to be back.

Mommy came home at nine, which was early for her. She was so happy to see me and started to cry. As we hugged, I could smell the beer on her breath and the cigarettes on her clothes mixed with the familiar scent of Evening in Paris. Mugsy was squealing again and running back and forth from the kitchen to the living room.

"My Sweetie is home, I missed you so much," she sighed, bending over to hug me.

With my hands around her, I felt bandages on the back of her neck. "What happened to your neck, Mommy?" I asked, startled.

Granny was explaining in Lithuanian, which I was starting to understand pretty well, that for no reason at all, someone in the building had thrown boiling water out of the window while Mommy was sitting on the backyard steps reading and getting some sun on her day off. No one saw who did it, but she thought it was the Polish woman on the third floor who was always making remarks about my mother when she or Granny passed her in the street.

My heart ached at the thought of Mommy being hurt by that mean old lady. I wanted to go right upstairs, bang on the door and scream at her. Even though I hated Mommy's drinking, I did not want anyone calling her names or hurting her. Instead I asked, "Are you okay, Mommy? When did it happen?"

"Two weeks ago, the blisters are gone now, but my neck is still a little stiff. Don't worry, I'll be fine."

Mommy and I talked for about an hour. I wanted to ask her about the divorce, but I felt it wasn't the right time. Instead I told her about my summer and that I would be watching Billy on Saturdays. Then I got ready for bed. Granny said she would unpack and wash and iron all my clothes the next day. "I would like to iron them myself," I said proudly. "Aunt Helen taught me to iron, and I ironed most of my clothes all summer."

It was difficult to fall asleep in the heat. There was no window to look out at the moon and stars; instead, as usual, the vigil lights eerily projected huge moving shadows of the saints onto the walls. I lay there thinking that one good thing about being back in Newark was that Aunt Helen and Uncle Bill were living on Downing Street. It was great having Aunt Helen nearby. Swatting at the mosquitoes that buzzed around me, I finally put the sheet over my head and with the sweat soaking my baby doll pajamas, I fell into a deep sleep.

Awakening to the smell and sound of Granny's coffee perking, I felt Mugsy still snuggled at the back of my folded knees in the dark bedroom. He groaned and snuggled tighter as I tried to get out of bed. My mother had left for work at Child's a few hours earlier. I missed Picky Pine with the sun shining into the windows, the rooster crowing, and the smell of Aunt Helen's bacon frying. Instead, the saw was already humming loudly from the yard next door.

It was hot. After washing off with hot water that Granny had poured from the kettle into the basin in the kitchen sink, I fumbled through my clean clothes that Aunt Helen had separated from the dirty, and chose a pair of rose pedal pushers with a matching rose and white checkered top. I wanted to look nice. I couldn't wait to run around the corner to Clover Street to see Elaine and the other kids. Granny helped me braid my hair. I approved of the image of myself in the bedroom mirror with my skin so tan. When I went to put on my size seven sneakers, they didn't fit anymore. My feet seemed to have grown, which I couldn't tell while running around barefoot or wearing sandals. I started to cry; I thought my feet were too big already. Granny said we would go to Ferry Street later and look for new sneakers. I reluctantly slipped on my worn out white sandals. After dunking challah into coffee, I left with Mugsy at my side. He had been scratching impatiently at the door to go out.

As soon as we went through the outside door, Mugsy lifted his leg by the tree then galloped down the street where I could see him turn right at the corner of Downing Street, headed to his dog lot. Walking down Jackson Street, looking at our neighbors sawing wood, walking under the railroad trestle where passing cars had flung their garbage into the weeds, made me break into a run until I reached the corner of Clover Street. One turn and the scenery changed to pretty two family houses with fences and flowers lining the street. Three houses down, I entered Elaine's driveway. I could feel my heart pounding with excitement as I yelled up to her second floor window. "Eeeelaine, Eeeelaine." I saw her appear and disappear, she came charging down the back stairs and seemed just as happy to see me. We hugged and jumped up and down. We had a lot to tell each other. Arlene arrived a few minutes later and we repeated the hugs and jumping. Elaine's mother yelled down from the window, "Katherine, how are you? Nice to see you. *Maaaaarrrrooone!*" she exclaimed, dragging out the Italian word she used often. "You are even darker than Elaine."

She was the only one beside the nuns who called me Katherine, but somehow when she said it, it sounded okay. Arlene, Elaine and I ran into the garage and didn't waste any time to start jumping rope. We played Double Dutch for quite a while, until Elaine's mother called us for lunch. We brought the ham with butter on soft rolls she had made for us down to the bottom of the steps and pulled over a wooden box from the garage to use as a table. I went back up to get the lemonade.

"Thanks, Annie."

"Good to have you back home, Katherine."

Arlene told me she was not going back to St. James School; in fact, she was moving the next weekend to North Newark. Her mother was going to marry the man she had been seeing. I sucked in my breath and blurted out, "Oh, no!"

"Don't worry, we will still see each other," Arlene said as she reached for my hand. "My grandmother is still here so we'll be visiting often, and you both can come to see my new apartment." My reaction of "Oh, no!" was mostly about her having a stepfather. I could not bear the thought of my mother getting married, but I didn't say that out loud to Arlene. I just nodded as she told us how excited she was about the fact that she was going to have her very own room. Stanley, that was her stepfather's name, was going to let her pick out her own furniture.

I told them that I thought my mother and father might be getting a divorce. Neither of them said anything. Just then we heard, "Look who's back, how are you?" Elaine's father yelled with his charming

Portuguese accent as his plumber's truck with its pipes and tools rattled into the driveway. He was very gray and very handsome, and was always so cheerful and nice to all of Elaine's friends; he gave me a big smile. I thought he looked like Ezio Pinza.

"Hi, Mr. Chunha," I waved, glad for the interruption. I wished I had Elaine's family. I liked her mother and father and her two older sisters. I thought she had the perfect family, with a nice house, a television, and a great cooked dinner that they all ate together. Her mother didn't have to work and she was always taking the girls shopping to buy beautiful new clothes.

After I left Elaine's house, I walked up Jackson to Downing Street to visit Aunt Helen. I walked up the three flights but when I knocked there was no answer, so I went down to the second floor and knocked on Aunt Elizabeth's door.

"Well, hello, honey. Charles, look who's here," she called to her son, my older cousin. He had the same kind of Virginian accent as Aunt Elizabeth. "Well, I'll be, if it isn't my sweet little cousin," Charles drawled. I didn't know him too well because he was in the Navy and not home very often. It was so strange to hear them speaking with that twang, since Granny was Aunt Elizabeth's sister and hardly spoke any English.

Aunt Elizabeth always served me tea and cookies. She told me how hot the summer had been here, how much she loved having Charles home, and all about the visit of actor Lou Costello of the Abbott and Costello team. Apparently, he had looked at the lot across the street as a possible site for a youth center. It was such exciting news that a movie star had been right here! Aunt Elizabeth said he bought all the kids ice cream and signed autographs. I was so sorry I missed his visit. We looked out the window at the lot and I could see Mugsy playing with another black dog a little larger than him. I yelled, "Mugsy, Muugseeey!" He looked up at the window. I went back into the kitchen to finish my tea and, before long, there was a scratch at the door; it was Mugsy, wagging his tail as we opened the door. He came in and smelled around the three rooms. "Hi there, little fellow," Charles clucked at him to come over. Mugsy loved to be petted, so he sat next to Charles for as long as he would pet him.

It was late afternoon when I went back home. Granny was singing while she worked the earth around the marigolds planted in the center of rubber tires. My clean clothes swayed on the clothesline in the slight breeze. Granny said as soon as she finished, she would wash up and take me for sneakers before the stores closed. Much to my dismay, the new white sneakers I picked out in size seven and a half at Goldfinger's store didn't fit, I needed a size eight. Aunt Helen always teased me that if I kept drinking so much fresh milk, my feet were going to grow. I also had been scooping the cream from the top of the milk bottles with a spoon. Boy, was I sorry now. It was embarrassing to be a size eight. Granny also bought me a pair of brown penny loafers for school. Most of the kids either wore loafers or brown and white oxfords with their uniforms. Granny had gotten my uniform out of the cleaners and washed and ironed my two beige blouses. I went into the stationery store and got a few pencils and a black and white composition book. Only two more days before the weekend and then school would start on Monday. I was ready for the fourth grade and anxious to get back to choir practice.

I asked Granny if she'd take my new shoes home so I could go to the movies. I read on the marquee of the PIC movie theatre that *Belle of the Yukon* with Randolph Scott, Gypsy Rose Lee, and Dinah Shore was playing. It started at six. I loved Randolph Scott and I loved that movie. I also had not gone to the movies all summer. Granny gave me twelve cents for the movie and ten cents for popcorn that she said I should buy since I hadn't eaten dinner yet. When the lights went out, I was so excited. It was great to be at the movies again! I watched and began my pretend game. I couldn't make up my mind if I wanted to be Gypsy Rose Lee or Dinah Shore, they both liked Randolph Scott, and so did I. He was the owner of a dance hall and was so handsome. The next movie was about dinosaurs. Normally, I would have stayed to watch, but it was late and I was getting hungry. Granny said she was going to make *kože*, her potato pie, so I left before it began. I thought I might come back on Saturday to see it and watch *Yukon* again, but it depended on what was playing at the Rivoli.

It was dark when I came out and I found myself running down the block. It was strange to be back in the city and I was just a little frightened by myself. When I entered our hallway, I could smell the potato pie. Mugsy greeted me with his squealing and wagging. Granny cut me a large slice, and then she went to sit in the parlor on the rocking chair to say her rosary. I helped myself to another piece and ate in the hot kitchen while I listened to *Fibber McGee and Molly* on the radio. The *košė* was so delicious. Granny really made this so well; the crust was nice and brown and the inside was so soft. I was now full and very tired. I wished Mommy would come home. I wanted to wait up but, by ten thirty, I went into the bedroom. Granny had already lay down in her bed. I said goodnight and I got ready for bed. Mugsy and I snuggled together again and I think I must have fallen asleep almost as soon as I hit the pillow.

CHAPTER 33

Sister Agnes

I was proud to be in the fourth grade. At St. James, grades four through eight were on the second floor. We were the bigger kids now, closer to the high school students on the third floor. We got to know some of them because they often acted as monitors. I didn't like our new teacher, Sister Agnes. She didn't seem to like me either. Actually, she didn't really appear to like any of us. Behind her granny glasses, her eyes remained stern under thick gray eyebrows. She looked older than most of the other nuns.

It was a relief to be part of the choir. The director, Sister Maria, whom we all adored, scheduled rehearsals three times a week for two hours, one that overlapped with the last hour of Sister Agnes's class. We were once again rehearsing the Christmas hymns I loved. Walking home for lunch on the sunny side of the street, feeling the warmth of the Indian summer sun, Elaine and I would sing together. Elaine would go to her house to eat and I to mine. I'd take the little charge book from Granny's icebox cabinet and go around the corner to Mimi's grocery store to pick out my lunch for the day. It was usually Chef Boyardee ravioli, macaroni and cheese, or chili in the can. Today Mimi told me she just received a shipment of Butoni's frozen lasagna, which I loved, but it took too long to bake at lunchtime, so I took one package for dinner. Sometimes Granny was home and sometimes not. I would just heat up whatever I bought, eat it, wash the pot and dish, and then head back to pick up Elaine for the rest of the school day. She always left at the last minute and we'd have to walk fast and sometimes run to make it on time. I sure didn't want to be late for Sister Agnes.

About a month into classes, I got into trouble. Our homework assignment was to write a letter to the classmate whose name we picked from a box of little papers Sister Agnes had folded. Then we were to mail it and each of us would bring in the letter we received. I picked Edward's name. He was not very popular in the class, but it just so happened that on the first Saturday of the school year, we saw each other at the Rivoli movie theatre. We started talking and found out that we both came by ourselves every weekend, so we decided to meet each Saturday and sit next to each other. My letter read:

October 15, 1948

Dear Edward,

 I really love meeting you at the Rivoli. Next Saturday whoever gets there first should save the two end seats in the second row of the mezzanine. Wasn't it fun last week watching Abbott and Costello Meet Frankenstein together? I'll see you next Saturday when Johnny Belinda with Jane Wyman is playing. The coming attractions looked so good.

Sincerely yours,
Kathy Persico

I smiled when Edward started reading my letter out loud, but my smile soon faded when my attention shifted to Sister Agnes. I saw that she had taken the pointer and began tapping it against her desk. This was the clue that she was very angry. By the time Edward finished, her face was beet red. Our names spewed from her lips, "Katherine and Edward, come up here this instant!"

Edward's smile also disappeared and we both walked anxiously to the front of the room.

"Put your hands out, both of you." Sister glared at me and swatted me hard on the knuckles, and then she swatted Edward. I felt the blood rushing to my face and held back my tears. "How dare you meet at the movies? It is a sin to watch those horrid movies. Didn't you listen in church when Monsignor read the list of movies banned by the Legion of Decency?" I thought she would burst right out of her wimple. There were snickers in the classroom and she screamed, "Be still or all of you will get your knuckles swatted."

She made me feel very guilty for going to the movies and worse for meeting Edward there. Edward and I did not look at each other, nor could I look at anyone in the class as Sister sneered through gritted teeth, "Go back to your seats, and from here on you will please address yourself as Katherine, Miss Per-see-co!" She always mispronounced my name. "Per-sic-co," I wanted to correct her, but I never dared. My friend Lucille ran her finger on my leg as I passed her desk. We were saved from further reprimands and abuse, because just then Sister Maria came to gather us for choir practice.

The next Saturday, Edward and I both went to the Rivoli, but just waved to each other. We didn't dare sit together for fear Sister Agnes would find out somehow. After that, I really didn't like her and wished that fourth grade would go by quickly. A few weeks later, we were practicing our Palmer Method with stick pens, making rows and rows of black circles within the lines of the composition notebooks. Sister Agnes was going up and down the aisles looking over our shoulders, sometimes taking someone's hand and guiding it to perfection. Suddenly I felt a whack across my cheek so hard I thought I'd fall off my seat. She just glared at me and grabbed the pen out from between my fingers and proceeded to make her perfect circles. I was stunned and embarrassed. A rage came over me and I had to restrain myself from jumping up and kicking her. I hated her so much at that moment. When I allowed my eyes to glance up, I saw all my classmates intently practicing their Palmer. It was so quiet in the room I thought everyone could hear my heart pounding. Sister Agnes never uttered a word; she just proceeded to glide through the rest of the aisles for what seemed like forever until the bell rang for recess.

I ran to the girl's lavatory. In the mirror I could see the imprint of her fingers on my cheek; there were four distinct welts and it really smarted. Lucille came over and offered me wet paper towels she had prepared. "I hate her so much," I wailed. "I wanted to kick her and pull off her habit. She is mean, so mean!" Lucille nodded in agreement.

When we went back to the room, Sister had put four math problems on each section of the blackboard. I was one of four that got called up to solve one. It was long division with fractions. I was very nervous but very good at math so I finished first.

"Excellent, Katherine, you may sit," she announced as though nothing at all had happened earlier. For some reason, from that point on she was pretty nice to me, or as nice as she acted to anyone, especially after I got my haircut. This definitely wasn't something I wanted to do. I loved my long, thick braids. However, the nurse examined our heads every few weeks and six of the thirteen girls in our class had lice in their hair, including me. We were required to leave school immediately to address the problem.

Up three flights I charged to Aunt Helen's, pounding on her door, holding the note the nurse had given to us stating we would not be allowed back into school until the lice were gone. I made such a racket that Aunt Elizabeth stuck her head out and called up from the second floor, "Honey, is that you?"

Aunt Helen opened the door and I ran into her arms sobbing. "Whatever has happened?" she asked quite alarmed.

"I have head lice," I burst out, almost choking.

"What is it, Helen?" Aunt Elizabeth yelled upstairs.

"She's okay. We'll tell you later." Aunt Helen kind of chuckled and said, "I'm so relieved; I thought you had been in an awful accident." She told me that in her beauty parlor, she often had to treat head lice. "Come on, we'll go to the drug store and buy a fine-tooth comb and I have some kerosene under the sink."

"I want to stay here; I don't want anyone else to know I have bugs in my head."

That afternoon, Aunt Helen spent a long time fine combing through my thick hair. She had spread a white sheet over the coffee table and combed and combed, each time bringing teeny black bugs to the sheet. She would then squash them with her thumbnail. She pulled out a single strand of hair and showed me little white spots. "These are the nits, the eggs, so we have to soak your hair with kerosene." The kerosene stank and burned; even though a towel was wrapped tightly around my head, my eyes burned and were tearing from the fumes.

"I bet I got these lice from that girl Geraldine, she is always a little dirty," I said stamping my foot.

"Now, now," Aunt Helen said, "if five other girls have them there is no telling who the first was."

"I want them out, out of my head as fast as possible," I shrieked.

"Well then, I think we'd better cut your hair, little Puddin'."

"No! That would be worse than having bugs."

"Puddin', if you really want to get rid of them, short hair will be easier to manage."

"No, I'm not cutting it, I'm not!"

After she washed out the kerosene my hair still smelled of it. I sat by the coal stove until it dried. I winced as Aunt Helen tediously combed out the tangles in my now brittle-looking hair, and then she braided it again. "You have so much hair."

"Are they all gone now?" I asked.

"No Puddin', the eggs will keep hatching, so we have to do this for quite a few days."

I could hardly believe I said the words, "Okay, cut off my braids."

"Are you sure?"

I just nodded. Aunt Helen went to get the scissors. I closed my eyes and felt the grating snip, snip of the scissors. When I was brave enough to look, Aunt Helen was holding my two braids in her hand. Then she combed out my hair and started to shape it into a feather cut. I looked into the mirror, but I did not see me. I didn't like my hair short, but it was done. I cried some more.

"As soon as we get rid of the lice, I'll give you a little perm, and your hair will look real purdy."

This was the most terrible day. I wanted my hair back. "What are you going to do with my braids?" I said as I looked at them sadly.

Aunt Helen had laid them side by side on the table. Aunt Helen went to the cabinet and took down a jar. "Here, why don't you put your braids in this jar until you're ready to throw them away."

"I'll never throw them out, I'm going to keep them forever." I gently lowered each one into the jar.

When I went back to school and walked into the classroom, Sister Agnes said, "Don't you look pretty, Katherine. Class, look at Katherine's new haircut, doesn't it look nice?"

I heard, "Yes, Sister," from several of the kids. I still didn't like my hair short, but at least it made Sister Agnes like me more. I took my seat behind Lucille. As I passed by, she slid her finger on my leg again and I knew from her big smile that she was happy for me.

CHAPTER 34

Meeting Margaret

Dear Daddy,

Here is a picture of me with my new feather cut. I didn't like it at first, but now I think I am getting used to it. It makes me feel more grown up. Do you like it? I am sorry to hear you were not feeling well again. I hope you are better soon. I got a good report card from my fourth grade studies. All A's and two B's. The B's were in Gym and Science. Our teacher is pretty fresh but she seems to like me because I pay attention and get answers right.

Thank you for the ten dollars. I will start saving for Christmas presents. Thank you for the picture of your dog Trouble. I will try to take a picture of Mugsy, but he never stays still, besides he looks the same. I'll keep Trouble's picture in my jewelry box. That's where I keep your letters. I will write soon.

Love,
Kathy

He didn't write anything about the divorce, so I didn't write anything either. Mommy told me about it one night. She said it was the best thing that they got divorced because she never wanted to see him again, if she could help it. "He is still your father so you should not let it change anything," she said over and over while sitting in the rocking chair, drinking her beer and taking long drags on her cigarette. "If he thinks it's going to bother me, then he has another thing coming. It doesn't bother me one bit," she slurred.

Well, I didn't think it was the best thing, but it seemed that it was going to happen anyway. She signed all the papers and sent them back to him. It was easy for her to say it shouldn't change anything for me, but I felt like he was divorcing me, too.

I was glad I was so busy. Their divorce had bothered me throughout the summer in Picky Pine. School every day, with lots of homework and choir practice three times a week, kept me from thinking about it.

On Saturday when I watched little Billy, I'd get up early and take the 34 Market bus to downtown Newark to meet Aunt Jean and Billy at the Lipple Dance School. He had some leg problems and the doctor said tap lessons would help. After class, we'd stop for breakfast at Hayne & Company, where Aunt Jean worked as a waitress at the downstairs food counter. We'd have pancakes or waffles with blueberry syrup and bacon or sausages. Then I'd bring Billy back to their apartment in Kearny until Aunt Jean came home at four o'clock. Aunt Mae worked two shifts at the GE factory and wouldn't get home until after midnight. She always made dinner and left it for Aunt Jean to warm up for all of us. Then Billy and I would take a bath. It was great to be in a modern bathroom with a real tub. They had a television set, so after Billy went to bed, Aunt Jean and I would watch a movie or a game show. Sometimes, we even would wait up for Aunt Mae. One night we watched all of *The Last of the Mohicans* together.

The routine on Sunday was to attend mass at St. Cecelia's Church. Then I'd take the number 40 bus home to Granny's. Most Sundays, I just stopped home, dropped my bags and headed to the Rivoli movie theatre. I had to get away because, as usual, my grandmother's friends would be there drinking and singing loudly in Lithuanian. When I got home from the movies, they were usually gone or ready to go. Once they left, I would study for tests that Sister Agnes always gave on Mondays.

A new tenant had moved in on the top floor. Every Sunday evening she would bring a big plate full of meat in spaghetti sauce and put it in the backyard for the stray cats. Mugsy would smell it, scratch to go out, and gobble most of it down. It looked and smelled so good, too good for the dogs and cats. One Sunday I opened the door just as the woman was coming down the stairs. "Hi," she said in a breathy voice with a slight accent. She was very pretty and young, maybe only twenty years old, wearing a blue cotton housedress and an apron. "My name is Margaret. What's your name?"

"Kathy," I smiled.

"I hope you don't mind if I put this out for the animals." I again noticed her accent.

"No," I said, "it always smells so good."

"Every Sunday I make gravy for the macaroni. Dominick, that's my husband, and my little boy Patrick will eat the meatballs and sausage, but not the beef and pork that I use for flavor. But my mother-in-law said it's not real Italian without the meat."

"Well, it looks pretty good to me."

"Would you like it? There is nothing wrong with it."

"Sure," I said.

"Here you go," she said as she handed me the paper plate. "Let me know if you like it and I'll bring it down to you next week." She went bounding up the stairs. Just the smell made my mouth water. It was delicious, so good. I shared some with Mugsy, who would have gotten most of it if she hadn't given it to me. Granny thought it was awful that I had taken food that was meant for the cats and dogs. She did not like Italian food, so to her it was distasteful and disgraceful. "Look what she's eating," she kept saying in Lithuanian and crossing herself as she swayed back and forth on the rocker.

The taste brought back memories of eating at Daddy's mother's house with his family, which seemed so long ago. I tried to picture my other grandmother and aunts, but I could hardly remember any of their faces. I liked going there and missed Uncle Tom singing after we ate. I wondered if I would ever see them again.

The following week, Margaret knocked at the door and asked if I wanted the dish. Did I ever! I could hardly wait for her to come downstairs. "Would you like to come up to my house a little later?" she said in her breathy voice. "On Sundays, Dominick always goes to play cards with his friends and Patrick goes to sleep, so it would be nice to have some company."

"Sure," I said, "right after I do my homework."

Once more Mugsy and I devoured the plateful. I did my homework and told Granny I was going up to Margaret's apartment. I knocked lightly, thinking her little boy might be sleeping already. She opened the door with a big smile and her breathy "Hi." The kitchen was so bright with yellow walls and a black and white linoleum floor. She had a gas stove and shiny pots hung over it. Starched ruffled white curtains framed two white Venetian blinds. "Your kitchen is so pretty," I said.

"Thank you, let me show you the rest." She spoke lower and put her finger to her lips, "Patrick just fell asleep." Their middle room was the parlor, which had a nice brown couch with fluffy orange and beige pillows, two matching beige chairs and a polished wooden coffee table over a really pretty carpet with swirling colors. Directly across from the couch was a television! The only people I knew who had a television were Elaine and my aunts. We walked through to the bedroom where Patrick lay sleeping like a little angel in light blue pajamas in his white crib. A full size bed in the middle of the room was covered with a white chenille bedspread with pink and yellow flowers in the center. Under my feet I could feel the thick softness of the blue carpeting. The room smelled sweetly of baby powder. I could hardly believe I was in the same layout as Granny's apartment. Margaret kissed her fingers and planted that kiss onto Patrick's forehead. Then we tiptoed out and back to the kitchen.

Margaret told me she was a Scottish war bride. So that was the accent. Dominick was in the Army and they fell in love in Scotland. He was very Italian, she said, and his mother was teaching her to make the food that he liked.

"Could you teach me to make that great spaghetti sauce?" I asked.

She took one of her breaths, "Sure, I'd love it, and I'm a good teacher, too. But the Italians call it gravy," she whispered as though she were telling me a secret.

I told her my father was Italian and that my mother and father were getting a divorce. Suddenly, I found myself crying. She came over and hugged me. I could smell the light scent of flowers as I let myself stay against her for a moment. When I moved away, Margaret got me a tissue.

"Whenever you feel like crying, you can come up here and cry."

I nodded. I always felt ashamed about crying, but somehow I was very comfortable with her. I told her about Sister Agnes, the choir, and watching Billy. She said maybe I could watch Patrick some night so she and Dominick could go to a movie. I said I could. The time went by very quickly and before I knew it was ten o'clock. "You'd better be going down to sleep, you have school tomorrow and I don't want to be the one to get you into trouble with that Sister Agnes," she said in her Scottish accent, which she made even thicker for emphasis. I knew I had found a friend and I looked forward to spending more time at Margaret's.

When I walked into Granny's kitchen, it seemed darker than ever. The black iron coal stove loomed out at me. Granny was in bed saying her rosary. I washed up, brushed my teeth and changed into my pajamas. I wasn't very tired, so I stayed in the kitchen studying my science for a while. Ronnie came home. He had been out with his friends. He helped himself to the pot of potatoes that Granny kept warm for him on the coal stove. I told him about Margaret. He thought it was great that I was going to learn to make sauce or gravy as Margaret called it. He laughed, "Don't you think it's pretty funny that you're going to learn to cook Italian from a Scot?" He started to imitate a Scottish accent giving me instructions. "First you roll the meatballs, lassie, then you fry them in olive oil…." He was doing the accent so well—we both started laughing.

Just then we heard the familiar sounds of the front hall door crashing open, the knocking against the hallway walls, and Granny commenting in Lithuanian, "Nu, Jau ateina, alaus prisilakusi," Oh, now here she comes full of beer.

Mommy was fiddling and fiddling with the key, until Ronnie jumped up impatiently and opened the lock. She looked startled as the door opened and she staggered forward, grabbing onto the icebox cabinet for support. Ronnie went into the parlor and closed the door.

"Well, hello to you, too," Mommy said waving toward the parlor. I wanted to run right after Ronnie. I hated seeing my mother like this, but I was afraid she would be angry with me. Granny kept saying things like, *"Puikus būdas atvykti namo!"* Nice way to come home. "If you don't die of drinking, the smoking will kill you." Mommy lunged forward again and somehow managed to make it across the room and plop down heavily into the rocking chair. "Hi, Sweetie. Your Mommy is very, very tired." She took out a Pall Mall and tried to strike the match. I got up and lit her cigarette. She inhaled so long on the cigarette, she starting coughing. I could hear Granny still praying in between saying, "*Puikus būdas atvykti namo.*" I was glad my mother didn't say anything to her because that would start one of their fights, which could go on for a long time.

"Mommy, I was just going to go to bed—Goodnight, Mommy," I said as I kissed her on the cheek. I almost gagged from the smell of beer and cigarettes.

"Good night, Sweetie."

I was so relieved that she didn't start in about Daddy or Ronnie, because then I would get caught and have to stay and listen. I climbed into my bed and snuggled next to Mugsy, who let out a little growl because I had to move him to make room for myself. No wonder Daddy wanted a divorce. When Mommy is that drunk, she is not like-able. But part of me felt very sorry for her. I thought that if her life were happier, she wouldn't drink. I said another prayer to St. Monica to help her stop drinking. The next thing I knew, through the flicker of the vigil lights in the darkness, I could see my mother in bed with Granny and hear her loud snoring. I put the blanket over my head. My movement sent Mugsy to go sleep with Ronnie. I thought of Margaret and looked forward to learning to cook."

CHAPTER 35

March Madness

During the winter, I busied myself with my usual activities—school, choir, movies, babysitting for Billy and, now, also for little Patrick upstairs. Margaret did teach me to make Italian gravy and I put the recipe in my jewelry box with Daddy's letters.

When Daddy got the picture with my new haircut, he wrote, *"What a beautiful young lady you have become. I wouldn't have recognized you if we passed on the street. How impressive—you've learned to make gravy at nine years old."* I imagined a day in the future when I would be so proud to make the gravy for my father.

I also found both a new interest and a new friend. In early March, the St. James High School students performed in a play called *Arsenic and Old Lace*. The upper grades were able to attend the annual high school senior production. I had never seen actors on stage before, except for the *Passion Play* and the dancers at Radio City. Although I loved pretending I was a movie star acting out the characters of a movie I had just seen, and enjoyed being in Elaine's garage plays, this was different; on stage were real actors talking to each other. Suddenly I knew I wanted to be a stage actress. I was so enthralled by *Arsenic and Old Lace* that I went to see it every night the entire week it played and two times on Sunday. I got all the actors to sign my program. They said I was their biggest fan. I felt like a big shot because for the rest of the term they waved to me in and out of school.

Aunt Jean's boyfriend, Frank, took her to see the Broadway show *South Pacific*. When I babysat for Billy, I would sleep over and each Sunday morning she'd play the record, over and over. Aunt Jean told me the story. I memorized the words to all the songs. I especially loved to sing *Younger than Springtime*. At home with a makeshift sarong, I'd pretend I was the young Polynesian girl with the handsome lieutenant so in love with me.

One late Sunday afternoon after I had seen *The Kissing Bandit* with Frank Sinatra and Kathryn Grayson, I used the low brick wall of the demolished building in front of the billboard across the street as my stage. With my eyes closed, I sang *A Kiss in the Dark* with all my heart and imagined that Frank Sinatra had just kissed me. Desperately trying to reach Kathryn Grayson's high notes, I heard laughter. Flashing me the biggest smile was a teenage girl wearing a bright red jacket, which stood in stark contrast with her very blond curly hair.

"I'm Sissy. I just moved into that building." She pointed behind the billboard. Instead of being embarrassed, I laughed, too, as I buttoned up my pea jacket to shield myself from the cold. We introduced ourselves and she was surprised to learn I was not quite ten years old. She was fourteen but we were pretty much the same size since I was big for my age. We talked about the movies and movie stars we liked. Then she invited me to come up to her apartment for a while. We used the back entrance and climbed up the worn, wooden zigzag steps leading to the second floor landing where they lived. She introduced me to her mother, father and brother Junior, who was two years older than Sissy. Except for all four having blond hair, Sissy seemed to have a look all her own; they were short and chunky, she was taller and shapely. Like us, they also lived in railroad rooms with a kitchen, two tiny dark bedrooms and a very small parlor. Their toilet was outside on an unheated porch and was shared with a family from another apartment. In comparison, Granny's little toilet off the kitchen seemed much more modern. I actually had to go to the bathroom but wouldn't because it looked all rusty and nasty, aside from being freezing cold.

Sissy was in her first year of high school, and I again felt like a big shot since she liked to hang out with me. Elaine was still my best friend, but very often at night I would walk across the street to Sissy's. In her room we looked at movie magazines or played "Name that Star." Giving each other clues, we'd try to guess the star's name. Occasionally, her friend Joanie, a sixteen year old high school junior, would hang out with us and all three of us would have fun playing the "star" game. I was the best at it.

About a week later on a Monday night, my mother came home very drunk. I heard her stumbling around in the bedroom and then call out, "Ronnie, shut that off and come in here now." He had been in the parlor listening to one of his favorite detective shows, *The Adventures of Sam Spade*. I was in the kitchen doing my homework when Mommy came in with a small brown leather book. She slid one of the kitchen chairs into the bedroom, almost breaking its leg as both she and the chair crashed through the doorframe. "Kathy, you sit right here," she cried, dabbing at her red eyes. Ronnie was sitting on Granny and Mommy's bed with Mugsy by his side.

"Ronnie, since you are gong to be sixteen in May, I think you should know about your father. It's all in my diary," she wept as she handed it to him. I went back to get my homework and Mommy took it away saying, "Kathy, I want you to pay attention and make sure Ronnie reads every word."

Ronnie and I just looked at each other. We knew that saying anything would just set her off. So I sat while Ronnie read. The overhead light was on. I noticed all the cracks in the yellowing wall and the rotting plastic covering on the large high window to the parlor. I thought about how clean and neat Margaret's house was in comparison. Mommy kept coming in and out of the bedroom, crying harder each time, blowing her nose and dabbing at her red eyes. She kept pointing at me and saying, "Kathy, you are in charge, be sure your brother reads every page."

Ronnie would raise his eyebrows at me whenever she left the room. I shrugged my shoulders apologetically at him but neither of us spoke a word. In the beginning, Ronnie seemed interested and sat against the back of the iron bed. What exactly was he reading? How much did she write in the little brown book? But after about an hour, Ronnie started skimming through the pages. I didn't tell on him. More time passed and we were both exhausted. Ronnie was now lying on his side, facing me with one arm supporting his head. My behind was hurting from sitting so long on the wooden chair. I decided I'd watch to see where my mother put the diary and read it without her knowing. Ronnie looked bored. Why didn't she just sit down and tell him about his father? After all, she made me sit and listen to the story so many times. Why shouldn't I read it, too?

Every time Mommy stumbled in and asked me, "Is he reading? Are you watching?" I nodded yes. Sometimes Ronnie saluted me. In the meantime, Granny had come home from church, where she was making a Novena. She came into the bedroom lighting the vigil candles on the two dressers in front of the saints' statues. Ronnie threw her a kiss. I could hear her murmuring in the kitchen as she washed herself at the sink. It was getting chilly; I got up to pull the blanket from my bed and wrap it around my shoulders.

I looked over at the statue of the Virgin Mary; she looked so peaceful. Around her neck, Granny had put the blue glass rosary beads I'd won as a prize for giving the most to the missions. The flickering of the candle made her eyes look as though they blinked at me. I silently begged her to keep peace in the house this night. In exchange, I promised to say two rosaries tomorrow.

After what seemed like hours, Ronnie closed the book. When my mother came in again and saw the diary closed, she asked, "Did you read every word?" Ronnie nodded. We all looked at each other. Suddenly, she reached over me, almost falling, and grabbed the diary from Ronnie's lap, startling Mugsy, who yelped, jumped off the bed and ran into the kitchen. I ran after him. My mother then charged into the kitchen, went directly to the round iron grate of the coal stove, opened it, and threw the diary into the flames. I gasped, "Mommy, don't." I could not believe she had done that after saving it for so many years. She was so drunk, I wondered if she'd be sorry tomorrow. Loud sobs came from her as she watched it start to burn, her life story turning to ashes. An acrid smell of burnt leather saturated the rooms. Sparks flew as she jabbed at it with the poker. Ronnie was now at the kitchen doorframe, shaking his head.

Granny yelled in Lithuanian, "Now she's going to burn the house down. Shut that grate." Mommy smacked at her arm where some sparks singed her. Granny got up, yanked the poker from her hand, then slammed the iron cover over the flame, yelling "*Rupūžė*," which is just about the worst name you can call someone in Lithuanian.

It was now eleven o'clock. Ronnie just kept shaking his head in disbelief and then marched to the parlor. Mugsy followed. The door slammed and the lights went out. Granny got ready for bed and so did I, but my mother stayed in the kitchen crying.

I wondered what, exactly, she wrote about Ronnie's father and how he felt reading it. I was angry with her for destroying the diary. "It's not fair, now I can never read it," I thought. I wished Mugsy hadn't gone into the parlor with Ronnie; I missed him snuggled into the back of my legs.

Mommy was off the next day. When I left for school, she was on the big bed snoring loudly. Granny had already left for church. After school, as soon as I opened the hallway door, I inhaled the wonderful smell of Mommy's cooking. When I entered the kitchen, she smiled at me. "Hi, Sweetie, I'm making breaded veal cutlets." I knew they were Ronnie's favorite, but I loved them, too. Veal was expensive so we didn't have it very often. She acted as if nothing had happened, but her eyes were red and swollen. We waited an extra hour, but Ronnie didn't come home for dinner, so Mommy said I could eat his cutlet. I felt guilty eating it, but I knew she would be upset if I said no. It would be like taking sides if I asked her to save it for Ronnie.

When he came home just before eight, he went straight into the parlor. A few minutes later, *Rhapsody in Blue* boomed loudly from the record player. My mother slammed down her glass of beer on the table and by the way she swung in the rocking chair, I knew she was getting more and more upset. I was glad it was Tuesday because I could escape up to Margaret's apartment. Every Tuesday night at eight o'clock, I was invited to watch Milton Berle in the *Texaco Star Theatre*.

When I came back downstairs, I could tell my mother had been crying. I was thankful that the only words she said were, "Kathy, I'm sorry I didn't save the diary for you to read when you are a little older." I nodded and kissed her good night. Exhausted, I went to bed. I was sorry too.

Recipe for Margaret's Sunday Gravy

2 large cans of peeled Italian plum tomatoes
1 large can of tomato puree
1 small can of Del Monte tomato sauce
2 small cans of tomato paste
4 cloves of garlic
1/4 cup of olive oil

1 pound of ground beef
8 Italian sausages (4 hot, 4 sweet)
2 pieces of pork on the bone
2 pieces of beef

Meatballs
Mix ground beef with 2 pieces of garlic (chopped small).
Add pinch of oregano.
Add 1/3 cup of parmesan cheese.
Add 1/2 loaf of Italian bread mashed with a little water.
Mix well and make into balls.

Put olive oil in large frying pan.
Brown remaining 2 pieces of garlic, cut in 4's (remove from pan).
Brown meatballs on all sides (remove from pan).
Brown sausage on all sides (remove from pan).
Brown pork and beef well (remove from pan).

Spoon out about 1/4 cup of oil from pan and put into bottom of a large
   pot.
Put in the two cans of tomato paste—sauté. Then add two paste cans
   full of water and let it simmer a few minutes.
Mash plum tomatoes from 2 cans and add to pot of paste.
When hot, add puree and tomato sauce and stir together, then simmer
   for about 1 and 1/2 hours, stirring occasionally.
Add all meat and let cook for another 1 1/2 hours or till thick.

Yum!

CHAPTER 36

The White Gardenia

I was now taking the bus by myself and, therefore, I could spend more time with my mother. I'd take the number 34 to Broad and Market Streets and then walk on Broad three blocks to Child's Restaurant, where my mother worked. I went mostly on Saturdays or during school holidays. She was really cheerful at her job. All the other waitresses at Child's seemed to like her and they treated me so well. I would have great lunches and then my mother would make me a big sundae for dessert. Vanilla ice cream with maple syrup, walnuts and whipped cream was my favorite, which she always topped with two maraschino cherries.

On other days, I'd go downtown after school and meet her at Beb's bar, which was around the corner from Child's. She knew almost everyone. Men and women bought beers for her and sodas for me. I spent a few hours with her, doing my homework at the bar. During that time, she talked and laughed and seemed to really enjoy herself. Sometimes, when watching the baseball game, she rooted loudly for the Brooklyn Dodgers. Even when drinking many beers, my mother never seemed to get drunk before I left. However, by the time she got home, which was ten o'clock or later, she could barely stand. Once in a while, she'd leave with me and we'd go for Chinese food at the Pal A Joy on Branford Place. We always had chicken chow mein. Those were the best times, sitting together talking like two girlfriends. She would tell me all the gossip from her job and I'd tell her about school. We stopped going there when we read in the paper that the Pal A Joy was fined and temporarily shut down for serving cat meat.

One of the highlights of that year was in early June when Olympic Park opened for the season. Since Tuesday was her only day off, she let me skip school so we could go to that large amusement park in Irvington, New Jersey. The day we went the weather was quite warm so I wore a new red and white pedal pusher set with new white sandals. My mother looked beautiful in her black and white cotton dress with an artificial white gardenia pinned in her shiny brown hair. She loved gardenias, so every Mother's Day I'd buy her a gardenia corsage. Granny said wearing a white flower on Mother's Day represented that your mother had died. Mommy didn't care; all she wanted was a gardenia, and so that was another subject for their arguments.

Off we went, taking two buses from Newark to Olympic Park. When we walked through the gates, the gravel got into my sandals and Mommy's wedges. As we sat to empty our shoes, the mixture of good smells drifted in the air. Looking up, I could see the Ferris Wheel and the Roller Coaster and hear the popping of the game guns over circus-like music. We went on most of the rides except the Roller Coaster since my mother was afraid. One of our favorites was the Whip, so we went on three times in a row, each time squealing as we gripped the bar to brace ourselves for the jolt to our necks on the end loops. We shared a pink cotton candy, laughing as it stuck to our lips and chins. Later, I ate the largest hot dog ever, with the most delicious tangy mustard. I could have eaten another, but Mommy was afraid I'd get sick since we were still going on rides; instead, I had a jelly apple. Then we went on my very favorite, the Swings. We sat near each other, Mommy in the inner ring, me in the outer; we could touch hands before it began. Once it started, we had to let go as the individual swings spun round, high and wide, the breeze cooling our warm bodies. I could look down and see the entire park from every angle. I wanted to swing forever.

"Let's go again, Sweetie." Mommy smiled as she reached into her purse for more money.

"Are you sure? It costs so much!" The rides were expensive and I knew we had used up our book of tickets. I noticed how much she was spending.

"Don't worry, Sweetie. I factored today into my budget. Plus, last week I won a little when I bet on a horse." She often placed bets with the Bookies at Beb's bar.

As the swings spun high again, I heard Mommy yell, "My flower!" I saw her still holding the place where it had been fastened in her hair. When the ride stopped, we started looking for it on the ground. A very good looking man came toward us holding out Mommy's gardenia. I could tell by the way he looked at her that he thought she was very pretty. I saw her blush as she thanked him, reached for my hand, and we trotted off. Mommy was very shy when she wasn't drinking.

"Come, Sweetie, we want to get a good seat in the bleachers to see the fireworks." They were held at the park's small stadium. On the way, I got a double vanilla frozen custard; Mommy said I could have it since we weren't going on any more rides. The fireworks were spectacular, ending with a red, white and blue American flag, while the band played *The Star Spangled Banner*. It was wonderful when everyone in the stadium sang the national anthem together. I sang with one hand over my heart, the other holding Mommy's hand. I felt a lump in my throat, as I usually did, when we came to "the land of the free and the home of the brave." We filed out slowly with the crowd and were unable to board the first three buses. After finally boarding the fourth bus but having to stand all the way to Broad and Market Streets, I realized my sandals had given me a few blisters. I was glad to sit when we changed for the number 34 bus to our house. The next thing I knew, Mommy was shaking me to wake up. It was our stop and my stomach felt a little upset.

When we walked into the house, Granny was already in bed. I was thankful because it was a great day and I didn't want it to be ruined by them arguing. I wanted Mommy to be as happy as she was at Olympic Park or at Beb's bar.

The next two weeks were filled with studying for the end of the term exams. I was promoted to the sixth grade; Sister Maria Williams would be my teacher. She had been my second grade teacher and led the choir, so I was really pleased.

I started packing for Picky Pine, and went to the library to take out my allotment of twelve books for the summer. The last week in the house was a nightmare. Mommy had gotten a letter from Daddy that made her very angry. Each night that week when she finally came home she kept crying and arguing with Granny. "See if I care," she kept saying to me, to Granny, to herself, and even to Mugsy, whose ears kept going down every time she said it. Mugsy could tell she was upset and stayed away from her; in fact, he would scratch to go out and not come back for hours. I managed to ask her what the matter was.

"Why don't you ask your father?" she snapped at me.

Some nights I couldn't fall asleep until I heard Mugsy scratch and I opened the door for him. Ronnie stayed out late more and more with his friends and, as usual, he left for Picky Pine one week earlier than I did to start caddying at the golf course. Mugsy and I would make the excursion in the rumble seat when Uncle Bill and Aunt Helen came to pick us up.

On one hand, I was glad to leave Newark, but on the other, I hated to see Mommy so upset and felt like I was deserting her. I looked everywhere for the letter to her from Daddy. I never snooped like that before but something in that letter really upset her and I wanted to know what it was. The night before I left, my mother had gone to bed very drunk. I waited until she was snoring and looked in her pocketbook. Sure enough—there it was. I went into the parlor to read it. I was terrified she would catch me, my heart was pounding and I could feel the sweat break out all over my back. I carefully slipped the paper out of the envelope. Attached to the top of the letter was a clipping from a newspaper; the bold print read: "**Divorce Decrees**." Half way down a list, "Persico, Joseph from Sonia" was underlined in pencil.

My hand shook so I had to hold down the paper to read.

Hello Tommy,

Just a few lines to let you know that my divorce has been granted. As I explained to you, there was nothing in the charges but what I wrote you. As for Kathy, there was a provision made for her support by me. She is not in real custody of anyone, so everything stands just as it is.

Hope you are all in the best of health, and best of luck to you. Give my regards to all.

Sincerely,
Joe

P.S. Tell Cathy I will write to her soon.

That was it, the divorce. The letter read like nothing much happened. "Best of luck to you," he wrote to Mommy. I felt like screaming. Was Mommy as upset about the divorce as I was? She always said she didn't want ever to go back with him. "I bet she's more upset about the letter itself. It sounds so casual," I thought. I wanted to run into the bedroom and tell her how sorry I was for her. I felt so angry with Daddy. Plus, I noticed he spelled Kathy with both a K and a C. Doesn't he even know I only spell it with a K? I sat there and read the letter over and over. What did he mean I am not in the custody of anyone... aren't I with Mommy? I wished I could talk about it with her but I couldn't let her know I had read the letter and, tomorrow, I was leaving for Picky Pine. Finally, I put it back into the envelope, tiptoed into the bedroom, and returned it to her purse. She was still snoring loudly. I looked at her with her mouth wide open, her hair wet with sweat; she looked like a wreck.

I lay awake tossing, not able to find a comfortable position, causing Mugsy to let out one of his disturbed groans and jump off the bed. I begged St. Monica to help Mommy feel better so she wouldn't need to drink. I decided that as soon as I was old enough to earn lots of money, I would find us a nice place to live. I thought that if she had a nice home, it would make her happy. I started dreaming about the kind of furniture we would buy; we could even get a telephone and maybe even a television. Somewhere during my fantasy decorating, I fell asleep.

I woke to find my mother bending over me. She was leaving for work. "Goodbye, Sweetie. You be a good girl." The tears started to run down my cheeks as I hugged her tight. "I'll miss you so much, Mommy."

"It will only be a few weeks and then I'll be coming to Picky Pine for your birthday." I nodded but couldn't say anything else. "I love you," she said as she waved and left the bedroom. Then I heard the kitchen door closing, her key locking the door, and her high heels clicking down the hallway.

I ran to the parlor window and watched her cross the street to the bus stop. It was not quite light out yet. Mugsy scratched and I let him out the front door. The bus must have come because my mother was gone. Granny went into the bathroom so I just went back to bed. Aunt Helen and Uncle Bill would be here by noon. I fell into a deep sleep. When I woke up, I was alone, so I started to get everything ready. When Uncle Bill beeped that horn, he did not like to be kept waiting.

CHAPTER 37

Ten!

Picky Pine was always a refuge. As glad as I was to be there, I thought about my mother every night and pictured her still very upset about my father's letter and the divorce. But in her first letter to me, she seemed okay and she was definitely coming for my birthday. I was very excited about turning ten: it seemed to be a very grown up age.

Aunt Helen was talking to me more like a grownup rather than telling me stories. She taught me how to hem curtains on her electric Singer sewing machine and how to iron more intricate things like dresses and blouses. I now cooked certain dishes by myself, like mashed potatoes and blueberry jam. I loved picking pots full of blueberries in the woods, singing to myself for hours, and then smelling their sweetness while the berries were bubbling in a pot on the stove.

This summer Aunt Helen said that instead of celebrating both birthdays together, I could have my own party, Billy's would be the next day. Uncle Bill's sister Jessie, and her husband Uncle Andy were planning to come, as was Uncle George. Billy was very excited; together we made signs for his fifth and my tenth.

A few days before my birthday, I took my daily stroll to the mailbox. The prickly sprigs of grass tickled between my toes as I walked barefoot across the soft carpet of newly cut lawn, delighting in its fresh smell and the sweet perfume of the hydrangeas. Aunt Helen, the guardian angel of all the plants and flowers, often whispered lovingly to them, like they were her little babies.

The red flag was up. In the very rear of the mailbox was a small package. It was for me! The return address read, "Joe Persico, 618 5th Street, Miami Beach, Florida." "From Daddy!" I heard myself exclaim out loud. When I started to use my teeth to pry open the securely taped package, I could hear Aunt Helen's warning in my head, "Never use your teeth, they have to last you your whole life." Quickly grabbing the other letters, I slammed the box shut, almost catching my finger as I flipped down the flag. With both arms extended, I took giant leaps toward the house, swerving back and forth, a small aircraft coming in for a landing. Dashing into the house for the scissors, I forgot to prevent the screen door from slamming. Aunt Helen's voice reached down from upstairs. "Puddin', you have to be careful of that screen door, Uncle Bill will have a fit if it comes off the hinges."

"Sorry," I yelled upstairs. Sticking the corner of the large scissors into the package, I also stuck my left thumb. A small trickle of blood was now on the package. Finally removing the brown paper wrapping, I sucked my thumb while the other hand held a small white box. I opened it, expecting to find a birthday present, a bracelet maybe. Instead, I found a small, green plastic telescope. Lifting it to the light, I saw a headshot of my father, looking very tan and sweaty. I stared at it a long time. He looked so different than I remembered him on my First Communion Day, three years ago. Is this my birthday present? I unfolded the enclosed note.

Hello My Darling,

> *I am sorry I have not been able to write sooner. I miss you darling and it has been very lonely for me away from everybody. I thought I was going to be able to save enough by June to take a trip home, but June is gone and I'm still here. I hope you are well. Take care*

of yourself. Someday maybe conditions will change. Give regards to all.

Love and kisses,
XXXXXXXX
Daddy

Not a word about my birthday. I squinted into the telescope once more. I read the note again and tried to imagine his voice, an affectionate Randolph Scott-like voice saying, "My Darling," but it didn't go with this picture, not with his thick black mustache, and his glasses were missing! It was like looking at a stranger.

"Was there any mail?" Aunt Helen yelled from upstairs.

"You have three letters, and I got a picture from Daddy."

"Oh, how nice, come up and show me."

Taking the stairs two at a time, I handed Aunt Helen the telescope.

"My, my, isn't this the cutest thing?" She raised it to the window's light.

"How handsome he looks, and you look just like him."

I thought, "Everyone says I look like him, just because we both look Italian." Going to the mirror above the dressing table, I saw my olive skin even darker from the sun. When Aunt Helen handed back the telescope, I peeked at him again. Our faces are both round and maybe the noses are the same. But I wanted to look like Mommy. We have the same shiny dark brown hair and high cheekbones.

"How is your father?"

I read the note out loud to Aunt Helen. My throat tightened when I read, *"It has been very lonely."* I thought that I should have gone to spend some time with him.

Aunt Helen stood behind me putting both arms around my shoulders like a cape; her scent of lilac cologne and cooking smells filled my nose. "I guess he really misses you. Three years is a long time." In the mirror, I noticed how different Aunt Helen and I looked. Though tanned, she, Aunt Mae and Aunt Jean were fair, blond and blue eyed like my grandmother, as was Ronnie.

"It's time for lunch. Why don't you go down and start putting out the fixin's for sandwiches while I finish straightening up," Aunt Helen said. After two sandwiches, one ham with mayo, tomato and lettuce, one liverwurst with mustard and then a slice of Aunt Helen's blueberry pie, I felt as stuffed as a bed pillow.

"Puddin', I'll clean up, go inside answer your father's letter. Tell him I said hello and how handsome I think he looks."

Moving into the dining room, I put a magazine down on the mahogany table so I wouldn't scratch the surface, took my blue Holland Linen writing paper from the desk drawer, and with pen in hand, I was a statue staring at the blank paper. He didn't write anything about the divorce. Should I? I doodled on the magazine and finally aimed the pen to paper.

Dear Daddy,

Thank you very much for your picture in that cute telescope. When I showed it to Aunt Helen, she said you look very handsome. She also said to say hello. I miss you too and hope I will see you soon. I am having a nice summer at Picky Pine. Uncle Bill is digging a well and soon we will have running water in the kitchen instead of the pump. Once they have water, they will build a real bathroom so we won't have to use the outhouse anymore. I wanted to answer your note right away and let you know I got the picture. I will write soon.

Love and kisses,
Kathy

I kept doodling so Aunt Helen would think I was still writing and I wouldn't have to help with the clean up.

Before I knew it, my birthday weekend arrived! Late that Friday afternoon, Aunt Helen, Billy, Mugsy and I went to Farmingdale to pick up my mother at the train. Aunt Mae and Aunt Jean would be driving down with Uncle Bill later that night. My mother never drove with Uncle Bill.

As always, when I heard that train whistle and the bells clanging to seal off the traffic, my heart started to pound with excitement. Billy was jumping up and down and Mugsy squealed and wagged his tail as my mother descended the iron steps of the train. She ran toward us.

"Mommy!" I burst out while running with my arms spread. I could see her red dress swishing back and forth, and thought she looked so beautiful and happy.

"Sweetie, my Sweetie," she said as she hugged me tight. With my arms around her waist, I welcomed her wonderful scent of Evening in Paris. Dabbing at her eyes, she kissed Billy and Aunt Helen. Mugsy jumped so high to get her attention that he bumped her in the nose with his snout; we all laughed as we went to the car. My mother sat up front with Aunt Helen and Billy. Mugsy and I jumped up into the rumble seat; Billy was still not allowed to sit in it. I wished Mommy were in the back seat with me because I couldn't wait to be close to her.

Back at the house, the first thing I did was to grab my mother's hand and proudly show her the curtains I had sewn. Aunt Helen took my mother's suitcase upstairs and we followed behind. Mugsy knew he was not allowed up there and barked for us the entire time.

Aunt Helen explained, "Eva, you sleep in Kathy's bed, Kathy will sleep with me, and Mae and Jean can sleep in the big bed with Billy."

"Can't I sleep with Mommy?"

"Mine is three-quarters and yours is twin, it will be awfully cramped for your mother."

"It's okay, Helen, we'll manage," my mother said stroking my hair. "Your hair looks very cute."

"Aunt Helen trimmed it and gave me a perm." Actually, I wasn't crazy about it. Too frizzy, I thought. Billy hadn't had his nap and fell asleep on the bed, sucking his thumb. My mother saw me eyeing the three wrapped presents she pulled out of her bag. "Two are yours and one is Billy's," she winked.

Downstairs we helped Aunt Helen prepare to serve the dinner she had cooked earlier. Mommy put the coleslaw on a plate, and I mashed the potatoes, adding milk and butter with Aunt Helen's special touch, a teaspoon of mayonnaise. My mother chatted away; she told us my grandmother was having problems with ulcerated legs. "Sweetie, Sissy and Margaret send their regards and Patrick misses you babysitting for him."

We three had so much to say that we kept interrupting each other. We told her about all the things I learned to do. Just as we finished setting the table, in walked Uncle Bill, Aunt Mae and Aunt Jean. Mugsy started squealing and wagging again. Everyone kissed everyone else—except for Uncle Bill.

"How is little Puddin'?" Uncle Bill boomed loudly, smiling so broadly you could see his gold tooth.

"I'm good," I said, reaching for my mother's hand.

All three of the newcomers went upstairs. I could hear Aunt Mae saying, "Well, look who's blowing his bugle, come my angel and give me a kiss."

"Shame on you, such a big boy sucking your thumb," Uncle Bill bellowed. Billy started to wail. "Mah, Mah, Mah, Mommy's baby, you're a Mah-Mah," Uncle Bill chuckled.

"Leave him alone," Aunt Jean said with real irritation in her voice.

"He is just teasing you," Aunt Mae then said reassuringly to little Billy.

When they came back downstairs, there was a huge pot roast on the table with dark brown gravy, carrots, coleslaw, string beans and my potatoes. Billy clung to Aunt Jean and would not look at Uncle Bill. Uncle Bill kept talking about the traffic and what work he would have to do to dig a new well this weekend.

"I have good news," he directed to Aunt Helen. "I've been promoted and will be transferred as branch manager to Brighton Beach in Brooklyn." He was just about to say more when Ronnie came in, kissed everyone's cheek, pulled up a chair and piled food on his plate. "How was the train ride, good?" he asked Mommy. Mommy nodded, giving him a big smile. Ronnie told us one of the rich golfers had given him ten dollars, which brought his tips for the day to twenty eight dollars.

"Pretty soon you are going to make more money than me," Uncle Bill beamed, giving Ronnie a thumbs up and talking with food in his mouth as he often did. Aunt Helen was very quiet when we were cleaning up. I could see she was upset.

"Helen, does this mean you have to move to Brooklyn?" Aunt Mae said quietly since Uncle Bill was sitting within earshot in the parlor.

"I'm so tired of moving around," she whispered, shaking her head and putting her finger to her lips. For a moment I thought she was going to cry. Then I got a pang in my stomach. If she moves, she won't be close to us on Downing Street anymore, but no one said anything more about it.

Afterward, Aunt Helen and Uncle Bill went out to sit on the swing. I could see them through the window; you could tell by their faces they were having an argument. We sat in the living room listening to Gabriel Heatter's news program on the radio. I was sharing the armchair with Mommy. Billy was sucking his thumb in between Aunt Mae and Aunt Jean on the couch. Ronnie hummed to himself while he swung back and forth in the rocking chair with Mugsy curled up at his feet.

We all went to bed early after taking turns to relieve ourselves in the grass. I lay happily wedged between Mommy and the window looking at the twinkling stars. Excited about my birthday party, I couldn't fall asleep. A cricket chirped somewhere in the house. My mother's soft breathing turned to a light snore. I could hear Aunt Jean and Mae breathing from the bed across from me, while Aunt Helen and Uncle Bill snored loudly. I hoped the sun would be out tomorrow so I could wear my new white dress and sandals. I wondered if Daddy would be thinking of me since I had not even gotten a birthday card from him.

The next thing I knew, Mommy was leaning over me, "Happy Birthday to you…Happy Birthday to you," she sang as she planted a kiss on my forehead. I couldn't believe it was already ten o'clock in the morning! I jumped up. The sun was shining, it was a beautiful day. I loved my birthday, especially this one. I was ten!

When I went downstairs, Aunt Helen was already finishing the dishes. "Well, Happy Birthday, you sleepy head," she chuckled. "I left some bacon and sausage on a plate, how would you like your egg?"

"Sunny side up for me. Where is everyone?" I asked.

"Ronnie's gone to the golf course and Mae, Jean and Billy went for a walk."

Mommy and I sat together. I could hear Uncle Bill and Mr. Carmer, who were just outside the dining room window, drilling for the well.

"How is the birthday girl? Ten! My, my, I remember the first summer you came to Picky Pine," Aunt Helen mused as she fried my egg. "You would say, 'I want to go home to my Mommy,' when you cried at night. I'd say, 'You'll have to tell me that in the morning, there are no trains now.' Then the next morning, you'd forget all about it until nighttime, and we'd go through the same routine for three or four days. Then you would be happy as a lark. Now here you are ten years old."

After I ate, Aunt Helen combed my hair, clipping it away from my face with a white barrette. "I want you to look real purdy today."

Just then Uncle Bill's sister, Aunt Jessie, walked in with her husband, Uncle Andy. After taking her usual deep breath before her words came pouring out, Aunt Jessie shrieked, "Helen! Look what happened!" Half laughing and half exasperated, she lifted her sundress and then her half-slip and displayed huge amounts of blood on her panties and upper thighs. "Aunt Martha decided to come full force on our walk over here. I guess I'm in the change...it's that time in life," she directed to my mother and me. Mommy put her hand over her mouth to stifle a giggle. We both just stared as Aunt Helen suggested, "Jessie, let's go upstairs to get you cleaned up and I'll give you some other clothes to put on." From the stairs, Jessie sucked in her breath and said, "Oh, Happy Birthday, Kathy dear." Mommy giggled again and turned to Uncle Andy, who just stood at the door looking embarrassed. He shrugged his shoulders giving me a wink and a bow, "Happy Birthday, my Lassie," he said in his Scottish accent before he scooted out to help Uncle Bill. Aunt Helen came down to get a basin of water. "I can't wait until we have a bathroom in this house, hopefully by the end of the summer." She was shaking her head and nodding her chin upward. "Jessie sure has her ways," she said. We all smiled at each other.

Mommy and I decided to walk to the fresh "spring barrel." It was out on the main road. Many cars stopped with buckets to fetch some of the cool, delicious spring water. Our feet crunched on the gravel as we strolled hand in hand. We each carried two large jars so we could bring water back. The thickness of the trees shielded us from the hot sun; a breeze sent us the sweet smells of honeysuckle. The day was glorious.

Late in the afternoon, Aunt Helen put out a spread of food with all her special salads—coleslaw, potato, and macaroni. A big roasted ham, kielbasa, sauerkraut, and cold cuts, including liverwurst and bologna, also sat on the picnic table. Uncle Andy brought a large bag of his little grape tomatoes. Aunt Helen set up a folding table outside by the glider swing. On one end were all my gifts. I didn't have to help because it was my special day. I ran upstairs to put on my white dress and red sandals.

Uncle George's wife Beulah came over. The men ended working on the well early so they could join us. Mugsy jumped up and down because he smelled the liverwurst. Aunt Helen sneaked some liverwurst to him so Uncle Bill wouldn't see. The last time he had shouted out, "That damn dog should eat dog food."

Everything tasted so delicious, better than ever. Then Aunt Mae and Aunt Jean came out with a big round butter cream pink and white birthday cake with my name on it and a big "10" in the middle and eleven lit candles. Everyone sang "Happy Birthday." Little Billy clapped his hands and said, "Make a wish, make a wish!" I felt like a princess. My wish was that my mother would be happy and stop drinking. Just as I blew out the last candle when everyone was clapping, someone put their hand over my eyes…it was Ronnie!

"Happy Birthday, Katie Did. I can only stay a short time. I have to get back to the golf course, so open my card first." He kissed me on top of my head. The card read, "To My Sweet Sister." As I opened it, eleven one dollar bills slipped out. "Just like the candles, one for every year and one for good luck," he beamed, kissing me again on top of my head while we picked up the bills together.

My mother handed me a gift, "Open this next, Sweetie. I think it will come in handy right now." This time Granny sent a little red patent leather shoulder bag. "It matches my red sandals," I squealed, tucking in the eleven bills. Aunt Mae and Aunt Jean let Billy hand me the next gift. He watched excitedly as I pretended I could not figure out that records were under the wrapping. "An *Alice in Wonderland* record!" They knew my old one was very scratched from playing it so much. "We will listen to it together, Billy, first thing Monday when everyone is gone." The other was the new Frank Sinatra album *Frankly Sentimental*. It had *Body and Soul* and *Laura* on it.

"Where is the Victrola, Aunt Helen?"

"It's in the attic; we'll take it out later." Aunt Helen had already bought me the sandals but she handed me a little box. In it was a silver bracelet with a number 10 charm on it. I gave her a big hug. Uncle Andy and Aunt Jessie gave me a card with five dollars and Uncle George and Aunt Beulah bought me a game of Chinese checkers… more hugs. Then Mommy handed me her two gifts. The first was a one piece blue bathing suit I had liked in Ohrbach's. The second was a Brownie Hawkeye camera. I wanted my own camera for the last few years. I jumped up to give her a big hug and kiss, as she wiped away happy tears.

"Thank you, thank you, Mommy."

We all had cake. Ronnie kissed me and ran off. Billy and I had cherry Kool Aid and all the adults drank beer. My mother showed me how to use the camera and I took a few pictures. Then I excitedly pushed in one of the little flash bulbs. After taking the first picture, I took the bulb out too soon and burnt my thumb a little. Aunt Helen told me to hold onto a cold can of beer; it took the sting out. Uncle Bill lit a small fire so Billy and I could roast marshmallows on long sticks. At sunset, the lightning bugs flickered all around us, the crickets chipped and you could hear the whippoorwills trilling. Aunt Helen and Uncle Bill glided back and forth on the swing. Uncle George, sitting across from them, told us more interesting stories while we all sat around him on lawn chairs. Smoke from the punks gave off a pungent odor and kept the mosquitoes away. Now and then someone would say how pretty I looked and how big I was getting. We stayed outside until ten o'clock. It was the best birthday I ever had.

After breakfast the next morning, Uncle Bill drove me, Aunt Mae and Aunt Jean to church in Farmington. Uncle Bill stayed in the car reading the Sunday paper. We picked up another cake at the bakery for little Billy; this one had blue and white butter cream frosting and the number "5" on it.

When we got home, it was time for lunch. We all ate sandwiches and leftover salads from my party. It was a hot, sunny day so I rushed upstairs to put on my new blue bathing suit. As I looked at myself in the mirror, I saw that my breasts created two round bumps in the soft material. I sucked in my stomach and thought I looked pretty grown up and shapely. My mother was just coming up the stairs and I modeled the suit for her. "Mommy, come down to the pond with me."

"Let me get my hat and I'll be right with you," she said.

When I came out the house door, Uncle Bill, Uncle Andy and Mr. Carmer, who were drilling for water, all started to whistle at me. I was both embarrassed and flattered that they noticed how nice I looked in my new suit. "Well, look at Esther Williams. All set to do some fancy swimming?" Uncle Bill chortled. Mommy came out followed by Mugsy and we three went down to the pond.

Mugsy charged into the water, but I had to edge in slowly because the water was cool from the fresh spring. Mugsy was doggy paddling back and forth looking like a sea lion. Once I got in, I doggy paddled beside him, back and forth, back and forth until he left the water and shook himself all over Mommy, who was sitting on a blanket. She shooed him away and he came dashing back into the water to doggy paddle with me some more. I don't know who loved the pond more. I swam underwater, flapping my legs to propel me forward, pretending to be Ann Blyth as the mermaid in *Mr. Peabody and the Mermaid*. Before long some of the local kids came and we played a game of water catch. Mugsy always tried to retrieve the ball when it floated on the water.

We left early so we could help Aunt Helen get ready for Billy's party. I loved walking back in my wet suit letting it dry in the hot July sun, a towel shielding my shoulders. My mother and I swung clutched hands while walking up the road. Mugsy ran ahead to the house. As we approached, I remembered the men's whistles and wrapped the towel around myself.

"Here comes our little bathing beauty," Uncle Andy winked as I passed.

Aunt Helen scolded as Mugsy tried to sneak past her. "You are not coming in the house all wet." He shook himself and plopped down on the grass by the men.

Just toward the end of Billy's party, a thunderstorm threatened and we ran inside just in time. It poured, the entire sky seemed to light up and the thunder crashed loudly. Little Billy started to cry when the lights went out for a while. Aunt Helen told him it was good luck. "Saint Peter is setting off fireworks to celebrate your birthday." That seemed to stop Billy from crying.

It was a great weekend. Uncle Bill, Aunt Mae and Aunt Jean left to drive back to Newark at six on Monday morning. In the afternoon, Aunt Helen drove my mother to the Farmingdale to catch the three o'clock train. When she waved from the window, I felt my throat constrict as the train disappeared from sight. I wouldn't see her again until Labor Day. It had been so wonderful to spend the last three days with her.

CHAPTER 38

Back to Newark Again

September came quickly. The day after Labor Day, we headed back to Newark. School would begin the following Monday. Little Billy left by train on Sunday with Aunt Mae. Mugsy and I boarded the rumble seat for the long ride home. Every year, coming off the highway onto the shabbiness of Market Street was so depressing. I already missed Picky Pine. However, I could hardly wait to see my mother. It seemed like forever since my birthday. Uncle Bill was very nice when he dropped me off; he even carried my bags into the house. "Well little Puddin', you are home, you behave yourself now." He winked as he waved good-bye. At the kitchen door, Aunt Helen kissed Granny then me. Granny gave me the biggest hug. Mugsy went charging into the house wiggling and squealing while Granny tried to pat him on the head. We all went to the parlor window to wave goodbye to Aunt Helen and Uncle Bill.

It was dinnertime already and Granny had made me some blinis. It seemed to be her "welcome home" dish. The room looked so tiny and smelled old and musty. The kitchen was very hot, small and crowded; the tiny table fan did not offer very much relief. I unpacked my records and separated my clean clothes from the dirty. I couldn't wait for my mother to come home. I listened to my new *Alice in Wonderland* album and then to some Frank Sinatra songs. I played *Body and Soul* over and over while Mugsy snuggled next to me on the studio couch.

Finally, at ten thirty, the front hallway door slammed and the familiar irregular footsteps made their way to the kitchen door. Mugsy lunged into the kitchen and as the door opened, he leapt up to greet Mommy, causing her to brace herself on the doorknob. He kept jumping in the air and squealing as Mommy slurred, "My Sweetie, I am so happy to see you, and you too, Mugsy," as she patted his head. I smelled the beer and cigarettes as she pressed me to her. Why did she have to drink tonight? I had to keep from pushing her away. I wanted to scream at her but instead I just hugged her back. "I'm happy to see you too, Mommy. I waited up for you but I am so tired I have to go to bed."

"You go ahead, Sweetie, we'll talk tomorrow night," she said as she lit a Pall Mall and plunked down hard into the rocking chair.

In bed I covered my head with the sheet. I slept like I was drugged.

The next day I ran around the corner to Clover Street to see Elaine. We had a lot to catch up on. Elaine had her wrist in a sling. She had broken it in on vacation at Seaside Heights. I was so jealous of Elaine's breaks, this being about the fourth. I had never broken anything. But it never stopped her from her activities. That week before school started, we met all our friends and played a lot of Kick the Can. Bobby, who lived across the street from Elaine, had a big crush on her. He was so cute. I could have had a crush on him but I stopped myself because he liked Elaine. Two sisters from Jackson Street, Rosary and Cecelia, also joined us that week. It was starting to be fun to be back.

The next Saturday, I took the bus to downtown Newark to meet Aunt Jean and accompany little Billy to a tap dance class at the Lepple School. Once again after class we stopped to eat at the counter in Haynes & Company, where Aunt Jean worked. Billy and I then took the bus to Kearney and I babysat him until Aunt Jean returned at four. Aunt Mae still worked two jobs, lunchtime at Uncle Don's nightclub, The Band Box, and the night shift at the General Electric plant. That particular Saturday, I stayed over because Aunt Jean's boyfriend Frank told her to invite me to come with them. They were taking Billy to see *The Wizard of Oz*. Somehow, despite all of my movie going, I had never seen it, although I knew all the songs and had read the book. Frank was

Aunt Jean's old boyfriend from high school, whom she met again a year after Billy's father died from a heart attack. I liked Frank very much.

I was excited to see the movie. Billy sat in between Aunt Jean and me and kept jumping in his seat, spilling popcorn all over until the lights dimmed. I was really disappointed to see that the movie was in black and white and was so surprised when it turned into Technicolor as Dorothy entered the Land of Oz. When Judy Garland sang *Over the Rainbow* I had to wipe the tears with the sleeve of my blouse. I heard the song so many times but to watch the expressions on her beautiful face made me want to be like her; I wanted be an actress more than ever. Toward the end of the film, Billy hid his face in Aunt Jean's lap, crying and begging to leave—he was terrified of the wizard. Then when the wizard was uncovered, Billy kept laughing and pointing. The girl behind him told him to "Shush up!"

While holding swinging hands, Billy and I skipped the entire five blocks back to his apartment house, merrily singing *We're Off to See the Wizard.* We waited with Frank for his bus to come.

"Thank you so much, Uncle Frank," I yelled as he boarded. We all waved to Frank as he waved back from the bus window.

Billy started to suck his thumb and whimper, "I'm tired, Mommy."

As soon as we got upstairs, Aunt Jean handed me some sheets to fix the couch for myself while she went into Billy's room to put him to bed. I put on my pajamas and washed my face and brushed my teeth in the bathroom. As I looked around at the pink flowered wallpaper, I wished I had a pretty bathroom like this. I went into the parlor and lay down on the couch; the room was so cozy and modern. The whole apartment smelled as sweet as roses. Aunt Mae usually came home about two in the morning, but I never heard the door open.

The next day it was lunchtime by the time Aunt Mae got up. She sat with us in the kitchen drinking coffee while Billy and I had Chef Boyardee Ravioli. Somehow they tasted like a special treat here.

"Did you know your father is getting married again?" Aunt Mae asked me.

Dropping my fork, I answered, "No! How do you know that?"

"He wrote me a letter a few weeks ago."

I was shocked; in his letters there was never any hint of a girl-friend. He always sounded sad, sick and lonely. I thought of the mean stepmothers I'd seen in the movies and I hated the whole idea.

"Does Mommy know?" I asked.

"Yes, she told me he wrote to her, too."

"What did she say?"

"I don't think your mother cares about what he does. Maybe next summer we can go to Miami Beach to see him if he doesn't come back to New York by then." I was stunned. I couldn't wait to get home later and reread my father's last letter, but I knew it didn't say anything about getting married or a girlfriend.

CHAPTER 39

A Fun Fall

A few nights later, while taking a big drag on her Pall Mall, my mother just said straight out, "Kathy, I just want you to know your father is getting married again."

"Do you care?" I asked hesitatingly.

"Are you kidding? God help her, whoever she is."

And that was that. Aunt Mae was right—she really didn't care. But I did. It all seemed so strange. I wondered if he would write to me about it or would just assume Mommy told me.

The weather was turning colder, so after school Elaine and our group spent more time indoors. Wilson Avenue Playground, which had a large playroom, was our favorite after-school hang out. Everyone loved Mr. Attanasio, the program director, who was the nicest man— chubby, cheerful, and always smiling. "Mr. A," as he liked to be called, set up a lot of different activities for us, such as Ping-Pong, Bingo, Checkers, Parcheesi, and a card table where we made crafts for various holidays. On Friday nights, he organized indoor roller skating in the gym, which was my very favorite. He brought in his own record player so we could skate to music. I loved skating to the *Strauss Waltzes*. Mr. A gathered together many pairs of skates for us to use, but they always pinched my toes. I put a pair of white leather roller skates on my wish list for Christmas.

Once a week, I would babysit for Patrick while Margaret and her husband went out to dinner. One evening, after putting Patrick to sleep, on the news President Truman revealed to the world that Russia had tested its first atom bomb almost a month before on August twenty-ninth. The frightening images of Hiroshima that I had remembered from the newsreels a few years ago flashed through my mind, filling me with terror.

The next week at school we started to have bomb drills. When the warning bell rang, we were instructed to get under our desks until the "all clear" signal sounded. Although it was a drill, I often got the feeling of impending doom. To me, the atom bomb meant burning to death—the image was so frightening, like the way the nuns described hell. I could attempt to be good and avoid going to hell, but I could not prevent being bombed. The newsreel images reached into my dreams at night.

I always looked forward to going up to Margaret's apartment on Tuesday nights for the *Milton Berle Texaco Theatre*. She always saved me the meat left from her pot of Sunday gravy. I pretended she was my big sister. On school holidays, I would sometimes take Patrick to the Rivoli movie theatre when they showed cartoons, and he'd pretend I was his big sister.

I became friends with a few of the girls from Elaine's class. They were one year ahead of me in school, but I knew them from the choir. Four of them worked at St. James Bingo games on Saturday nights. I went for an interview and was hired to work every other Saturday. You had to be twelve but I looked big for my age. So now, every other Saturday after I took Billy to the Lipple dance school then back to his house, I left at four o'clock when Aunt Jean came home. I'd go home to Newark and get dressed for Bingo in the required black skirt and white blouse; they supplied a little black apron with big pockets that held the boards and money.

Bingo was held in the St. James School auditorium, where long tables and folding chairs were set up. In the corner behind a small partition were two electrical burners. A giant pot with hotdogs simmered on one, and the other had a smaller pot of sauerkraut. The smell would tease my taste buds and, by the end of the night, I was sure to have a hotdog on a roll with sauerkraut and lots of Pulaski mustard. My job was to collect the money and give out the boards. We earned ten cents on each board. If you had a winner, you often got a tip of one to five dollars. Sometimes I made as much as ten dollars.

It became routine that on Sunday the "Bingo girls," Phyllis, Concetta, Margie, Grace and I, would meet at the Italian restaurant Santa Lucia on Jefferson Street. Margie was very funny and always kept us laughing with her stories and imitations. I'd always have Veal Parmigiana and a tortoni for dessert. We would talk about our crushes on boys; they all had one and so did I—Anthony, who sat next to me in the sixth grade. I told the girls that Anthony and I had started to pass notes back and forth until Sister Maria Williams caught us. We were punished and had to stay after school to write on the blackboard one hundred times *"I MUST NOT PASS NOTES DURING SCHOOL."* Sister would leave and come back in occasionally to check on us. We dared not speak because if we were caught, we would have to come back the next day as well. After she inspected the boards, we had to erase and wash them, then pound the erasers out the window. The chalk dust would fly back into my nose and on my hair. Although we didn't pass any more notes, during class when Sister was writing on the blackboard, we would touch feet across the aisle.

Somehow this story seemed very funny and made us girls laugh so hard that the waiters started to laugh as well. After dinner we'd all go to the Rivoli. One time when we went to downtown Newark to the RKO Proctor movie theatre to see *Samson and Delilah,* we ate at a Chinese restaurant and all ordered egg drop soup. Margie put on a very serious face and carefully dunked her fingers into the soup as though it were a finger bowl, then very slowly wiped each of her fingers with the cloth napkin. We all broke up and all the Chinese waiters laughed the entire time they were serving us. Margie was such fun to be with. Sundays were now great because I didn't get home until long after Granny's old drinking buddies had already left.

I was glad to be busy so I didn't have to spend too much time in my house. Late that fall, Ronnie quit high school to take a full time job at Otis Elevator Company in Harrison. He was hardly home anymore. I missed seeing him for dinner. After work he went out with his friends. The entire family tried to talk him into going back to school, but he refused. At seventeen, he was old enough to quit without permission.

Aunt Helen and Uncle Bill were especially upset. The first Saturday after he quit school, they came all the way from Brighton Beach to try to talk to him, but with no luck. Ronnie was now coming home even later than Mommy, or on some nights he slept at the apartment of one of his friends, Mike or Tony, who were a few years older than he was. Neither of them had a job. I only saw them from the window when they'd beep for Ronnie in a beat up green car. Ronnie would jump in the back seat and wave to me; they'd wave also. The driver was blond and the passenger had black hair and a mustache. I didn't know which guy was which. I wasn't sure where they went or what they were doing, but my aunts referred to them as "bad company." No one in the family liked these two guys. My aunts said Ronnie was spending his money foolishly; he should be putting some in the bank. Actually, once in a while Ronnie borrowed a few dollars from me and paid me back when he got his next paycheck. "It's our secret. Okay, Katie Did?"

The only time I spent with Ronnie was on holidays. At Thanksgiving dinner that year, he sat next to me. When my aunts started talking to him about the company he was keeping, he just laughed and said they worried too much. I knew he was upset because I could feel his leg shaking under the table, which he always did when something was bothering him. Mommy was the only one who never criticized Ronnie.

Christmas Eve was the next time that Ronnie and I spent time together. After I returned from singing at the midnight mass, Granny and I waited until nearly 2 a.m. for Mommy to come home from the bar. Ronnie arrived shortly after. In the cold parlor, layered in sweaters, we exchanged gifts sitting around the tree that my mother had decorated on her day off. She did her usual happy weeping as we opened our presents, especially when I opened my main gift. "White leather roller skates! Thank you, thank you, Mommy!" My mother gave Ronnie two really nice sweaters in different shades of blue, his favorite color. Granny loved the religious pictures I gave her. I also bought her some extra vigil lights and new pearl pop beads. Ronnie bought my mother a beautiful necklace with blue stones He must have spent at least twenty five dollars on it. She kissed him on the cheek and thanked him, but I could tell she really didn't like it. I knew she didn't like blue very much. I think he could tell, too, because when she opened my gift, a leopard scarf, she made a big fuss over it. She loved anything leopard. I felt good for me but bad for Ronnie.

On Christmas day, we again went to Aunt Helen's for dinner. Ronnie came and it was great to spend time playing with little Billy and his new Lionel train additions. Later at dinner, the subject of Ronnie's friends came up again.

Uncle Bill turned to Mommy and in a gruff voice said, "Eva, you should make your son go back to school." Mommy looked startled that Uncle Bill had spoken to her so directly. We all got quiet for a few minutes until the turkey came out, then everyone started helping themselves and the talk turned to how good the food was. After dinner, Ronnie left early and did not stay for coffee and cake.

Then Uncle Bill addressed me, "Talk to your brother, otherwise he is going to grow up to be a bum." I nodded and went back into the bedroom to play with little Billy and his trains.

CHAPTER 40

Mary

After Christmas, our choir started practicing for Easter. I began to hang out with Mary, who was in my class and in the choir. At first we'd meet after lunch, each one of us racing home then returning fifteen minutes early so that we could practice our choir hymns while walking around the block that surrounded St. James School. She was a high soprano with a voice as sweet as an angel and we'd sing two part harmony to my favorite hymn, *Panis Angelicus,* in our respective parts. Singing together was so soothing. We also started to study together some days after school. I would go over to her house. Both of her parents worked so we studied in her parlor. Everything was sparkling and spacious with modern furniture, without throws and doilies. The linoleum floors were new and shiny. With the sun shining through the window, her house was so bright and cheerful.

Sometimes if we finished our homework early, Mary would put on her pink tutu, play her *Teddy Bears Picnic* record, and dance for me, doing the routine she learned in her ballet class. She was blond and slender with blue eyes and was so graceful she seemed like a beautiful butterfly dipping in and out of flowers. I longed to be like her, dance like her and look like her.

I remembered with a heavy heart that when my mother signed me up for dancing lessons at age five, my father forbade it and made her pull me out after only one lesson. Having watched so many Technicolor musicals, I wanted to be a dancer and still fantasized about it. I envied little Billy taking tap lessons, especially since he hated his classes. I would give anything to study dance, but it was too expensive. It was during those times of watching Mary dance that I decided I was going to try to lose weight.

One day when I was browsing through Woolworth's, I came across a tiny red book called *Joe Bonomo's Calorie Counter*. After paging through, I saw it offered the possibility of losing a pound and a half per week if you followed the diet. Using the chart provided, I calculated what my ideal weight should be. I could lose fifteen pounds in about twenty weeks! I paid the twenty five cents for my guide to a new figure.

Sister Maria asked for volunteers to help in the convent twice a week for about half an hour at lunchtime and another hour after school. Mary and I both raised our hands. We decided to bring our lunch from then on and eat in the school cafeteria, a room with a few tables which was generally used as a study area.

At the convent, the nuns were so different than in the classrooms. They laughed and seemed to have a lot of fun with each other. At lunchtime, Mary and I helped to do the dishes and, after school, we assisted in chopping vegetables for dinner. I learned how to make a tuna casserole, which I only attempted once at Granny's because it was too much for one person to eat. Since Granny and Ronnie didn't like it, I wound up eating far too much. It was very difficult to stick to Joe Bonomo's daily suggestions, but I definitely was trying to cut down on my eating.

I had such a good time with the nuns. The convent seemed like the college dorms from the movies. Mary and I both talked about maybe becoming nuns, but I was really torn between entering the convent and becoming an actress. It seemed more likely for Mary to be a nun. When she walked down the church aisle after receiving Holy Communion, she looked like a delicate saint. Her hands would be in a prayer position pointing toward heaven, her eyelids lowered reverently, and everyone seemed to be looking at her.

CHAPTER 41

Easter Vacation

The rumble seat was not much fun when the weather was chilly. I emerged from under the blanket as we turned into the tiny gravel road to Picky Pine. Everything looked so bleak without leaves on the trees and without the white and blue hydrangeas around the houses. All three houses had been boarded up for the winter. Without their colorful awnings, they looked run down. I chose to come down for Easter vacation because Aunt Helen needed a hand, plus I missed her since she moved to Brighton Beach in Brooklyn.

When we went inside the main house, it smelled musty and was dark and dreary without sun shining through the bare windows. I began to regret coming. After unpacking our things and the groceries, Aunt Helen got right to her cooking. I peeled potatoes and carrots while she braised some beef. Delicious smells took over the kitchen. Aunt Helen ruffled my hair saying, "It will be so much fun when you visit me in my new apartment in Brighton Beach. We can walk together on the Boardwalk to Coney Island. A weekend in June would be a good time, just before we come to Picky Pine for the summer."

She told me about the Parachute Jump and many of the rides in the Steeplechase. I had never been to Coney Island and was excited about visiting her there. The movie *Coney Island* with Betty Grable singing *Cuddle up a Little Closer* popped into my head. I found myself singing it for the next few days. Aunt Helen knew the words and sometimes joined in while we did lots of chores together. There was so much to do. The two little bungalows needed to be readied for renting the last week in June. All the storm windows needed removing; they were heavy but the two of us managed. Aunt Helen told me all about Brighton Beach while we pulled out and aired the bedding, hung curtains, swept, and waxed all the floors and furniture. She told me, "On the next corner from my apartment is Mrs. Stahl's Knishes. Not only do they have potato knishes, but also cheese, kasha, cherry, cabbage and many other kinds." Her description made my mouth water.

Outside, the landscape between the houses was filled with old twigs and dead leaves. Together we raked and, with picks, loosened the packed ground around the trees and plants, and then Aunt Helen nursed all her babies with fresh fertilizer.

Aunt Jessie and Uncle Andy had also come down to their house. Uncle Bill talked Uncle Andy into giving him a hand painting the outside of the main house. Aunt Jessie was not too happy about it. "Andy, we have a lot of work to do on our own house," Aunt Jessie said shaking her head.

With his Scottish accent and pipe hanging from the side of his mouth, he winked at Aunt Jessie. "Jessie, my lovely girl, your 'Handy Andy' will get it all done, now don't you worry your pretty head."

She gave him a little make believe punch. They really seemed to love each other so much. I could never understand why Uncle Bill didn't like Jessie, his own sister. But that was Uncle Bill; he sure didn't like too many people. He was always so gruff. He had been a circuit judge. I think he believed that he was better than everyone else.

Except for dinnertime, I really didn't see too much of Uncle Bill. During our dinners, he was very nice and asked a lot of questions about my schoolwork. I was surprised he was talking to me and even more surprised when he said, "You seem to be a very smart girl." He also thanked me for helping Aunt Helen. It was really something to ever get any compliments or a thank you from him. I was flattered and felt like he was starting to like and include me instead of ignoring me, except for when he wanted me to do something like help him dig the cellar.

It was pretty cold both outside and inside the house so we had to layer in sweaters. Within two days, the house started to lose its musty smell and became filled with the aromas of freshly waxed floors and Aunt Helen's cooking. The sun now shone through the thin ruffled curtains we hung. Night times were especially cold. I missed Mugsy in my bed, but since we'd be here for only a week, he didn't come with us. Two thick wool blankets and sheer exhaustion made sleep come quickly and easily.

We were going to leave to go home on Sunday evening. Late Saturday afternoon, I began to feel really sick. After not eating much stew for dinner, I forced myself to eat the rice pudding Aunt Helen made because she knew it was my favorite and worked hard to make it; but it sat heavy in my stomach. After doing the dishes, I went to bed early.

Sunday morning we needed to put everything away and close up until June. I helped for a few hours, but my legs felt weak, I was dizzy and, in spite of the chill in the air, I broke out in a clammy sweat. By early afternoon when I could barely stand, I told Aunt Helen how awful I felt. She said to go upstairs and lie down. My entire body was shaking. I didn't remember ever feeling so sick. Aunt Helen took my temperature and said I didn't have one, but she gave me an aspirin anyway. When Uncle Bill heard I was lying down, he came up and sat on the edge of my bed. He started to rub my back and reached over with the other to feel my head, "You are just tired of working, what a faker! Boy, you sure found a way to get out of working."

I yanked my body away and said, "I am not faking."

Just then Aunt Helen yelled up, "Leave her alone, Bill. She's doesn't feel well."

He got up and yelled down, "You said she doesn't even have a temperature, there is nothing wrong with her." As he got up he bellowed, "You are just a big faker." I was so upset I wanted to punch him.

I slept on and off until it was time to go. In the rumble seat, I buried myself in the blanket. I was freezing and my teeth were actually chattering as I shook all over. It seemed like the longest ride of my life to get back to Granny's house.

"The little baby's home," Uncle Bill smirked when we finally arrived.

I screamed at him, "I am really very sick and you don't even care!" I felt tears stinging my eyes.

"Listen to her screaming," he said in his pompous tone to Aunt Helen. "I don't believe it for a minute. Mah, Mah, what a crybaby!"

Now I knew how little Billy felt when Uncle Bill started the "Mah, Mah" stuff on him. I ran into the house, so glad to be home. I ran right past Mugsy, who was squealing and jumping, and past Granny, who did not understand why I was crying. I just threw myself onto my bed. I didn't even take off my clothes. "Hi, Mugs," I said as I dove deeper under the covers while he wiggled under with me. Granny insisted I drink a few sips of hot tea she made with the elixir she always put in it when we didn't feel well. The tiny bottle was very scary with the skull and crossbones on it that said, "Poison for external use only," but she said a drop or two wouldn't hurt me and it did always seem to help whatever we had.

When Granny woke me for school the next morning she told me Mommy had come home last night and already left for work while I slept right through. I was so sorry I missed seeing her. Granny told me she gave me a kiss and handed me a note.

"I'll see you tonight, Sweetie. Hope you feel better."

XOXOXOXOXOXOXO
Love,
Mommy

I took off my wrinkled clothes. Granny saw them at the same time I looked into the mirror: Red marks all over me…I had the measles! So much for school for today and the next ten days. Part of me was so happy because now Uncle Bill would know I was not faking. I wished he were here to see all the spots. I felt absolutely awful. Granny said I had to stay in the dark or be scarred forever, so while lying in bed, I couldn't even read. Instead, my comfort was listening to radio programs. I especially loved the soap operas *The Romance of Helen Trent* and *Grand Central Station*. Being confined to the bedroom for over a week, I listened to the radio and my *Alice in Wonderland* record over and over.

CHAPTER 42

Ronnie Joins the Army

It was May 24, 1950, the day after Ronnie's eighteenth birthday. I rushed home from school to do my homework so I could then head out to Wilson Avenue Playground to join my friends in a game of stickball on this beautiful afternoon. Passing the parlor window, I heard a tapping. Looking up, I was surprised to see Ronnie home at three thirty; he usually worked until six o'clock at the Otis Elevator Company. Putting my books down on the kitchen table, I went right into the parlor.

"Hi, Ronnie." He had a very strange look on his face as he rocked back and forth.

"What's wrong?"

"I waited for you, Katie Did. I wanted you to be the first to know."

I panicked. "Know what, what's wrong?"

"Nothing is wrong," he offered, flashing his charming smile. While getting off the rocking chair, he announced, "You're almost eleven and old enough to know I just came from the recruiting office. Your brother just joined the Army. I'll be leaving for boot camp in about a week." As he moved to sit on the studio couch, he gave it a pat for me to sit next to him.

"What? Why?" My knees started to shake. I sat down. "Ronnie! Please don't go," I sobbed in someone else's voice. As we sat there, he hugged me against his shoulder. "The Army!" I said shaking my head. Images from the movie *Battleground* flashed through my mind of Van Johnson in World War Two. He was scared, tired and in danger, bullets were flying all around him and his friends were being killed. "Will you be fighting in a war?" I heard myself whisper.

"There is no war now. Don't worry, Katie Did. I'll write to you a lot and I want you to write to me, too. I'll be your regular pen pal," he said, gently rocking us side to side. Rising up he said, "I have to go back to work. I promised I'd put in extra time until Friday, which will be my last day." Don't say anything to Mommy and Granny yet, I'll tell them tonight," he said as he lifted me on my feet and gave my chin a play punch. "Promise?"

I nodded.

"You keep that chin up and don't worry your little head about me, it's for the best. You okay?"

I nodded again.

He winked and out the door he went. When the door shut, I stopped myself from running after him. I hadn't seen much of him lately, but I never thought there would be a day that he would leave home, that my big brother wouldn't always be there. I just sat staring out of the window. Thoughts of the atom bomb's giant mushroom kept recurring. I couldn't do my homework, and certainly didn't feel like going to the playground. I played Ronnie's record of *Rhapsody in Blue*, that I had come to love, resetting the needle over and over. I lay on the studio couch, smelling his scent, thinking that when Ronnie left, I'd sleep here in the parlor on his bed. Mugsy had been outdoors and scratched to come in. When I opened the door for him, he jumped up on the couch; as I lay back down he curled up beside me—I fell asleep. I woke up to my grandmother calling my name as she took the scratching needle off of the record. It was already dark.

When Mommy came home that night she had been drinking, as usual. Ronnie came in soon afterward. Granny was also in the kitchen. Ronnie just came right out and told them, "Mommy, Granny, I joined the Army today and I am leaving for boot camp in about a week." Mommy loudly sucked in her breath. Granny got frightened and asked Mommy to translate what Ronnie said. When Mommy did, Granny blessed herself and ran right over to the statue of the Virgin Mary and started to pray. My mother began to cry, her mascara running down her face. She started waving her hand with the lit cigarette between her fingers saying, "To each his own," acting like Ronnie had just insulted her.

"Mommy, let me tell you why," he pleaded. I knew Ronnie was upset at the way she was behaving. I felt so sorry for him but I felt badly for her, too, and worse for me.

"Why?" she finally asked between sobs as she took a gulp from her glass of beer. He said his life was nowhere; he wanted a change. He thought the Army would be good for him. He could go back to school and then to college on the GI Bill.

Mommy was more mad than sad and still kept saying, "To each his own." Waving her hand like she was waving him away, her cigarette went flying across the table. Granny mumbled something in Lithuanian as she quickly picked it up and snuffed it out in the ashtray. Granny also seemed really upset. She loved Ronnie so much and kept saying how much she would miss him. She reached for her rosary beads. I knew Ronnie hated emotional scenes. He said he was very sorry they were both so upset, but it was a good thing, they should be happy for him. Nobody said anything for what seemed a long time. My mother lit another cigarette. Ronnie said he was very tired and had to get up early so he was going to bed. He gave Granny a kiss goodnight, then me. I wrapped my arms tight around his waist and he patted my head. Then he tried to kiss my mother but she turned her head. He and Mugsy went into the parlor; the door closed behind them. I kissed Mommy and Granny and went to bed, too. I dreaded that Mommy would start to rehash old things and I would be captive.

The next day at school, I couldn't think of anything except Ronnie going into the Army. I wished he had joined the Navy. I thought of Frank Sinatra as a sailor having so much fun in *Anchors Aweigh*. But scenes from the movie *Battleground* kept cropping up in my thoughts—images of Van Johnson trying to cook an egg in his helmet while in the trenches, sweating in the heat of the jungle. I also remembered Joseph Cotton coming back shell shocked in *I'll Be Seeing You*.

Every time Sister called on me, I hadn't been paying attention to the lesson, so I was punished and had to stay after school and write on the blackboard one hundred times, *"I MUST PAY ATTENTION IN CLASS."* Not only did I have to write it, but it also had to be in the best script. It was difficult to write well because my eyes kept clouding over with tears, so Sister smacked my hand a few times and thought I was crying because it hurt. I decided that day I was definitely not going to St. James High School after I graduated from the eighth grade. I wanted to be in public school like Sissy. I vowed I would go to East Side High.

When I got home that day, I started to write a letter to Ronnie. I planned to give it to him the day he left. I told him how much I loved him and how much I loved having a big brother and how desperately I would miss him. I told him I was sorry for all the times I was bratty and made him so angry. I forgave him for hitting me during those times with a rolled up newspaper. I went to my pink ballerina jewelry box where I kept my St. Christopher medal. After "*Hugs and kisses, your loving sister, Katie Did,*" I wrote, "*P.S. St. Christopher will keep you safe,*" and I tucked the medal into the letter.

CHAPTER 43

Coney Island at Last

On the Friday of Memorial Day weekend, as promised, Aunt Helen came to Granny's to take me to Brighton Beach. Ronnie stayed home until she came so he could tell her about the Army himself. I saw her very blue eyes cloud over but she did not cry. Ronnie explained all the reasons he joined while she listened attentively. She agreed it might be the best thing for him since he had quit high school.

"I just wish you had waited until the fall. This summer Picky Pine will not be the same without you. You've been coming every year since you were three. Everyone will miss you." She opened her purse and gave him some money. "Be sure to write."

Ronnie seemed relieved about Aunt Helen's approval. "I love you, Aunt Helen, you're the best."

Before we left, Aunt Helen told Granny that she had been very worried about him. He was always such a good kid. She thought it was best that he was getting away from the rough crowd before he got into some kind of trouble. We took the Hudson Tubes to downtown Manhattan, and then the subway to Coney Island. During our travels, I told Aunt Helen how upset I was and that I didn't think Ronnie should have joined. "I don't want him to be in any danger," I frowned.

She said Ronnie was very smart, he would probably have a desk job and never be exposed to shooting and bombs, and besides there wasn't a war going on. The Army offered a great opportunity for him to finish school and go to college. She then patted my leg reassuringly. Her approval of Ronnie's decision made me feel a lot better, too, and I also didn't feel as frightened for him. But I already missed him, even though he wasn't leaving until the following week.

When we finally got to the Brighton Beach elevated stop, I could see and smell the ocean from the platform. It was a warm afternoon so Aunt Helen promised that after dinner, we could walk on the Boardwalk. The apartment building was on Brighton's 11th Street, just one block from the subway stop. When Uncle Bill got home from work, he seemed really glad to see me.

At dinner, Aunt Helen told Uncle Bill that Ronnie joined the Army. Ronnie was always special to him and was one of the few people Uncle Bill always treated really nicely. I never saw Uncle Bill look sad before. Then his jaw tightened and he bellowed, "It's her fault, if she was half a mother, she would have stopped her damn drinking." As he resumed eating once again, the subject of Ronnie's current friends came up. They discussed Ronnie's opportunity for finishing high school and the GI Bill. Uncle Bill stopped eating and took a deep breath, was quiet for a long time, then finally said, "Maybe it is for the best." Then he seemed to make a complete turnaround. "So, the little Puddin' is going to Coney Island?" His tone had gotten so loud I actually jumped.

"What do you think of our apartment?" he asked with his mouth full while chomping on his steak.

"It's really nice," I offered, not wanting to be too chummy with him after his remarks about my mother. In my heart I knew Mommy's drinking always bothered Ronnie a lot. But I really did love their apartment. It was even more modern than Aunt Jean's, with a kitchenette separating a real eat in dining area. Aunt Helen had the rest of the furniture Aunt Mae had kept in storage since her divorce from the Golden Goose, Uncle Pete. Their parlor was like a department store showroom. The plush brocade couch of gold and maroon was wedged between two mahogany end tables with a cut glass lamp with tasseled shades on each. A matching coffee table sat on top of a thick carpet in gray with maroon flowers all over it.

I would sleep on that couch. There was only one bedroom. Although they always had had twin beds, I noticed there was a full sized bed covered with a white chenille bedspread. The matching headboard and dressers were also mahogany. Aunt Helen proudly announced that she had made all the drapes and valences on the windows.

While Aunt Helen was doing the dishes, I was very quiet and didn't know what to say as I sat across from my uncle. I think he noticed I wasn't acting very friendly toward him. The next thing I knew he was smiling as he patted my hand, "I heard you had the measles after the Easter break. I am sorry. I had no idea you were so sick when we left Picky Pine. Friends?" I nodded but wanted to say, "I kept telling you how sick I felt," but it made me feel good that he apologized.

Just then Aunt Helen said, "I'll get dressed while you dry the dishes and we'll go for our walk."

From the Boardwalk, which was only one block away, I could see the Ferris Wheel and the Parachute Jump, about ten blocks away where Coney Island started. Aunt Helen said we would get frozen custard for our dessert. I loved vanilla, she liked chocolate. It was absolutely the best custard I ever had. During the walk to Coney Island, we held hands while the breeze blew through my hair and brought with it the smells of cotton candy and hotdogs. As we approached the Ferris Wheel, it looked gigantic, like a hulking dinosaur. After hearing Aunt Helen talk about it so many times, I was excited. She said we could go on it right now. When our car reached the very top of the Ferris Wheel, you could see the ocean, all over Coney Island, and all the way down the long Boardwalk and into the Steeplechase. As our car slid diagonally down very fast to the center of the wheel, I squealed—it took my breath away. I loved it! After a few more spins and slides, the ride was over. It was everything Aunt Helen had described to me.

"Can we go again?"

Aunt Helen replied that because it was late, we had to head back but, come tomorrow, we'd have one more ride on the Ferris Wheel and then spend the rest of the day at the Steeplechase. Walking home on the Boardwalk, I thought Aunt Helen looked exhausted but I could have stayed out all night. On the way, she bought me a huge pink cotton candy; some of it stuck to my hair so, when we got home, she washed it away.

I slept soundly on the couch. I was startled to wake up in the morning to Uncle Bill sitting beside me. Instinctively, I pulled the sheet up to my chin. "So, the Puddin' is going to the Steeplechase," he said smiling wide with his gold tooth showing. Just then the sound of Aunt Helen's voice reached us from the kitchen where the smell of bacon and toast drifted to my nostrils. "Yoo hoo, sleepy head, breakfast is ready." We both headed for the kitchen. Aunt Helen's breakfast was always a treat, but I could hardly wait to be through and head out to Coney Island again.

As promised, we took another ride on the Ferris Wheel; it was just as much fun as the first time. Aunt Helen paid and we went into the Steeplechase. It was a dream come true, just as she always spoke of it. There were lovely flowers and so many rides. The first I chose was actually called "The Steeplechase." You sat on a beautifully painted horse which dipped and curved around the edge of the park on a single track to the finish line. It was actually a race and, much to my surprise, I won! They gave me a ticket to pick out a prize on the way out. I rode on so many rides and you didn't have to pay because it was all included in the price of admission. On my favorite ride, the Swings, Aunt Helen joined me, but on other rides I went alone. Flying high in a circle we could see all the way out to the ocean. It was spectacular. We then headed for the fun house. It was a very scary walk through the dark and I held Aunt Helen's hand very tightly. We screamed and then we laughed at each other for being so frightened of the creatures that jumped out at us. The most fun was exiting the funhouse. You had to walk through a big spinning barrel while trying to keep your balance. This led you into a large cage with metal jail bars, and you had to find the rubber bar to get out. Then came the final prank: a clown holding a long electrical stick with air pressure that blew your dress up over your head. I was glad I had on pedal pushers. Even though Aunt Helen knew what was coming, she screamed as she tried to hold her sundress down. All of this was happening on a stage. There was a large audience watching and laughing, as people did not expect to be on stage when they exited the fun house.

Aunt Helen and I joined the audience and laughed and laughed as we ate hotdogs and drank root beers. One lady did not have any underwear on, and, boy, did her face get red. I couldn't believe she had no panties! Afterward, when Aunt Helen thought I had digested the hotdogs, I went on more rides. On the way to the gate was the stand to retrieve the prizes. I picked out a key chain to give to Ronnie. It was the shape of a shamrock and said "Good Luck" in the middle with Coney Island printed on the bottom. With this and the St. Christopher medal, he was sure to stay safe.

It was a wondrous day. By the time we started walking home the sun was going down. There was a slight chill in the air so I had a hot chocolate. Because it was getting late, Aunt Helen said we would stop at Mrs. Stahl's Knishes and take some home. We bought potato, kasha, spinach, blueberry, and my favorite—cheese. At home, Aunt Helen heated some barley soup and put out the plate of assorted knishes.

"Boy, you two were sure stepping out. I'm hungry as a lion," Uncle Bill said laughing and winking at me, while he loudly slurped his soup.

The next day was hot and sunny and Aunt Helen took me to the beach, but not before we bought knishes to go for our lunch. I felt a little guilty about eating so much. During the last few days, I had not followed Joe Bonomo's calorie counter diet. Aunt Helen said, "You're on vacation, start again on Tuesday." It was wonderful to be with Aunt Helen. One more month and school would be out and I'd be back with her in Picky Pine for the entire summer.

CHAPTER 44

Death of the Car

The weekend after school was out, Aunt Helen and Uncle Bill came from Brighton Beach to Newark to pick me up for another summer at Picky Pine. Mugsy and I happily settled into the old maroon car and we had our usual fun ride in the rumble seat. When we weren't bumper to bumper in traffic, he loved to let his ears blow in the wind.

The big house at Picky Pine had many new improvements. Most wonderful was an inside bathroom with a tub, shower and hot and cold water. No more being attacked on my behind by mosquitoes in the outhouse. Aunt Helen now had a washing machine as well so we wouldn't have to go all the way to town and spend hours in the hot Laundromat.

I was so glad to be here. However, it wasn't quite the same without hearing Ronnie whistling or singing as he came home from his caddy job at the golf course. All week long, it was just my little cousin Billy, Aunt Helen, and I until Uncle Bill came on the weekend.

Both of the little bungalows were rented out, mostly for two weeks at a time, so each time it changed tenants, there was a lot of work to do getting it clean for the next renter. I loved seeing my country friends and going to the pond with them and Mugsy. I often walked to the other end of Carmersville to visit Aunt Jessie and her sweet husband,

Uncle Andy. She always had homemade cookies and lemonade. We'd all sit on the porch and talk and talk, Aunt Jessie with her big intakes of breath and Uncle Andy with his Scottish brogue. Uncle Andy would always send me home with a bag of his grape tomatoes from the garden, but I ate most of them before I got back to Aunt Helen's.

Of course, at night I would walk down to the orchard on Uncle George's property where he would tell his fascinating stories about life in the olden days. For some reason, I just realized that summer that Carmersville was named after him, George Carmer. He was the first to settle in these woods that slowly developed into this tiny village with no more than twenty houses. I still looked forward to picking blueberries and, on cloudy days, reading my library books. I was now reading teenage romance novels.

One afternoon, Aunt Helen and I were in the car going to shop in Farmingdale. We were on the dirt road between highways when a very loud "clunk" brought the car to a sharp, sudden stop. Good thing Aunt Helen always drove very slowly, otherwise we may have been hurt. Aunt Helen was very shook up; we were in the middle of nowhere, and it was hot! After a long while a car finally came along and stopped to ask what the trouble was. He was headed toward Farmingdale and offered us a ride to Walter's, the only garage in town. Aunt Helen wanted to stay with the car so he said he would tell Walter where we were stuck. Aunt Helen didn't often get nervous but she seemed a wreck during our long wait. We both had to go the bathroom, so we took turns going behind the bushes on the side of the road. Finally, the owner Walter himself came with a tow truck. He said it appeared that we lost an axle. We rode in the truck's cab with him, our little maroon car hitched behind us, rolling along on its hind wheels. At the station, Walter said we had to leave the car and he would see if there was anything he could do. "It looks kind of bleak for that there little baby," he said as he drove us home.

The next day he came to deliver the bad news, "Your little car is dead, Helen." He had one of his guys driving a car behind him. "I can lend you this car till you get one." Aunt Helen asked how much she owed him. "No charge, Helen. How long have we known each other, twenty five years or so? You and Bill come over to the garage when you can. Maybe you can find a used car you like. You know I'll give you a good deal." After he left, Aunt Helen was very sad. I even think she went into the bathroom to cry.

When Uncle Bill arrived that weekend, he drove Aunt Helen, little Billy and me to Walter's garage. Uncle Bill picked out a second hand dark blue four door car. All the way home, Aunt Helen kept telling him, "Slow down, Ducky, you are driving much too fast," but Uncle Bill paid no attention. Little Billy started to cry and Uncle Bill started to mimic him, "Mah, Mah, the Mah, Mah is starting." Little Billy grabbed my hand; with his other he thrust his thumb in his mouth. Now that he was almost six he didn't do that too often, only when he was nervous.

Aunt Helen got a little cross, "I said slow down, Bill." At this point he let up a bit on the gas, but just a little. I had been a bit nervous also. Their other little car could never have gone this fast. Suddenly, I felt very sad; gone were all the wonderful years in the rumble seat.

Aunt Jean's wedding, Aunt Mae is Matron of
honor her husband Pete is best man

My First Holy Communion (7 years old)

Me after Aunt Helen cut off my braids

Me, my cousin Billy and Ronnie at the pond in Carmersville

My father's picture in the telescope

Thanksgiving at my Aunt Jean's in Kearney

Ronnie in the Army (18 years old)

Uncle Bill

Me at 11 years old in front of the car with the Rumble seat

My confirmation Day (12 years old)

Wedding picture of my father with his 4th wife "Mike"

My half sister Louise

Aunts Mae, Helen, Jean and my mother (1972)

Part III

CHAPTER 45

Childhood Ends

The month of July seemed to go fast. I was excited to get my first letter from Ronnie. I missed him very much. I had already written to him several times. He wrote he was happy and met a lot of nice guys, wished me a happy eleventh birthday but said to forgive him; he couldn't shop for a card. I tucked his letter away with my father's in my jewel box. Daddy sent me a really nice birthday card and twenty-five dollars but didn't write a note in the card. My mother was unable to get off work for my birthday this year. Aunt Helen had a very small party for both Billy and me. I could hardly believe he was already six. He was becoming quite a nice little companion.

The Sunday after my birthday, Uncle Bill offered to drive me to church. I was surprised because he made it seem like such a bother when Aunt Mae and Aunt Jean needed a ride. I would always go when he drove them, but he had never offered to take just me. Aunt Helen winked at me, saying, "You are really starting to rate with Bill." I knew it pleased her—and me too. I had spent every summer with them since I was five; Uncle Bill never seemed to like having us kids around, except for Ronnie. I guessed that's why they never had children. On the other hand, Aunt Helen was like a second mother, and I felt she really enjoyed having me and Billy spend summers with them.

I'm not sure why Aunt Helen never went to church, but she didn't. I always felt sinful about missing mass and asked God to forgive me, so today I was thankful to be going. It was a clear, warm Sunday morning: a perfect time to wear the pretty new pink dress my mother had sent me for my birthday. Feeling quite grown up, I slipped into the front seat of Uncle Bill's newly purchased used Chevrolet. He gave the horn a toot and I waved goodbye to Aunt Helen as we exited the driveway. After the car turned onto the long stretch of country road toward Farmingdale, Uncle Bill reached over and patted my hand saying, "So the little Puddin' is eleven years-old." He then kept his hand on mine, which was on my lap, giving it an occasional squeeze. Part of me wanted to remove it, but I felt that since he was being so nice to me I didn't want to insult him. I was relieved when he took his hand away, until I heard the sound of a zipper. Then his hand grasped mine and pulled it over to his exposed and erect penis. I jerked my hand away, but before I could turn my head toward the passenger-side window, I caught a glimpse of his penis sitting in a bed of gray and black hair sticking up several inches out of his fly opening. The only other penis I had ever seen was my little six year-old cousin's. I was shocked that a penis could be so big and stiff. Suddenly, it seemed the entire car smelled of Uncle Bill's sweat and for a moment I thought I might vomit. I opened the window a crack. I heard his voice—low, hoarse, and pleading.

"Come on, don't be such a baby, it's not going to bite you, let me have your hand."

When he reached for my hand again, my dress crept up above my knees. Pulling it down quickly, I yanked my hand away and heard myself shouting in anger, "No! I will not! Put it away!" I was also frightened and remembered the movie *Johnny Belinda* with Jane Wyman, when she was raped and no one believed her.

"What's the harm in a little touch?" he was saying in a low voice I hardly recognized.

I pressed myself as far against the car door as possible. I wanted to jump out but we were moving, and there was nothing around us but woods. If I got out of the car, then what? Where would I go? What would I tell Aunt Helen? I knew I wouldn't say a word since I knew it would devastate her. She was such a happy person. Suddenly, I thought of my mother and how much she disliked and stayed away from Uncle Bill. I just knew he must have tried to put her hand on his penis, too, and because she drank he thought he could make her do it. I bet he would never try this with Aunt Mae or Jean, they would belt him one. When we came near the main road, I heard him shifting around. Out of the corner of my eye I saw him zip up his pants. I hated him and wanted to punch him. We drove the rest of the way in silence.

The car barely came to a stop in front of St. Catherine of Siena Church when I flung the door open and jumped out, nearly tripping on the running board. Uncle Bill shouted after me as he got out to shut my door, "I'll get the paper and meet you after mass in the parking lot." He acted like nothing had happened.

Repulsed, I ran to the bathroom and scrubbed my hands. I barely returned the smile from the older lady at the sink next to me. I felt so ashamed about what had happened. During mass I begged God and my namesake, St. Catherine, to keep him from doing anything again. After church I got into the car and slammed the door. I would not look at him. I silently pleaded to St. Catherine, "Please…please!"

"I picked up some cheese danish at the bakery," he smiled and winked as he handed me the box. I knew he knew they were my favorite. I gave him a dirty look, said nothing, put the box on the edge of my lap to weigh down my dress, and tucked both hands under the string.

We drove in silence. When we turned onto the road through the woods I wedged myself so close to the door that the handle dug into my side. I sat wooden, terrified that he might unzip again, but he didn't that day.

CHAPTER 46

What to Do!

The rest of the summer was not the same. I dreaded Uncle Bill coming on the weekends; he made me so uncomfortable. Aunt Helen thought it was great that Uncle Bill enjoyed my company. She kept encouraging me to accompany him on his car trips to town. I tried to avoid going whenever possible, but because I didn't want Aunt Helen to suspect anything, I couldn't say I wouldn't go to church on Sundays. On each ride I was extremely tense and tried to sit as far away from him as possible. Once again he took my hand and tried to put it between his legs, but I quickly yanked it away.

"Oh, come on, I'm not going to make you do anything you don't want to do. What's the harm in a little touch?" He tried this during several more rides but, thankfully, he never unzipped his pants again. The thought of seeing that big hairy penis again made me gag.

It wasn't how I had envisioned a man's penis. I thought back to when I had been shocked to see Mugsy's penis. Mugsy and I had gone to Mimi's grocery store to get his quarter pound of liverwurst. He always sat and watched as Mimi sliced, wrapped and bagged it. On the way back to the house, he was trotting along beside me with his pretzel tail wagging. Just before we turned the corner to Jackson Street, a small dog ran out from a hallway where a group of little boys was playing. Mugsy and the dog started circling around each other and, the next thing I knew, Mugsy had mounted the little dog and was humping her. The dog started to cry out like she was hurting and the boys began yelling at Mugsy and then screaming at me to get my dog off her. I tried to wave the bag I had in my hand to get Mugsy away, but he starting squealing loudly and seemed to be hurting as well. He also seemed unable to pull out of the little dog. Now both dogs were really yelping. I was so embarrassed and very frightened; I didn't know what to do. A lady ran out from the hallway with a pot of cold water and threw it at the little dog's backside. Mugsy got free, jumped away and ran home whimpering like he was in pain. The boys were now laughing. I could feel my cheeks getting red as I ran home and found Mugsy waiting by the door. When we got inside, he kept licking his penis. It was long and pink and smooth, and I thought that was what all penises looked like. I was worried whether Mugsy was going to be all right. After a while he stopped licking himself and fell asleep curled up in a ball on the couch.

Another day when I was in the car with Uncle Bill and he was pulling my hand to touch him, I blurted out, "I'm going to tell."

He just chuckled, "Oh, what a baby you are."

But he let go of my hand; at least he didn't force me. I knew I wouldn't tell, and who was I going to tell anyway? I wanted to say, "I'll write to Ronnie so he won't like you anymore," but I knew Ronnie adored Uncle Bill. It would just cause a lot of trouble to tell Ronnie, or anyone else. I wondered if Uncle Bill would have behaved this way if Ronnie were here this summer. I realized for the first time that having an older brother was having protection.

Now I was always uncomfortable at breakfast and dinner when Uncle Bill acted very jolly toward me. I hated the mornings when he stopped by my bed to give me a pat; I'd pull the sheets up over me. He mostly did this in front of Aunt Helen, which was good because I felt safe, but I also realized that if I ever told, he would just make everything sound as innocent as those friendly pats.

I no longer went to the pond without having a cover-up over my bathing suit, and dreaded each weekend more and more. By mid-August, I knew I wanted to cut the summer short, before Uncle Bill came for his two week vacation. So I started planning to go home with Aunt Mae. I knew Aunt Mae was going to Aunt's Helen's apartment in Brighton Beach for Labor Day weekend and I was pretty sure if I asked her, she would take me with her. She was coming to Picky Pine with Uncle Bill the following weekend, before his vacation began, and Uncle Andy was going to drive her home on Monday morning.

The Saturday night before, at dinner, Uncle Bill asked Aunt Helen, "When I take little Puddin' to church tomorrow, do you want me to pick up anything from the market?" My stomach did a flip; I couldn't even eat the blueberry pudding that Aunt Helen made especially for me. I hadn't slept the night before anticipating Sunday. Should I tell him I'm not going? But Aunt Helen would wonder why. Noticing my full dish of pudding, she asked, "Kathy, are you feeling all right?" That led me to say, "No, I think I'm coming down with something." Now I had a plan; when I get up in the morning, I will say I don't feel well and can't go to church, and that's exactly what I did.

The next weekend, Aunt Mae beat me to it; she invited me to come with her to Brighton Beach and I quickly said, "Yes!" Uncle Andy would be happy to drive both Mugsy and me back home. This was a perfect excuse to leave Picky Pine. It would be such a treat, too. I sadly realized I could no longer go to Brighton Beach if Uncle Bill was there.

Aunt Helen was sorry to see me go. I really had such mixed feelings about leaving her. Little Billy was crying when we drove away. I also felt badly about leaving him. Looking back at Picky Pine, I sorrowfully wondered when, if ever, I would come back. Yet, I also felt like a weight had been lifted off of me.

CHAPTER 47

Doing It

There were still two weeks until Labor Day. August in Newark was depressing and sweltering; on most nights, I couldn't sleep. Ronnie's studio couch, where I'd been sleeping since he left, was only a separated from the open window by the rocking chair. One night, after Mugsy started to growl and I heard a noise behind me, I jumped up in terror to discover two boys boosted up on their elbows, giggling and looking in on me from the window. I ran screaming into the bedroom, while Mugsy kept barking at the window. My grandmother and mother jumped out of bed and came running into the parlor. Mommy held me until I stopped shaking. I refused to go back into the parlor that night. My grandmother promised she would nail the half-screens to the side of the windows so no one could slide them open.

On nights that followed, even if there was a slight breeze, I couldn't feel it. I now pulled the shade down, except for an inch, so I could see if anyone was lurking. Because I felt exposed sleeping in my baby dolls, I wore long pajama bottoms with a sleeveless shirt. Besides that incident, on the wall the couch was against, there was a round opening for hooking up a pot-belly coal stove, which was sealed off by a thin circle of aluminum. Often during the night, I was awakened by fluttering inside the wall, which could have been mice or even rats. Granny assured me that it was just the wind and besides, she said, it was sealed tight and nothing could get inside. I felt a little less threatened with Mugsy beside me. Even with all that, I still thought it was better being alone in the parlor than being in the bedroom and hearing my mother snoring loudly, moaning most of the night and smelling like stale beer.

News programs were filled with details of the war in Korea. I was so relieved to get a postcard from Ronnie.

Katie did,

A quick note to say, don't worry your little head about me. Although American soldiers are now being shipped out to fight in the Korean War, I have been given orders to be stationed in Frankfurt Germany. Will write soon.

Your loving brother,
Ronnie

Elaine was still away and so were Margaret and Patrick. I spent most of my time with Sissy. Several times in those two weeks, we went to Hayes public pool by the Ballantine Brewery. It was a large city pool but the entire area smelled of malt from the beer. When you lay down on your towel to sunbathe, the strong malt odor, which even permeated the cement, seeped through. There was a White Castle directly across the street from the pool so, on the way home, we'd buy a few burgers at ten cents apiece. They were yummy, but I kept thinking I had to get back to Joe Bonomo's calorie counting. At night, Sissy and I would sit on my stoop or on the broken wall below her building, giving each other hints in the game *Guess Which Movie Star.* I usually guessed right on the very first hint.

Sissy would blurt out, "Legs."

I'd answer, "Betty Grable."

"Trolley Car?"

"Judy Garland." I definitely knew my movies and movie stars.

One night Sissy and I were hanging around reading movie magazines. They were filled with pictures of Frank Sinatra and Ava Gardner, who were arm in arm and all smiles while attending the Joe Louis—

Ezzard Charles world-heavyweight championship bout at Yankee Stadium. This incident, I read, caused his wife Nancy to file for a legal separation.

Just then Sissy told me that her friend Joanne was going to have a baby. I sucked in my breath and jumped up, causing all the magazines to fall onto the floor.

"How could that happen when she isn't even married?" I asked in absolute astonishment.

Sissy laughed as she bent over to pick up the magazines. Shaking her head she told me how it happened. "Joanne and her boyfriend were 'doing it.' That's the only way you get pregnant."

"Joanne 'did it'?" I was appalled.

Sissy just stood there still nodding her head. Then it hit me. I could barely get the words out, "Not my mother, my mother would never 'do it' with my father!"

Sissy laughed, "Of course your mother and father 'did it.' You wouldn't be here if they didn't. That's the only way you can have a baby, and Joanne was 'doing it' with her boyfriend," Sissy said wide-eyed. "I'm sorry to be the one to tell you."

I knew about intercourse. My school friends and I also called it "doing it." Somehow I had never connected it to having babies. I knew where babies came out from Aunt Jean but not how they got in. I just hadn't made the connection. Somehow I had thought that after you married, God planted a seed. This was such a shock! I certainly didn't lead a sheltered life and thought I was quite worldly having visited all the bars with my mother over the years. My father had also moved on to his fourth wife.

That night I waited for my mother to come home. I kept looking at her. I could barely speak to her; she had fallen into the category of those who "did it." With this new awareness, I kept picturing her and my father "doing it." My stomach turned upside down and I felt queasy.

"Are you all right, Sweetie?" Mommy slurred as her head bobbed loosely while she swung back and forth in the rocking chair.

"I'm okay. I'm just very tired." I went into the parlor without kissing her goodnight. In bed, I thought about the stories my mother told me about Ronnie's father. It had been like a love story from a movie, now it seemed different. I wondered what she had written in that diary, how much did Ronnie read? Did she write about "doing it" with him?

To me, love was romantic and sex was dirty. Then I visualized my father "doing it" with his new, young wife. I felt disdain for both my mother and my father. I thought about all my aunts. It was hard to believe that they all did it, except for Aunt Helen who apparently stopped "doing it" long ago. I now remembered one night in Picky Pine. I was lying awake in bed upstairs and overheard my three aunts talking about what I now realized was having sex. My Aunt Mae stated that her ex-husband "the goose" always wanted to get her into bed. I heard my Aunt Helen say she couldn't be bothered with that anymore, that's why they had twin beds. While thinking about this, I became upset with Aunt Helen. If she let Uncle Bill "do it," maybe he wouldn't have tried to make me touch him. Just for a moment I felt sorry for Uncle Bill. My romantic images from the movies made me think he felt Aunt Helen did not love him anymore. Instantly, the other part of me was glad she didn't let him because I could still see his disgusting penis sticking up out of that nest of curly gray hair.

I couldn't fall asleep for a long time because images kept coming of my mother, father, aunts and Joanne all "doing it." My stomach turned upside down at the images that came to mind. I felt both curious and disgusted. I pulled the sheet up over me in case the boys tried to look in the window again. I was so glad tomorrow was Friday when Aunt Mae would come to pick me up and take me to Brighton Beach for the Labor Day weekend.

CHAPTER 48

Aunt Martha's Visit

It wasn't quite as exciting going to Brighton Beach with Aunt Mae as it had been with Aunt Helen, but I was glad to get away for a few days. We arrived at the apartment early on Friday so we were able to spend quite a few hours at the beach. I welcomed the sun beating down on my shoulders. I pulled myself way out into the ocean to the end of the ropes and held on while singing *Summertime* and *I'll be Seeing You*, over and over, as each wave lifted me gently up and down, temporarily washing away all the events of this past summer.

Afterward, sitting on the beach blanket, Aunt Mae and I ate the knishes from Mrs. Stahl's. Turning to lie on my stomach, the swish of the waves and beach chatter lulled me to sleep. When I opened my eyes it was almost sunset. Exhausted from the trip and the sun, we went to bed early, planning to spend the next day at the Steeplechase.

We slept late on Sunday and, after a late breakfast, walked on the Boardwalk to Coney Island. Even though I had just eaten, when we passed the pizza stand, I couldn't resist getting a slice; Coney Island was one of the few places you could get pizza by the slice. After enjoying all of my favorite rides, we sat and laughed with the audience watching the people come out of the funhouse, struggling through the spinning barrel and trying to escape from the rubber bars, just as Aunt Helen and I had done.

The day went by so quickly and, on the way back, I was starved. Aunt Mae bought me two more slices of pizza, juicy with sauce and lots of mozzarella cheese. I agreed they would serve as my dinner. I was stuffed and vowed to start calorie counting once again the day after the holiday.

The next morning was Labor Day. I woke with very bad cramps and red stained undies. At first I thought it was because I had eaten too much pizza. I was very cranky and didn't feel like having the bacon and eggs Aunt Mae had prepared. Aunt Mae remarked, "By the way you're behaving, you'd think 'Aunt Martha' had come to town."

Then it dawned on me...I got my first period! Aunt Mae clapped her hands and congratulated me. I was miserable. To me this didn't seem like a happy event at all, the cramps were awful and I didn't want to sit for fear I would stain Aunt Helen's chairs. Aunt Mae said she would run to the drug store and get me the supplies I needed, but in the meantime, I should pad my panties with wads of toilet paper.

She soon returned with a sanitary belt and a box of Kotex. Through the locked bathroom door she explained how I should fasten the long gauze strip of the Kotex onto the hooks of the belt. It took several attempts to get it to stay firmly in place. I felt so uncomfortable with this big pad between my legs. She said I was very lucky to know in advance about the monthly period. She was twelve when she started to bleed, and didn't have any idea about what was happening to her. She thought she was dying and spent all day in church crying and pleading with God to save her life. Aunt Mae said her prayers were answered; her period went away and didn't come back until she was sixteen. I felt neither very happy nor very lucky.

It was a beautiful day and Aunt Mae suggested that we go to the beach; even though I could not go in the water we could enjoy the sun for a while. I didn't even want to go out since I felt everyone could tell I had my period. She offered to take me to the movie theatre that was just on the corner. I refused since I was afraid to stain my pedal pushers. I just wanted to stay in and lie down. Aunt Mae also bought me some Midol, which she said would help with the cramps. I took one and fell asleep for a short time.

"Let's just go back to Newark early today," Aunt Mae suggested when I woke up.

I agreed. The cramps felt a little better, but I dreaded having to travel with this Kotex on. I kept trying not to snap at Aunt Mae but I felt very irritable. The trip home by subway, train and bus seemed to take forever. I stood up most of the time, constantly asking Aunt Mae if anything was on the back of my pink pedal pushers. I remembered Aunt Jessie with her dress all stained. Once home, I immediately ran into the bathroom to change the Kotex. While I was in the bathroom, Aunt Mae told my grandmother.

When I came out Granny was lighting a candle. "Why are you lighting a candle?" I snapped as she blessed herself in front of the Virgin Mary's statue. Granny tried to put her arm around me and I just ran off into the parlor and lay down on the couch. Mugsy was glad to see me and jumped up onto the couch. When he started sniffing between my legs, I shoved him away, put him out of the parlor, and closed the door. School was going to start next week and I was glad that this period would be over by then.

Tomorrow I would tell Sissy that I got my period. At least I had Kotex. Sissy's mother ripped up old sheets into strips, and then folded them as a substitute for sanitary napkins. Sometimes she even washed them to use again. My grandmother ripped up old sheets also, but only to use to blow our nose and we always threw them away afterward.

When my mother came home, Granny told her about my period. I had been asleep but woke to Mommy leaning over me, kissing my forehead. The smell of beer was overpowering as she said, "So Aunt Martha came to visit my Sweetie today."

I just nodded and turned over, pretending I was not quite awake. She crashed into the table as she tried to tiptoe out of the room. Mugsy came running in and snuggled up beside me. I kept petting him on the head saying, "I'm sorry, Mugsy, you know I love you, you're the best dog in the world."

I stayed home all the next day, taking Midol every few hours and listening to my radio programs. After dinner I decided to go across the street and see if Sissy was home. She was. She told me her father bought a piece of property in Lake Parsippany and was going to build a house there. She said if I wanted to I could take a ride with them the following Sunday.

"I'll miss you so much," I told her.

Sissy hugged me, "It will take a long time because my father and Junior are going to do all the building themselves."

We talked about movies. She had just seen *All About Eve* and told me some of the plot and how great Anne Baxter was in it. She said I mustn't miss seeing it. About an hour later I was finally able to say, "Guess what Sissy? I got my first period yesterday."

"Right on Labor Day?" she laughed. I nodded and laughed as well. "I was also eleven when I got my first period. Wow, on Labor Day," and she laughed again. Her loud belly laugh brought her mother into the room.

"What is so funny?" she asked.

"Kathy got her first period on Labor Day."

Now all three of us were laughing. I was feeling a little better about getting my period. Sissy's brother Junior came into the room with a questioning look on his face. I threw Sissy a 'don't-you-dare-tell' look. Junior was fair and blond like Sissy but not outgoing like her. He was seventeen, had pimples over his face and pretty much kept to himself, always tinkering with a short wave radio in the parlor.

When Junior left the room, Sissy said, "Kathy, I think you should be wearing a bra." Her mother nodded. Sissy went into her bedroom and handed me one of her bras to try on.

"It will be too big," I protested.

"Try it on," Sissy insisted. I went outside to that nasty bathroom on the porch. Because the apartment had railroad rooms without doors, I didn't want Junior to walk in on me. The bra was white cotton, a Maidenform with many rows of circular stitching forming the cups into cone shapes, size 34 B. After finally managing to fasten the hook in the back, I called Sissy into the bathroom; she said the bra fit me perfectly.

"Since it fits you so well, you can keep that bra. Let me show you an easier way to fasten the bra in front, then turn it around." She also insisted on giving me a belted yellow shirtwaist dress. In the mirror I suddenly looked like a young woman.

"I can't keep your dress." Sissy assured me it was too tight on her. I elicited a loud whistle from Junior when he came into the kitchen. My arms flew across my newly uplifted, pointed breasts and the blood rushed to my face.

At home that night, though I'm not sure why, I was reluctant to tell my mother about Sissy giving me the bra, but when I did, she noticed the size of my breasts and agreed I should be wearing one. I told her I would need more of them and that this bra fit comfortably. Writing down the size and style, my mother said she'd buy me a couple more Maidenforms.

"My little Sweetie is all grown up," she cooed. "You got your period and your first bra all in a few days."

I was proud and embarrassed at the same time.

CHAPTER 49

Winter Coats

My mother and I shopped in Ohrbach's for a first day of school outfit. I picked out a yellow and red plaid wool skirt with a pleated cummerbund and a white blouse with dolman sleeves; we also bought two Maidenform bras and a new set of day of the week panties. For the first week of school we were allowed to wear our regular clothes, then it was back to the dark green uniforms and beige blouses.

I did start back on the Joe Bonomo diet, and after only five days of 1200 calories a day, I felt flatter and shapelier wearing my new outfit on the first day of school. The diet called for small portions of meat, vegetables and fruit. My Grandmother was upset that I wouldn't eat her blinis and potatoes. Except for us girls getting together at Santa Lucia's on Sundays, I definitely was going to keep up the diet.

When walking home from school on Ferry Street, I passed our dry cleaners. There was a sign on the door "GONE OUT OF BUSINESS." My navy blue pea jacket, long coat, Mommy's imitation leopard jacket, and Granny's black wool coat had all been stored there for the summer. It was September and would be getting cool very soon. My mother was so upset when I told her; I knew she did not have the money for new coats. She said there was probably nothing we could do about it.

Next to the Wilson Avenue Playground was Sal's candy store where Elaine and I hung out after playing kickball, ping-pong, Parcheesi, or checkers. We'd buy a double dip ice cream cone; Elaine always got chocolate and I vanilla.

Elaine didn't come out at night but I would go back to Sal's after dinner and play the jukebox or pinball machine. Sal had many Frank Sinatra selections as well as some Italian songs. I played *Come Back to Sorrento* or *O Sole Mio.* I remembered many of the Italian words since my father often sang those songs in his bar. Sal was Italian; his nickname was "Gooch." I told Gooch about my coats at the cleaners. He said I should call the Bureau of Bankruptcy in Washington, D.C., and they could tell me where my coats were being stored. He found the number for me.

I spent many dollars in coins in the public phone booth at Mimi's grocery store. Telephone calls had just doubled from five cents to ten cents for a local call. Mugsy would trot along beside me because he never missed a chance to go to Mimi's, the source of his liverwurst. He knew Mimi would always give him a slice. Mugsy sat outside the phone booth for a while. Several of the customers greeted him since they knew him from the neighborhood and from coming into the grocery store with me and Granny. After a while, he'd lost patience and scratched at the door to go out. Frequently being put on hold, I kept feeding the phone more coins. Finally, I got through to the correct person who gave me the location and phone number of a dry cleaner in Bloomfield, New Jersey, where the coats were being stored. When I told Gooch, he said he would get someone to drive me there. It was already October and we really needed those coats. On a Saturday morning, Jerry, one of the older guys that I knew from hanging out in the candy store, volunteered to meet and drive me there. It was about a half-hour away. Jerry and I chatted during the drive. He told me he thought I was a very smart young lady to track down the coats. At the dry cleaners, when I handed the clerk the receipt, sure enough he presented me with our four coats. The charge was more than I expected so Jerry loaned me the rest of the money.

I felt so accomplished and proud when I arrived home with all our coats. My mother and Granny were really excited. Mommy could not believe that I had actually tracked them down. She gave me the money that I owed Jerry. I began to realize that if I didn't do things myself, they would never get done.

Several letters arrived from Ronnie. He loved the army, was happy and had many buddies. He kept reassuring me that he would continue to be stationed in Frankfurt, Germany and that it didn't seem very likely he would ever be transferred to Korea. Germany seemed so far away. I missed him so much but was glad he wouldn't be in any danger. Mommy also received letters from him. Every time she heard the song *P.S. I Love You,* she would sing along and cry for Ronnie. *"Dear, I thought I'd drop a line...."*

One day Ronnie wrote telling her he made arrangements for his allotment check to be sent to Aunt Mae, so she could put it in the bank for him. Ronnie said he thought he would save Mommy the trouble of going to the bank since she always hated doing anything detailed. However, she thought he didn't trust her with the money and was offended and very distraught over this. It started a new emotional subject for her. She felt betrayed and humiliated for him to designate Aunt Mae instead of her. She'd cry and dwell on this subject over and over again every night. If I tried to defend and justify Ronnie's actions, she'd get furious at me, just like she used to about my father. "Go ahead, stick up for your brother, see if I care." I stopped trying; she was so hurt and beyond consolation.

The fall flew by. I was still working at Bingo, baby sitting for Billy and Patrick, going upstairs to Margaret's for the *Milton Berle Show* every Tuesday night, rehearsing with the choir for the Christmas mass, getting A's in my classes, and going to dinner and the movies on Sundays with my St. James girlfriends. Except for Sundays, I stuck to the Joe Bonomo diet and, by Christmas, I had lost four pounds with ten more to go. I actually dropped from a size fourteen to a twelve. I had been 134 and was aiming for 120 pounds.

In late November, Aunt Mae decided to take a trip to Miami Beach. She visited Daddy while she was there and brought back a picture of him with his new wife, Michelle or "Mike." She was young, blond and slightly plump; she was only twenty four years-old but looked older. Actually, she was one year younger than my father's daughter, my half-sister, Louise. I couldn't believe this young woman was his new wife. Although Aunt Mae said Daddy still very much wanted me to come to Florida and stay with them for Christmas vacation, I wouldn't dare to go so soon after Mommy's upset over Ronnie. My mother would have never forgiven me and definitely would have felt betrayed by me as well.

It was sad not to have Ronnie home for Christmas. Mommy, Granny and I still exchanged gifts after midnight mass. On Christmas Day, the three of us went to Kearney for Christmas dinner at Aunt Jean and Aunt Mae's, but the thrill of Christmas was gone. In Kearney, I was glad to see Aunt Helen. She said she was looking forward to my spending the summer with her at Picky Pine, and asked if I was coming for Easter vacation. I told her I couldn't. I fibbed and said I volunteered to help the nuns that week because the convent was being painted. I said I would be in charge of packing up all the books and covering the shelves.

It was very uncomfortable with Uncle Bill there. He acted like nothing happened. I sat at the opposite end of the table and as soon as we had dessert, I headed for little Billy's room to play with him and the new additions to his Lionel train set. I also knew I wasn't going to go to Picky Pine that summer, but I didn't want to tell Aunt Helen. I would have to come up with a good excuse later on.

CHAPTER 50

Alyea Street

At Wilson Avenue Playground, Elaine and I often played stickball with kids that went to school there or other nearby schools. I developed a big crush on a boy named Henry, who was in the eighth grade at Wilson Avenue. Henry was tall and well built for his age; most of the boys my age were still pretty short, or at least shorter than me. He always seemed to linger where I was, whether playing ping-pong, stickball or checkers. Whenever he spoke to me, he looked right into my eyes, and I was aware of the blood rushing to my face.

On the weekends at the Rivoli movie theatre, Elaine and I always sat on the right side aisle next to the wall. We liked it there because not too many people chose that area and we were able to eat the sandwiches we brought without disturbing anyone. Henry and his friend Charlie started to sit in the row in back of us and during intermission, we'd all talk. After a few Saturdays, Henry and Charlie came to sit in our row. Henry sat next to me and halfway through the movie, he put his arm around the back of my seat. It would sometimes brush the back of my neck and made me tingle all over. After a few weeks Henry turned me toward him and gave me my first kiss. I thought I would melt right into the seat and my heart would burst out of my chest. I thought I was now his girlfriend.

Actually, it wasn't my first kiss but it was my first kiss that wasn't part of a game. My classmate Joey had been inviting a group of the more popular kids in our class to his house after school while his parents were still at work. There were always eight or ten of us. We brought soda, chips or peanuts and sat around in a circle on the floor of his tiny living room playing spin the bottle, anxiously wanting to be the bottle's chosen one. Each couple would get up and kiss in the adjoining little alcove that led to his kitchen, so our kissing was somewhat private. The girls always wished the bottle would stop at two of the boys, Richard and John. They were especially good kissers, and kissing them in the alcove lasted slightly longer. Otherwise the girls didn't pay much attention to them other than in the game. At 4:30 or 5:00 p.m., we all went our separate ways.

Kissing Henry was different: it felt so good, so stimulating, and after several Saturdays of an occasional kiss, we began kissing throughout the entire movie. While I was sorry to miss the movie, I was more interested in our smooching. One Saturday after Henry left the Rivoli to go home for dinner; I actually stayed to see *Born Yesterday* with Judy Holliday and didn't get home until after seven.

When we saw each other at the playground, Henry was now standoffish and didn't pay any attention to me. But when we met again in the movies, he would slip into the seat next to me and act really affectionate. Then I started to see him walking a girl named Eleanor home from the playground. I didn't know what to think because he would still seek me out in the movies. This behavior was very confusing and hurtful since I thought that he really liked me, that I was special.

After a few more Saturdays of kissing, I finally told him I didn't want him to sit next to me anymore, even though I really did want him to and loved kissing him. I knew he was still walking Eleanor home from the playground. Meanwhile, Eleanor told the girls that she let Henry know that she wasn't the least bit interested in him. I was waiting for him to talk to me again and maybe start walking me home. I kept trying to bump into him. Henry and his friends did not hang out at Sal's candy store, but a different one on Alyea Street, which was at the back exit of Wilson Avenue Playground.

One night after the playground closed at nine o'clock, I decided to exit on Alyea Street in the hope that I might happen to see Henry. It was very dark, one side of the street was Wilson Avenue School and the other a few small houses and closed businesses. I was totally alone on the street until I saw a man turn the corner from East Ferry Street and walk toward me. He was tall in a green plaid jacket, walking at a normal pace. When he was near, he suddenly stopped, looked right into my eyes and with a crooked smile asked in almost a whisper, while he patted the zipper of his pants, "Honey, how would you like to make a few dollars?"

I panicked, I thought he was going to reach out and grab me and force me to do something with him. For a moment I felt trapped, then I bolted diagonally across the street into the candy store where I had been hoping to see Henry. I was shaking all over. No one was in the store except the old Polish lady who I knew was the owner. She was cleaning the glass on the candy counter. I wanted to tell her about the man, but I was too embarrassed. Instead, I asked for change of a quarter. She reached into her flowered apron pocket and with an accent counted out five nickels on the glass of the display case. It was sweltering in the little store. While unzipping my red corduroy jacket I tried to say thank you but the words caught in my throat. It seemed like she frowned as her eyes focused on my tight V-neck angora sweater; I quickly pulled up the zipper of my jacket. The pinball machine was parallel to the storefront window. I put the nickels in one at a time. Normally when I played, I would get a free game or two, but I was so nervous and looking out the window so much that the balls just dropped into the side gutters. My five games were over much too quickly. I was terrified that the man might still be outside waiting for me. I knew I didn't have any money left but took a few more minutes to browse though the movie magazines on the wall shelf. About to open one with Frank Sinatra on the cover, the old woman said, "You buy? I close now." I shook my head and returned it to its proper spot. I dreaded going outside.

Opening the store door very slowly and barely looking down the block, I ran as fast as I could toward East Ferry Street, where it was well lit, then continued to run home for the entire six blocks. By the time I reached my front stoop, I had cramps in my side and was sweating and out-of-breath. Once inside the hallway, I pressed my back against the door and tried to catch my breath so Granny wouldn't see me so frantic. I started to shake again and was frightened. I thought the man might have run after me and now know where I lived. When I calmed down, I got up my nerve to open the door and look down Jackson Street; no one was there. I walked down our hallway and unlocked the door into the kitchen. Granny was saying her rosary in the rocking chair; she gave me a nod and continued praying with whistling whispers. I went into the parlor, moved the shade aside very slightly, and looked out to make sure the man wasn't lurking about. When I took off my jacket, my back was soaking wet under my white sweater. I undressed in the dark and tried to shake off the image of that man's crooked smile. The sound of his hoarse whisper brought back the incident with my uncle and I started to cry. What is it about me that make these men think I might be willing to do things with them? I thought I might vomit as sourness came into my throat. How angry I was at myself for going down that dark street looking for Henry, who was no longer the least bit interested in me. I vowed never again to walk down Alyea Street or any street alone at night. I got into bed and buried myself under the covers.

CHAPTER 51

Twelve

With school out for the summer, it was strange not going to Picky Pine. Elaine had gone to Seaside Heights with her family, and the neighborhood seemed deserted. Even many of the dogs that Mugsy played with in the lot must have been away with their owners.

I began spending more time upstairs at Margaret's and taking little Patrick to Riverbank Park and the movies since he now had a baby brother, Barry. Margaret and I started to become close buddies and she often asked me to accompany them on their Sunday outings in the Orange Mountains with her husband's family. I enjoyed going, but I missed Picky Pine, my summer friends, Uncle George, and the pond, but most of all I missed Aunt Helen. I think Mugsy missed going there also.

The days were long and hot. The nights were even hotter in our house and it was difficult to sleep. I still kept the shades down on the windows to protect me from the peeking boys, and couldn't get any air. I bought a small electric fan, which helped a bit. My mother's drinking and crying over Ronnie at night seemed even more depressing with the summer heat. The smell of beer and noise from the corner bar's windows, which opened into our backyard, pervaded our kitchen.

I had received a typewritten letter from Ronnie; it was great to hear that he was pleased to have been given a new position as the right hand man to the lieutenant in Frankfurt. He had learned to type and, during his time off, he was able to see a lot of Germany and Switzerland.

I spent many nights across the street sitting with Sissy on the broken foundation under the billboards. Sissy was in town for the summer. Her father was still building the house in Lake Parsippany. They would move when Sissy graduated from East Side High School, where she was now in her junior year. I sometimes went along with them to the property. It was in the middle of the woods, and Sissy and I would pick blueberries while her father and brother worked on the house. On the way back we always stopped for burgers at White Castle. Sissy, Junior and I would sit in the back seat of the car, each eating at least three burgers. Sissy's father told us about the new 45 RPM records that RCA had developed; they were made of vinyl plastic and were much smaller than 78 speed, but you needed a different record player. That was something I definitely wanted to look into.

Once or twice during the week, Sissy and I would go to Hayes Pool and again stop at White Castle. It was so hard to stick to my calorie counting. I was losing weight, but more slowly than I would have liked. I had to skip a week of going to the pool because I started to shave my legs. The first time seemed so easy until I ran the razor over my shinbone and completely sliced off a layer of skin causing a painful wound that developed a thick ugly scab. During that time I went to the library and borrowed a new book, *The Catcher in the Rye* by J. D. Salinger, and I read it twice. Holden Caulfield seemed to be talking directly to me.

Wilson Avenue Playground was dead. Henry must have been away as well; I was glad I wouldn't have to see him. Mr. A., my favorite recreational director, was working there for the summer and I volunteered to assist him with the crafts workshop for some of the younger kids. Patrick came on occasion and had such a great time making macaroni sculptures and finger paintings for his mom and baby brother. We would stop at Jane Logan's on the way home for ice cream. Mr. and Mrs. B., who owned it, were charmed by Patrick and talked with us in between customers. It was a busy place with a long counter and many booths along the wall. One day Mrs. B. asked if I would be interested in working part-time at the counter. She said the job would pay fifty cents an hour plus tips. The idea of it really appealed to me, but I said I would let her know. It would be a great way to save up some money, plus it was air-conditioned.

In the meantime, Aunt Mae was going to go to Picky Pine for the week of little Billy's birthday and asked if I wanted to come. I jumped at the chance because with her there I knew Uncle Bill would not dare approach me, plus he would only be there on weekends. It would be terrific to be there once more, and for my twelfth birthday, too. We planned to go on a Friday and stay a week until the following Sunday. Fortunately, Uncle Andy was going to drive us down. Although I wished I could bring Mugsy, we weren't sure if we were coming home by train or car, because the following weekend both Uncle Bill and Uncle Andy were starting their two-week vacation. Before I left, I stopped into Jane Logan's to tell Mrs. B. I would begin part-time work at the counter when I returned. She gave me a hug and a free ice cream cone.

I got a letter from Daddy. He wrote that his dog Trouble ran away again and she was so happy to see him when he finally found her at the city pound. *"This was the third time she ran away. She really lives up to her name."* He said he would like me to meet Trouble and his new wife, Mike. It would be wonderful if I could come to Florida for a visit. *"Maybe during summer vacation?"* I wrote back that I couldn't because I now had the job at Jane Logan's. Of course, I knew the real reason was still to avoid hurting my mother. I also wasn't so sure I wanted to meet his young wife.

When I got out of Uncle Andy's car at Picky Pine, Aunt Helen hugged me tight. Snuggled into her chest, the smell of fresh flowers and her cooking swept over me. I surprised myself by bursting into tears and buried myself in her embrace. Little Billy was hugging Aunt Mae and also crying.

"Dear, dear," Aunt Helen laughed, "is this what happiness is?"

Aunt Jean had to work on Saturday so she came down for little Billy's birthday by train; we picked her up on Saturday evening. I was right; Uncle Bill stayed away from me and only talked to me at the dinner table. "So I guess we should be honored that the Puddin' decided to come visit us," he said winking at me. I cringed but feigned a smile.

On Sunday he drove us to church but Aunt Mae sat in the front with him. Aunt Jean, little Billy and I sat in the back. Billy was going to make his First Communion next spring and now went to church as well.

We celebrated our mutual birthdays afterward; I could hardly believe I was twelve. Aunt Jean said her gift to me was a trip to Washington, D.C., the weekend before Labor Day. I was so excited since I had always wanted to go there.

Uncle Bill's departure on Monday morning filled me with relief and made the rest of the week glorious. I felt closer to Aunt Helen than ever and I think she felt the same way. "Why don't you stay for the rest of the summer?" she asked as the next weekend neared.

I was glad to have a solid reason. "I promised to start working at Jane Logan's as a counter waitress."

"That is just wonderful, good for you. I'm very proud of you, Puddin'." She smiled and gave me a big hug. "I want you to know that I really missed you the last month. It's not the same without you."

"For me either. I love you, Aunt Helen." I hugged her back.

It was hard to leave the next Sunday. As it turned out, we did get a car ride back to Newark with Uncle Andy's nephew, Charles, who had spent the weekend with Aunt Jessie and Uncle Andy. Though I hated to leave Aunt Helen, I was looking forward to starting the job at Jane Logan's.

CHAPTER 52

Jane Logan's

Working three days a week at Jane Logan's gave me a very grown up feeling. My friends would stop in for ice cream cones. When Mr. and Mrs. B. weren't looking, I'd fill their cones up before topping them with a hearty scoop. Mrs. B always told me not to make the scoops too large but Mr. B. would say, "Put in a little extra so they will come back again." I had to be aware of which one was watching and make the cones accordingly.

A boy named Mickey, who I knew from Elaine's class and lived across the street from Jane Logan's, came in often. Sitting at the counter while eating a gigantic sundae that I had fixed extra special, Mickey started to flirt with me. He asked for my phone number but since we didn't have a phone, he gave me his. He was nice looking with brown slicked back hair and a twinkle in his eyes. He became my new crush.

On Saturday mornings, I would go around the corner to Mimi's grocery and call him from the public phone booth. It was so hot in there but I kept the door closed for my privacy, putting more coins in each time the operator came on the line. Sometimes I stayed in there for half an hour unless someone was waiting to use the phone. Mickey said he had a girlfriend but he really liked me and was trying to decide between us. Whenever he came in to Jane Logan's, I felt so fluttery. I was crazy about him. I could hardly think of anything else. One night I wrote a love poem and gave it to him after a few weeks of calls. Then he stopped coming in Jane Logan's. When I phoned him next, he told me he'd decided not to break up with his girlfriend and that he was very sorry he led me on. I felt very foolish about having given him my poem. It seemed I had no luck with boys.

The Washington, D.C., trip was the next weekend. Was I ever glad to go away and try to forget Mickey. Aunt Jean and I went by Greyhound Bus. It was the longest trip I had ever taken. We left about noon on Friday and arrived at our hotel around dinnertime. I had never stayed in a hotel before; I felt like a character in a movie. We washed up and went to dinner. After dark, with the Capitol all lit up, Washington looked so impressive, spacious and clean. Back at the hotel, Aunt Jean said, "We have to sleep fast, because tomorrow we are really going to be stepping."

We saw so much the next day. I was absolutely fascinated by the Smithsonian; my favorite exhibit was the Wright Brothers' airplane. There was so much more to see. "I wish we were going to be here longer," I sighed.

"We'll just have to come back again," Aunt Jean smiled as she draped her arm around my shoulder. I could see she was pleased that I was enjoying everything so much. It was a fabulous weekend and I really did get my mind off Mickey.

Labor Day was the next weekend, and once more I went with Aunt Mae to Brighton Beach. It was great going back to the Steeplechase, the beach and Mrs. Stahl's knishes. Having gotten my weight down, I went easy on the knishes and the pizza. Although I thought I was going to hate this summer, it turned out all right after all.

I was anxious to get back to school. When it began, I saw Mickey again; I was too embarrassed to look at him. I still felt very foolish about having written that poem for him, and was glad he was in Elaine's class and not mine. I never told Elaine about my summer crush on him.

In the seventh grade classroom, I was having trouble seeing the blackboard from my seat in the third row. I mentioned it to Sadie, the girl in front of me. She had just gotten new eyeglasses with a stronger prescription. "Try these," she said as she handed me her old glasses.

They were royal blue with a cat's eye shape. I put them on and was amazed.

"Wow! I can't believe how clear everything is."

Sadie said, "Keep them, they are no good to me anymore and they look good on you." So I had my first pair of glasses. I only wore them in class to see the blackboard.

I kept working at Jane Logan's after school three afternoons a week. Between that job, watching Patrick and little Billy, working at Bingo and doing my homework, I was very busy. I still met the girls on Sundays at Santa Lucia's and went to the Rivoli movie theatre afterward. I started to wear Sadie's glasses in the movies when I realized they made the images much clearer. The newsreels were filled with clips of Frank Sinatra's marriage to Ava Gardner on November 7, 1951, only seven days after his divorce from Nancy. I was happy for him. In the past few months magazines had been filled with stories of his despair over their constant breakups. Every time I heard him sing *I'm a Fool to Want You*, I felt his pain. I was so happy for him now.

Now that I was earning quite a bit of money, I made an appointment with Elaine's dentist, Dr. Mellon. I had only been to a dentist once before when Aunt Helen bribed me by taking me to Radio City. My second front tooth was growing over my baby tooth which had not come out on its own and had to be extracted. I remember getting so sick from the gas. Much to my surprise, Dr. Mellon discovered eighteen cavities. Appointments were made for me to come in once a week until the work was completed. I decided not to tell my mother. I would pay for the work myself.

Before I knew it, it was Thanksgiving and, of course, we went to Aunt Mae and Aunt Jean's. It was the first time I saw Aunt Helen since the summer. Uncle Bill didn't speak to me at all; it bothered me, even though I couldn't stand him. I kissed Aunt Helen goodbye and said we'd see each other at Christmas.

With all of my jobs, I had saved quite a bit of money and I wanted to buy everyone really nice Christmas gifts. For my mother I found a beautiful full-length black coat trimmed with a leopard collar which had been on sale for forty dollars at Lerner's. I thought she would absolutely love it—and she did. I picked out two new housedresses for Granny and even bought Mugsy a little green sweater for the very cold weather. He was not too happy; squirming away, he refused to let me put it on him. A large box arrived the day before Christmas Eve. My father sent me a very stylish, crimson-belted fitted coat. I was surprised at how great the fit was. I had lost fifteen pounds and had gotten down to 120 pounds, thanks to Joe Bonomo. Except for missing Ronnie, Christmas was okay. I was so happy for Ronnie though; from his letters he still seemed very content. I was also very thankful that he was stationed in Germany and not in Korea. Daddy had written that his sister's son, my cousin Louis, had been killed in Korea. "*He was blown to bits and they could only find a few pieces of him to send home for the funeral.*" I remembered him from when I was little; he was so handsome. I never know anyone young who had died. I felt very sad for his mother. The horror of it stayed with me for a long time with nightmares about Ronnie.

When I saw Aunt Helen at Christmas, she asked if I would be coming for Easter vacation. This time I told her I had religious instructions Easter week because I was preparing for Confirmation, which was partly true except we didn't have classes that week. The week after Christmas, Aunt Mae took me to see the Radio City Christmas show. The Rockettes danced to the *March of the Wooden Soldiers*. I was familiar with the tune from our record and the Laurel and Hardy movie. It was dark afterwards when we walked on Broadway. All the lights always dazzled me and once more I could not take my eyes off of the *Bond* sign, with its waterfalls constantly pouring down from the walls of the building between the two large statues dressed in neon lights. We went to Romano's on Forty Second Street; I ordered meat ravioli but had the discipline to leave two on my dish.

When school began, we received all the materials to study for our Confirmation. Confirmation Day was in May, which seemed like a very long time away.

CHAPTER 53

A Hole in My Heart

It was a freezing cold evening in February. Mugsy was snuggled into the back of my legs as I lay on the studio couch in the parlor under two blankets, listening to my Frank Sinatra records and reading about my new favorite actress, June Allyson, in *Silver Screen* magazine. June Allyson won the Golden Globe award for Best Actress in *Too Young to Kiss* with Van Johnson. I loved that movie and saw it three times. I attempted to imitate her throaty voice, but it was difficult.

Mugsy squirmed out of the covers and scratched on the parlor door to go out. Reluctantly, I emerged from the blankets to open the door to the hallway. As I opened the outer door to the street, I was hit in the face with a gust of frigid wind causing the door to crash against the wall, while I struggled to push it shut. Through the curtained glass of the street door I saw Mugsy relieve himself on the tree. Expecting him to dash right back, I waited shivering, but despite the cold he went trotting off for his usual walk.

I ran back inside and slid under the covers. At eight o'clock, I turned off my record player and clicked on the radio to listen to one of my favorite programs, *The Shadow*. I loved how the Shadow began by Lamont Cranston saying, *"Who knows what evil lurks in the hearts of men. The Shadow knows."* His evil laughter followed. Right in the middle of the story, the outside door slammed and running footsteps pounded along the hallway, followed by persistent knocking at our kitchen door. I heard Granny open it and I could hear boys' excited voices. Granny was saying, "Jesus, Jesus," as I entered the kitchen. The two teenage boys from next door were both talking at the same time. Leroy was crying and his older brother Freddie had his arm around Leroy's shoulder.

"Leroy, what's the matter?" I exclaimed.

Wiping his eyes with his coat sleeve he said, "We saw your dog get hit by a bike. He ran off yelping. We think he might be hurt real bad."

My heart stopped, I charged out the front door calling, "Mugsy, Mugsy!"

With the boys behind her, Granny came running after me, my coat over her arm. I put it on while heading in the direction the boys were pointing, yelling, "Mugsy…Mugsy!" The older brother yelled after me, "He was crossing under the railroad trestle when some boy on a speeding bike hit him."

I ran down the street, crying and sweating despite the cold, turned left on Clover Street and rang Elaine's doorbell. Elaine's mother stuck her head out the second floor window.

"Katherine? What's wrong?"

"My dog was hit by a bike, did you see him?" I shouted up to both her and Elaine, who had just come to the window.

"Kathy's dog got hit," I heard Elaine yell into the room.

"My father said he is coming down to help you look for him."

"I'm going to the vacant lot," I yelled up and ran across Jackson Street and turned onto Downing.

"Mugggggssssssy!…Mugsy! Please come out. Where are you?"

The lot was empty. Just as Granny caught up to me, Elaine's father turned the corner holding a flashlight.

"Mr. C., I can't find Mugsy, the boys said they think he is badly hurt."

"If he was hurt he probably wouldn't go very far and might try to find some shelter."

My head and my hands were freezing and I was shaking all over from cold and panic. I turned up my collar, buttoned my coat and plunged my hands into my pockets. We all went back down Jackson

Street past our house to Market Street and circled the entire block. Mr. C. shone the flashlight in all the doorways and alleys while I kept calling Mugsy's name, praying he would appear from somewhere any minute.

"Where can he be?" I cried.

"Don't worry, it was a bike and not a car so he's probably just scared," Mr. C. reassured me as he put his arm around my shoulder. We circled both blocks twice and the next time we passed our house my mother was just getting out of a cab.

I ran to her, "Mommy, Mugsy was hit by a bike, and we can't find him anywhere." Now I really burst out crying, the tears stinging my frozen face. My mother held me close and said she would help us look for him. She was staggering a bit and I hoped Elaine's father didn't notice.

"Mommy, why don't you stay here in case Mugsy tries to get in the house, and we'll keep looking."

The boys came out of the next house. Leroy asked, "Did you find him?"

It was ten thirty, we were all bitterly cold, and there was nowhere else to look. Mr. C. said we should go home. "Someone probably took him in and will nurse him or return him in the morning. Everyone in the neighborhood knows Mugsy."

Back in the parlor, wrapped in the blankets, I kept looking out the window. Every so often I went to the outside door and called out, "Muggggsssy, Mugggggggsssssssy!" I fell asleep sitting next to the window in the rocking chair.

It was barely light out when Mommy and Granny came into the parlor. They were both crying.

"WHAT?" I screamed, jumping up.

"I am so sorry, Sweetie. We found Mugsy at the backyard door, he is not alive." Mommy started to sob and hold me.

Pulling free, I grabbed her hand, "Where is he? I want to see him."

"We never looked back there because he couldn't have gotten over the fence unless someone lifted him over," I heard her saying as I ran through the rooms.

I opened the door to the backyard. There was Mugsy rolled in a ball, his snout snuggled into his hind legs the way he sometimes slept.

I bent down to pet him. It was like touching ice. I thought, "*He was here, waiting for us to open the door, if only we looked here. He must have been alive to be in this position. He must have frozen to death!*"

"Oh, God," I sobbed out loud. Was he whimpering the whole time we were looking for him, waiting for us to open the back door? "Mugsy, how did you get over the fence?" I looked at the fence—it was at least six feet high.

"Oh, Mommy. I can't…I can't."

At the thought of him lying here waiting, my chest felt like it would tear open.

"I can't," was all I could stammer.

I got up and put my arms around my mother's waist. I could feel my body shaking. "I can't, Mommy, I can't."

"I know, I know, Sweetie."

Granny had gone to get a small blanket, gently wrapped Mugsy in it, picked up his body, and moved it into the hallway. She said she would ask Leroy's father to help her dig up the frozen earth so we could bury him in the backyard.

"No! I don't want to bury him, I can't…I can't." I sat on the hall-way floor with my head resting on Mugsy. I could feel his cold body through the blanket. "Oh, Mugsy. Mugsy, I'm so sorry. I didn't know you were there. I love you, Mugsy."

Wiping her tears, Mommy said, "Sweetie, I hate to leave but I have to go to work and I'm already very late. You don't have to go to school today. Why don't you go back into the house?"

"No, I'm going to stay here with Mugsy."

Granny came out to the hall with a blanket for me, and I stayed next to Mugsy with my back propped against the wall.

"I can't…I can't," I heard myself saying over and over.

When my mother came out to leave, I wrapped my arms around her legs as she stroked my head and then kissed the top.

I must have fallen asleep, because the next thing I knew, Granny was tapping me on the shoulder. Mr. Jenkins, Leroy's father, was at the back door holding Mugsy in the blanket. The cold air smacked at me, making my breath smoke. I thought again of Mugsy freezing to death.

Granny handed me my peacoat and boots. I put them on and wrapped a babushka around my head. We walked to the far corner of the yard. A pick and shovel lay on the ground. Leroy's father had already dug a deep hole. Granny had lined the hole with a pillowcase where he gently lowered Mugsy's body, still wrapped in the blanket. Granny lifted the blanket from Mugsy's head and we all looked at him. Granny blessed herself and kept nodding while she prayed. In English she said "Good dog," and I could understand the word heaven, *dangus,* in Lithuanian. I petted Mugsy's head once more; nothing seemed real.

"I can't…I can't," I wept as Granny covered his head.

We all stood silent for a moment. Then Mr. Jenkins nodded, picked up a shovel and put the first pile of dirt into the hole. I had to turn away and leave. I saw Leroy and his brother Freddie looking over the fence. Leroy ducked as I looked his way. He ducked! A thought exploded in my head. The other side of the fence was their backyard. Did they put Mugsy over the fence? But why wouldn't they bring him to our door? Did one of them hit Mugsy with his bike? Running into the house, I threw myself on my old bed, going over all the ifs in my head while sobs racked my body.

I woke up in the early afternoon. The bedroom was always dark and it took a few minutes before I realized it wasn't just a bad dream. The thought of Mugsy's death consumed me. Going into the kitchen, I looked out the frosted window. The winter sun shone bright gold in the sky. In the back of the yard, I saw the mound of fresh dirt. Granny had put two sticks in the ground to make a cross. I blessed myself and said a prayer for Mugsy. Again my chest began to swell in pain.

"I can't."

CHAPTER 54

Moving Forward

I carried the heaviness of Mugsy's death with me for weeks. Both my mother and grandmother were also still very upset. We often cried when we spoke of him. The image of him snuggled frozen at the back-door haunted me. I wrote to tell my father and Ronnie. Daddy's reply was so understanding and consoling. He wrote that he also grieved for Mugsy, who was born a year before I was. Mugsy was the pup of his dog, Tiny. He remembered how sad he felt when Tiny had died. He said if anything happened to his dog Trouble he would be devastated, so he knew how awful I must feel. Ronnie wrote a letter back saying his heart was broken...he, too, loved Mugsy.

In his condolence letter, Daddy also wrote, as he had before, that he would like me to meet Trouble and his new wife, Mike. "*It would be wonderful if you could come to Florida for a visit. Maybe Easter vacation?*" I wrote back yet another excuse; I couldn't because I was beginning classes for my Confirmation.

I threw myself into my Confirmation lessons and took the preparation for receiving the sacrament very seriously. It was necessary to choose a sponsor. This person must be someone to educate and prepare you for the sacrament, stand with you in church during Confirmation, and guide you for the rest of your life in the faith. We learned Confirmation is the gift of the Holy Spirit, the mature commitment to and deepening of the Catholic faith. I thought the ideal person to choose as my sponsor would be Patrick's mother, Margaret. She had become like an older sister to me and, besides, with her living upstairs it would be easy for both of us to study together. I was so pleased when she accepted. Since Confirmation was not until May, we had plenty of time to prepare. I had to choose a Confirmation name. Although it was customary to take your sponsor's name, I asked Margaret if she would mind if I chose Monica after St. Monica, to whom I always prayed to help my mother stop drinking. Margaret said just the fact that I had chosen her was already an honor.

Besides watching the *Milton Berle Show* and babysitting for Patrick and baby Barry, I was spending more and more time at Margaret's. After Margaret helped me study for Confirmation, we'd spend time cooking together and I would stay for dinner. She was aware of my calorie counting and helped me not to overeat. This was difficult to do on pasta night, which was every Wednesday. Sometimes I cheated a little but, in spite of it, my weight was still going down.

On other nights, I'd go across the street to Sissy's, where we would just hang out and talk about movies or boys. I wasn't seeing too much of Elaine after school since I was attending Confirmation instructions and choir rehearsals in preparation for Holy Week and Easter Sunday. This would be the second Easter vacation I didn't go to Picky Pine. When I thought about that, I became furious with Uncle Bill since it was his fault that I couldn't be with Aunt Helen. I missed her so much.

Easter hymns were my second favorite to Christmas carols. I belted out the "Alleluias." Proudly strutting down the aisle to receive Communion, I wore a new, very fitted three-piece beige suit, size ten, that Mommy and I had shopped for together. On Ferry Street, I found a pink blouse with a ruffled collar that I liked. It was a very grown up outfit. My mother had to work at Child's on Easter so after church I took a bus to Kearney and met Aunt Mae. We went to Kearney Park together with Aunt Jean and Billy and took pictures by the yellow and scarlet tulips. Aunt Jean, her boyfriend, Frank, and Billy were going out to dinner at Schrafft's and invited Aunt Mae and me to join them. It was a special treat to eat at such an elegant restaurant; the pink linen tablecloths matched my blouse.

Easter Monday was a big day for Italians and Margaret invited me to an outing with all of her in-laws in the Orange Mountains in South Orange. It was a little chilly but we ate outdoors and feasted on all their leftovers from Easter Sunday dinner. Patrick was thrilled to have me along. We played ball together with a couple of other little kids.

Being off this week gave me a chance to hang out with Elaine and play some kickball and kick the can in the street. I had missed seeing her. Her family was so warm and friendly. When I saw her father, I thanked him for coming out on that cold night to search for Mugsy. They had no pets but he said he still remembered his dog, Greco, that he had as a boy. I especially missed Mugsy this week. He would have been hanging out with us, too. People in the neighborhood inquired about him since they hadn't seen him for a while. They also knew him because he always went in search of my mother or grandmother in the bars or the grocery store. Elaine's father said I should get another dog, but I couldn't think of replacing Mugsy.

After Easter vacation, school was very busy again. On the afternoons I wasn't working at Jane Logan's, I'd go downtown to meet my mother to shop for a Confirmation dress. Some size tens were still too tight. We shopped at Ohrbach's, Lerner's, Klein's, May's Department Store and even at Hayne & Company, which was a more expensive store. After shopping, I'd join my mother at Beb's bar for a while, do my homework, and then leave to take the bus home alone.

Finally, one afternoon at Ohrbach's, we found a mint green organdy dress with a peter pan collar, belted with a gathered shirt in a size ten that fit perfectly. Another day we bought white leather Mary Jane shoes at A.S. Beck & Company, and a white patent leather purse in Klein's. I told my mother I was sorry our shopping was over; it had been nice to meet her so often. She suggested that, from now on, I come downtown and meet her once a week at Beb's after school.

Confirmation day was very exciting. The night before, I set my hair with bobby pins. When I took them out my hair was all fluffy and looked great. I thought my green dress, with the white shoes and bag, was perfect. My mother took a corsage of white gardenias that she had hidden in back of the refrigerator and pinned it on my shoulder. All of us headed out to Saint James Church for this important day: My mother, grandmother, Aunt Mae, Aunt Jean, Aunt Helen, little Billy and, of course, Margaret with little Patrick. I wished Ronnie could have been there, too.

It was an honor to have the Bishop visit and administer Confirmation. When he anointed me on the head with holy oil, Margaret stood behind me holding a big bouquet she had gotten for me and her other hand gave mine a big squeeze. Afterwards, I went to the H. Slarek Studios, the photographer on Ferry Street, for formal pictures. When I arrived home everyone was eating. My grandmother made a big ham and Aunt Mae brought her delicious potato salad and cole slaw. Mommy bought a big iced butter cream cake at Cushman's Bakery that said *"Congratulations on your Confirmation."* I was so surprised by Margaret's gift; she gave me a ruby ring with a cameo engraved in the stone set into a gold band. I never had a ring before and absolutely loved it. Everyone else gave me money, except my mother, who bought me a sterling silver cross for my neck.

A week later when we saw the photographer's proofs, we thought they turned out well and ordered one for each of my aunts, one for Ronnie, and one to send to my father. I had not heard from him in a while. After he received the picture from me, he wrote:

> *Dear Daughter,*
>
> *Received your last two letters also your Confirmation picture. You look beautiful; my little girl has certainly grown into a young lady. I could hardly believe it. It made me very happy to get your picture. I will get one taken of me soon and will send it to you.*

I guess he didn't know Aunt Mae had shown me the picture of him and his new wife. I did wish I could see him. Maybe I will consider going to Florida sometime during the upcoming summer vacation.

CHAPTER 55

Catherine

Elaine graduated from St. James and was going to go to East Side High School in the fall. I wished I were going to East Side now, but after the summer I'd be entering the eighth grade, my last year at St. James. I liked the nuns but I hated all the restrictions and guilt.

Just before school was out, I had seen the movie *Showboat* with beautiful Ava Gardner. I was so angry with her for breaking up with Frank Sinatra. All the magazines were filled with stories of his torment over her. How could she not love him? One day when our class was cutting through the school courtyard going to a Novena at the church, I started singing the song from *Showboat* very softly to myself. *"I love him, because he's..., I don't know..., because he's just my Bill."* Sister Helen tapped me on the shoulder saying, "Katherine, sometimes I think there is something wrong with you." The class started to laugh and I felt humiliated. I was glad we were nearing summer vacation.

Once more I was going to work at Jane Logan's for the summer. Catherine, who was in my class at St. James since second grade (in fact, she was the snooty girl that Sister Maria made me share a desk with when I first moved from the Bronx), would often stop in Jane Logan's with her boyfriend, Joe Costa. She had always been skinny with glasses and was unattractive. But somehow this summer with her blond hair long and loose and a cute little figure, she had blossomed into a lovely young woman. Joe was from Portugal, tall and handsome, spending the summer "Down Neck" with his uncle. They seemed so perfect together, holding hands and always laughing; you could tell they adored each other.

One night when I went to the movies alone, *Come Back Little Sheba* was playing. Shirley Booth kept calling for her dog *Sheba* and it made me cry for Mugsy. I just couldn't stop wiping my eyes and crying through most of the movie. Catherine and Joe were together a few rows behind me and Catherine came over and asked me to join them. After the movie, I told them about Mugsy and they said they now understood why I had been crying. We started spending time together at night and became a threesome. I wished I could have a boyfriend as nice as Joe. Catherine was so upset about the fact that he would be going back to Portugal.

I missed Picky Pine; however, the weeks went by quickly. I turned thirteen with a birthday celebration lunch at Child's with Aunt Mae, Aunt Jean, and Billy. I usually sat at the counter, but we sat at a table. My mother waited on us and at the end the manager and all the waitresses gathered around and sang happy birthday to me while my mother held a strawberry cheesecake with lit candles.

I had received birthday greetings and quite a letter from my brother.

Dear Kathy,

Received your letters, it seems that during this period you have advanced quite rapidly from what was once my sweet little sister to a sweet, inquisitive young lady, when a girl of thirteen becomes quite aware of the world around her. I am speaking of sex. I realize that you are probably familiar with all that helps make up sexual behavior. But I shall try to enlighten you a little more. To begin with, please remove any thought from your mind that sex is either a dirty thing or evil. Under the right circumstances, generally consisting of one man and one woman who are in love, intercourse can truly be the most wonderful thing in the world. It is an expression and appreciation of each other's love.

The first thing I will say is that every guy you go out with will try in some manner to have intercourse with you. Now it will be up to you to size these guys up, which I know you will be able to do. I don't want to know about your personal life—it is your own business and I am sure you have conversations with your girlfriends about sex. I can go into detail about many things in reference to sex, but you can find them all in books which can tell you far more than I. I want you to be able to protect yourself.

This may be the most important letter that I have written to anyone, as a brother who loves you very much; I just want you to be equipped with all the facts and information. May I say that if there are ever any questions on your mind about anything, no matter what, remember your brother will always be glad to advise you or help you. I hope this letter was some help to you. You are now a lady, but I did so very much like the little sweet fresh sister of mine. I wish you all the luck in the world. The world is yours to have and to hold, do what you think is right, be what you want to be, and love as you want to love. There will be a person who will always be around to love that little sweet fresh gal and who will end this letter with just one word.

Thanks.

Your loving brother,
Ronnie

He seemed worried about me. I was embarrassed when reading the letter, but comforted by his concern. I felt he truly loved me. I wasn't going to tell him that I used to think sex was dirty. I now felt differently; when a fade-out followed a passionate kissing scene in a movie, I now visualized and fantasized about the love making that would follow. I thanked Ronnie for writing that letter to me and assured him I would be careful and take care of myself. I also thanked him for being such a caring brother.

Margaret had been away for a few weeks. When she returned, she told me they were looking for a house—the apartment had become too small for them with two children. I was so upset, I couldn't imagine her not living upstairs anymore. "Don't worry, you will come and spend weekends with us," she assured me. "I will miss you more than you can imagine."

I watched Patrick a lot more since she now had little Barry. Mostly Patrick and I went to the movies on my days off from Jane Logan's. During the summer, the Rivoli had a lot of cartoons, shorts like *The Three Stooges* during the day and the regular movies at night. I still hated *The Three Stooges* but Patrick liked them and I was getting paid to watch him.

One night when my mother didn't come home, I stayed awake frantic. Every time the outside door slammed, I waited to hear her footsteps, but it was always someone else going up the stairs. After midnight there were no footsteps at all. I kept remembering the time in the Bronx when she had fallen into the pit after drinking heavily and had broken all her teeth and split open her chin. I stayed awake all night, terrified. She started work at 6:30 a.m. but Mimi's grocery store didn't open until seven. I was waiting at the grocery store door when Mimi opened the store and dashed to the phone booth to call Child's. "May I please speak to Sonia Persico?" I asked. "One moment, I'll call her to the phone," a woman's voice replied. Mommy was there! Someone was calling her to the phone. She said, "Hello?"

"Mommy, are you all right?" She said she slept at a friend's and since we did not have a phone she was unable to call us. I was so relieved but very mad at her causing me to have such an awful night. Of course, I didn't tell her how angry I was because I didn't want her to be angry with me.

Daddy wrote again and asked me to visit. I felt really bad about not going but I just couldn't upset Mommy. However, once again I wrote that I had committed to my summer job, but for sure I would come for Thanksgiving or for Christmas vacation and I meant it. I imagined my father and me walking down the streets among the palm trees arm and arm as he showed me Miami Beach.

When school began, it was strange not to be walking to and from school with Elaine. I couldn't wait to go to East Side High the following year. I was really thankful that Catherine and I had become close friends during the summer. Joe had gone back to Portugal and wrote to her almost every day. She would bring in the letters and share them with me. I also became closer to a few more girls in my class. The group I used to go to Santa Lucia's for dinner with on Sundays had graduated. I managed to get two of my classmates, Lucille and Josephine, to commit to Sunday dinner and the movies. I loved going to the movies with girlfriends. After so many years of going alone, I no longer enjoyed the movies by myself. Now that I was thirteen and was allowed into the movies at night, my mother and I started going on Tuesday nights since Tuesday was her day off. I was anxiously waiting to see *From Here to Eternity* next year. I had been reading about Frank Sinatra making a comeback and being so terrific in the role of Private Angelo Maggio. I was so happy for him. Mommy promised to take me as soon as it opened, even if we had to go to New York City to see it.

Choir resumed and I went back to working at the Bingo games on Saturdays. I cut down to two afternoons at Jane Logan's because homework was heavy in the eighth grade and I wanted to continue getting good grades until graduation. I could hardly wait for the year to pass and begin high school.

CHAPTER 56

The Phone Call

It was late in the afternoon on a very hot Indian summer day in October of 1952. I was home alone sitting in the parlor next to the open window doing my eighth grade long division homework when I heard heavy footsteps stomping through our hallway and then a loud pounding on the kitchen door. I ran through the bedroom to the kitchen door and asked, "Who is it?"

A man's voice said, "There is a phone call for a Kathy at the Esso station."

My heart was racing. I was afraid to open the door and also wondering who could possibly be calling me. We didn't have a telephone, but we'd never gotten a call at the gas station before. "She'll be right there," I yelled loudly.

When I heard the footsteps walk away and the front door slam, I unlatched our door, grabbed my key and locked up. My blouse and uniform were sticking to me as I dashed down the stairs and ran toward the office at the gas station. An older man in coveralls was counting change by the gas pump. He looked at me and thrust his chin toward the office. I ran in and picked up the earpiece, which was hanging down from the public wall phone. Standing on my tiptoes, I spoke into the mouthpiece. "Hello?"

"Kathy, this is Aunt Jean."

"Hi," I said, my heart pounding in my ears. There was a long silence.

"Hello, Aunt Jean?"

Her voice broke into a rasping sound as she said, "I'm sorry to have to tell you this, Kathy, but your father is dead."

"What?" I ran my hand through my sweating hair. The gas station man came into the small office and gave me a little wink and a smile. As I tried to send him a "thank you for calling me smile," my mouth twisted into a quiver. I noticed he stopped smiling.

Aunt Jean repeated in a louder voice, "I said that your father is dead."

At the same time I was saying, "Yes, I heard what you said. What happened?"

Aunt Jean was still talking, "Your Uncle Johnny called me to say your father died in Florida. They're shipping his body back to the Bronx. It will be here tomorrow, tell your mother and Granny."

"Okay," I said in someone else's voice.

"I'm so sorry, Kathy, we will talk more tomorrow. Aunt Mae will be coming to take you to the Bronx."

I guess we said goodbye. As soon as I hung up, I gave the man a quick thank you wave and ran back to the house. I could barely see the keyhole because I could no longer control the tears from gushing. Once inside, I went back into the parlor and just let myself cry. I was shaking all over and wished Mugsy was still here. I then cried for Mugsy. Mugsy was with me my whole life and now he was gone. I thought of all the letters Daddy had sent to me asking me to come to Florida. When was the last letter he wrote…when did I write…what did I say in my letter? When was the last time I saw him? At my Communion? That was five and a half years ago. I went into the bedroom, opened the jewelry box with all of my keepsakes, and took out the little telescope with Daddy's picture that he sent me a few years ago. I squinted with one eye and looked into it. There was that headshot of Daddy looking very tan. I looked at his thick black mustache and realized I never saw him with it in person. I tried to hear his voice but I had forgotten what he sounded like. I realized I didn't really know him; now I never would. My daydreams about our future time together would never happen. Sitting by the window for the next two hours, nose running, eyes tearing, I thought of Mugsy, then Daddy, then Mugsy. I began thinking about Mugsy even more than Daddy. My stomach began to feel as though there were a large hole in it.

When I heard my grandmother walk down the hallway, I ran to the kitchen door and opened it even before she had time to put in her key in the lock. "Granny!" I startled her; she took a step backward. I saw a reprimand coming, but I just blurted out, "Granny! Aunt Jean called me on the phone at the gas station to tell me Daddy died."

"Jesus, Jesus," Granny said as she blessed herself. She stepped into the kitchen, put down her pocketbook, and lit a vigil candle in front of the statue of the Scared Heart of Jesus that was on top of the refrigerator. She whispered in her prayer voice and told me I should pray for my father, too. Then she went into the bedroom and lit all the vigil lights in front of every saint on her dressers. She motioned for me to kneel beside her on the little red velvet-padded stool, which she kept by the dresser near her bed for praying. I knelt there but prayers would not come, nor could I cry anymore. After a time I made believe I was finished praying, blessed myself, and got up. She got up also and went into the kitchen to start dinner, while she kept muttering in Lithuanian about Daddy dying too young and asking Jesus to save his soul. He was only fifty one years-old.

I went back to the parlor and sat by the window until it got dark and my radio programs came on. Granny had brought me in some blinis that I must have eaten because when she came to get my plate, it was empty. She said I shouldn't be listening to the radio because my father had died. I didn't want to argue with her and hear a lecture about the devil, so I shut it off. There was nothing to do except go to bed. I lay there in the heat watching the shadows of the saints flickering on the walls. I wished Mugsy were nestled up beside me.

After a short time, I heard my mother stumbling down the hallway and then fumbling with her key in the door. I was coming out of the bedroom as she entered the kitchen. Granny was already telling her in Lithuanian that Daddy had died. I ran to her thinking she would be very upset. She slurred, "I'm sorry for you, Kathy, that's all I can say, I am very sorry for you, Sweetie." She then asked Granny, "What happened?"

Granny told her that we didn't know yet, that Aunt Mae would tell us tomorrow, and that his body would be shipped up to the Bronx. Mommy repeated many more times, "I am sorry for you, Kathy, I am very sorry for you, because he was your father." She cried a lot and said it was because she was so sorry for me.

I felt very sorry for her; I hated to see her cry. I sat next to her holding her hand. "Mommy, I'm all right, honest." I looked at her and realized she cried like a little child, mouth open, nose running, wiping her face with the sleeve of her dress. I got her a handkerchief.

She looked at me and said, "I'm sorry to tell you and I hope you understand, but I will not be going to the funeral, after all, his new wife will be there." Until now, it hadn't occurred to me that she wouldn't be going. I nodded as though I understood, but I felt abandoned.

CHAPTER 57

The Outsider

I woke up the next morning, my eyes red and swollen. I think I dreamt about Mugsy all night. I still felt that hole in my stomach. The smell of wax lingered, mingled with the smell of oatmeal that drifted into the parlor. My grandmother usually made oatmeal every morning. I hadn't any idea what time it was, but I knew I wouldn't be going to school today or Wednesday, and probably not for the next few days. "Good thing," I thought, "I never finished my long division." I wondered when Aunt Mae would come for me. My mother had already gone to work; she usually left at six. When I went into the kitchen, I saw that it was ten o'clock. It was already very hot so hot oatmeal was not very appealing. I decided to take a bath and wash my hair. My grandmother helped me pull the oval aluminum tub out from under her bed, and then fill it with warm water. I asked if she would please leave the room, she shook her head mumbling in disbelief, since she felt no shame standing naked and washing herself at the kitchen sink, lifting each big breast and washing under it, with me in the room. I washed my hair while in the tub, but I had to throw a towel around me to rinse it with clean water under the kitchen sink faucet and towel dry it the best I could. I hoped I'd have some time to set it into pin curls with bobby pins.

Funerals were not new to me. I'd gone to many when my grandmother's friends died or my friend's grandparents died; some were in funeral parlors, others had their loved ones laid out in a coffin right in their home. I knew I should wear black. Looking through my metal closet, I chose my black taffeta skirt with a cummerbund and a see-through white dotted Swiss short-sleeved blouse. I always liked that the cummerbund made me look much thinner. I looked in my drawer. Thank God Granny had just washed and ironed my white full slip.

When Aunt Mae arrived at noon, I was dressed except I still had to take the pins out of my hair. I sat out in the sun, on the back stoop to let my pin curls dry. I looked over at the spot where Mugsy was buried. Except for the wooden cross, it was now just a patch of grass. I still couldn't erase the image of him freezing to death. "Oh Mugsy," I whispered.

Aunt Mae wept as she told Granny and me that Daddy had fallen on the slippery boards behind the counter where he worked as a short order cook and had broken three ribs. He refused to stay in the hospital, caught double pneumonia and died. Aunt Mae kept dabbing at her eyes, her blue eye makeup smearing. She fixed it while I combed out my hair. "Take a jacket," she advised.

Hurriedly, I grabbed my new red corduroy jacket. We left for the funeral parlor at 12:30 p.m. Aunt Mae said the first viewing was from two o'clock until four. The trip was long. We took the bus to Penn Station Newark, then the Hudson tubes to Fulton Street, walked four blocks to the No. 4 Woodlawn subway, and got off at Fordham Road, where we took another bus to the funeral parlor, arriving just after three.

The burning in my stomach got worse as we entered the crowded viewing room of the funeral parlor. The smell of roses permeated the hot air and the cigarette smoke hung over all the figures in black, giving the room a spooky look. Suddenly, I became aware that I had the red jacket folded over my arm. I hung it on the coat rack, pushing it deep between the many dark-hued jackets. As Aunt Mae pulled me by the hand and led me to the coffin, I felt the oatmeal from breakfast come up to my throat and go down again. When I knelt next to Aunt Mae, I heard my name accompanied by loud sobs. I looked at the man in the coffin, this man that was my father surrounded by white satin, his head resting on the pillow; he looked like the man in my telescope. I was surprised to see how short he was; his hair and mustache blacker than I remembered. I thought how Italian he looked. His hands were clasped together on the lap of his dark blue pin striped suit. Again I made believe I was praying and when Aunt Mae blessed herself and stood up, I did the same.

As we turned, several ladies and a gentleman in black came toward us. The women were my father's sisters, my other Aunt Mae, Aunt Bridget, and Aunt Ola. The man was my Uncle Johnny, my Godfather. I noticed how much they all looked alike. The women with their glasses, hair in buns, and deep black circles under their eyes, made them all look like sad raccoons. Aunt Bridget put her arm around me and led me to the coffin again. I felt as though I were sleep walking. She started to talk to my father.

"Joe, Kathy is here. Look what a big, beautiful girl you have," she sobbed while stroking my hair, as if I were the one crying. "Why didn't you listen to the doctor? Now we won't see you anymore. Joe, Joe, my baby brother…. JOE, JOE," she shrieked.

Thank God, Uncle Johnny came to guide her to a seat. I thought I should be crying; they probably thought I didn't care. I looked around for Aunt Mae, who was talking to some people nearby. As I walked toward her she said, "Kathy, this is your sister, Louise." I said, "I know," but I really hadn't recognized her right away. It had been five and a half years since I had seen her.

Louise was tall and, even without makeup, you could see how good looking she was. She pushed her long dark hair away from her tear-streaked face. Trying to smile, she began hugging me saying, "Of course Kathy remembers me, don't you, honey?" She was speaking to me as though I was five. Just then her two little children ran over. "Helen, Frankie, this is your Aunt Kathy." It sounded funny to hear me called an aunt. We looked at each other. I was a stranger to them, everyone was a stranger to me, and even my father seemed like a stranger. Then Aunt Mae told me she was going back to Newark. I would stay at Louise's house until after the funeral on Saturday, and she would come back to bring me home on Sunday.

"We Persicos have to stick together," Louise was saying as she patted me on the head. "He was our Daddy," she said as she started to shake and cry some more. I tried to look very sad; I wished I could cry. Louise introduced me to many relatives and others who came to pay their respects. "This is Kathy, my father's other daughter and my other sister." I was reintroduced to all my cousins. Louise referred to my Aunt Bridget as her mother and Bridget's children as her siblings, since she lived with Aunt Bridget when her mother left my father. It was all very confusing to me. Most people cried when they met me. It was like a bad dream. I just kept going around kind of stunned. When Aunt Mae and I were alone, I asked, "Do I have to stay? Please don't leave me alone."

"You are not alone, they are your family, and it is your father's funeral, of course you have to stay. They are all so nice and you will be with your sister and her husband."

Until now, I hadn't met Louise's husband. Then I heard my sister tell my aunt that Mike, my father's last wife, had just arrived. Everyone seemed impressed that she had driven all the way up from Florida to pay her respects. I discovered that she had already been separated from my father, and I also heard them saying that her boyfriend was waiting for her outside in the car.

As she walked in, my aunts, Louise, and my cousins started to sob out loud again. "Mike" was dressed in a black trumpet-style dress trimmed with black fur around the bottom and also on her three quarter-length sleeves. The slanted black tam over her blond shoulder length hair made her look like the actress Dagmar. When Louise regained her composure, with her arm around my shoulder, she veered me toward her and introduced us.

"Mike, Kathy is my father's other daughter. Kathy, Mike is Daddy's last wife."

Mike started to cry. She held out her red manicured hand to shake mine, her large mascaraed brown eyes looking deep into mine. "Sorry we have to meet under these circumstances. I am so sorry about your father, Kathy."

"Hello," I said, nodding. I didn't know what else to say. Louise was asking about her drive up. While Mike talked, I noticed how tall she was and tried to picture her with my father. They just didn't seem to go together. When she went up to the coffin, the sobs in the room got louder. The family all seemed to like her; they were hugging and kissing her. Aunt Mae embraced her as well, since she had met her on her trip to Florida.

Helen, my little niece, was holding her brother Frankie's hand while asking me where I lived and how come she didn't know me before.

"Well, I live in another state, and my mother used to be your grandpa's wife."

"I thought Mike was grandpa's wife."

"Yes, she was his last wife." I tried to change the subject. "How old are you?" I asked. "I just turned six," she beamed as Frankie burst out, "Two!" He demonstrated with two fingers. Helen wrapped her arms around my waist and cooed, "I'm glad you're my Aunt."

I hugged her back and tried to hug Frankie, but he ducked behind Helen. Helen and I held hands for the next few minutes. Then the funeral director announced that we should pay our last respects since the viewing was over, and that the room would reopen between seven and nine o'clock.

Everyone started moving toward the coffin. This time I went up to it with Helen and Frankie. "Grandpa is sleeping," Frankie whispered. I knelt down again and performed my pretend praying. I looked at my father. I couldn't believe this was happening. I heard sobs starting again in the room.

"Let's go," Helen said, pulling at my skirt. I blessed myself and got up. Louise was right behind me, now shaking and sobbing loudly.

"Kathy, take the kids outside, I'll be there in a minute."

Aunt Mae walked out with us. I took my red jacket from the rack and draped it over my arm, hoping no one would notice it. The air outside felt good, I could breathe again. Aunt Mae said she'd better get going; she didn't want to travel too late. She would pick me up at Louise's house on Sunday. "Be a good girl," she said, hugging me tight. I saw that her blue eye shadow was all smeared again. When she got to the corner the bus came right away. She waved from the window as the bus passed.

"Daddy, Daddy," Frankie screeched at the car that had just pulled up. A tall, dark man came around to the curb and Frankie jumped up into his arms. Helen kept holding my hand and said, "He's my Daddy. This is my new Aunt Kathy, Daddy." He winked at me, holding Frankie in one arm he reached out his free hand to greet me, "Hi, Aunt Kathy, I'm Frank, Louise's husband. Sorry about your father."

"Hello. Thank you." I thought he seemed nice.

Louise said goodbye to everyone and then to Mike. I watched as Mike walked down the street, her hips swaying slightly. I wanted to see her boyfriend. I didn't think it was right for her to come with her boyfriend, but she turned the corner and was gone.

Louise got into the front seat of the car and put Frankie on her lap. My newfound little niece, Helen, sat in the back seat, still holding my hand. Once the car started moving, Louise asked, "What kind of macaroni do you like?"

Somehow I thought this was not a subject we should be talking about. The solemnity of the funeral parlor still remained with me; asking me about macaroni seemed far too casual.

"Do you like Ziti or Rigatoni? she asked. "I made a big pot of gravy with meatballs and braciole."

"Whatever everyone wants is okay with me," I said.

"You're the guest," she said. "If you like another kind of macaroni, we can stop at a store to pick it up."

I found myself getting angry about this small talk, but I kept it to myself. "What do YOU like?" I asked Helen.

"I want Ziti," and Frankie joined in. "Ziti, Ziti, Ziti," they both chanted.

"Then Ziti it is," I said as I gave Helen's small hand a little squeeze.

After two more afternoons and evenings at the funeral parlor, my father was buried at Saint Ramón's Cemetery in the Bronx. That morning the weather had changed drastically; it was sleeting and freezing cold. Louise's neighbor lent me a gray winter coat and boots. Thank God I didn't have to wear my red jacket. Although I had been to many wakes, I had never been to a cemetery. I stood there numbly watching as my father's coffin was lowered into the ground. Moans and sounds of absolute agony accompanied my Aunt Bridget's screams; my uncles had to support her collapsing body. I held a hanky to my eyes and hoped no one could see I could not cry. I felt so alone.

CHAPTER 58

After the Funeral

Having missed several days of school, there were so many lessons to catch up on. I also had to let the principal know if I was going to attend St. James High School. When I informed her I had registered at East Side High, the principal and several of the nuns tried to dissuade me, but my mind was made up; I was definitely going to the public high school. I didn't want my marks to go down, therefore I threw myself into my studies, getting almost all A's. It helped to fill the emptiness I felt without Mugsy and my father. I couldn't believe my father was dead. I hadn't realized how much I had looked forward to receiving his letters. I prayed that he would forgive me for never having gone to Florida to see him. I paid for and attended several masses that were said for him.

When I finally caught up with my schoolwork, one Sunday afternoon I opened my bottom drawer, where I now kept all of my father's letters. It took me the entire afternoon to read them; there were many over the last five and a half years. In each letter, he wrote that he loved and missed me, and in almost every one he apologized for only sending me five or ten dollars because his business had gone bankrupt and he was broke. Many asked me when I would be coming to visit him in

Florida. In his early letters, he wrote that he was lonely and not feeling very well.

Maybe I should have been happy for him when he married Mike. The thought of her sent a surge of anger through me remembering she had her boyfriend waiting in a car outside the funeral home. I wondered what happened to my father's dog, Trouble—so many letters expressed his love for her. Should I try to locate his dog? Whom would I contact? I didn't know anyone he knew in Florida and Mike was off somewhere with her boyfriend.

For the first time since the day I was told of my father's death, it hit me. I cried. I cried for him. I cried for his dog Trouble. I cried because I had always postponed visiting him. I cried remembering how awful it was to get the phone call from my Aunt Jean at the gas station. I cried because my mother didn't seem to care that he died. I just cried and cried. It felt good to finally let go.

When I was returning the letters to the drawer, I came across the little green sweater Mugsy refused to wear, and cried again for him. Then I noticed a small cloth bag tied with a drawstring. Opening it, I discovered my little teddy bear, Poochie. I couldn't remember when I had packed him away, but I was so glad to find him. I decided to put Mugsy's little green sweater on him. Though it was too big, he looked adorable. I pressed him to my chest as I did when I was a young child, and silently thanked him for being with me on the nights I was alone and frightened. I sat him down on top of my dresser near the phonograph, right in front of my *Alice in Wonderland* record that I hadn't played for a while. I remembered how I used to pretend I was Alice lost among all those strange creatures, but in the end she always woke up outside of the rabbit hole. I realized that I had come out of the rabbit hole, too.

I sat quietly for a while on the rocking chair. Then I thought of one thing I could do tomorrow. I would call the telephone company and have phone service installed. I'd pay for it myself. There would be no more phone calls to the gas station or sitting in Mimi's phone booth, and my mother could call me if she's going to stay out all night.

That decided, I was beginning to feel better. I went into the kitchen, washed my face and got ready to meet Lucille and Josephine at Santa Lucia's for dinner. Tonight the revival of *Anchors Aweigh* was playing. I remembered my excitement of seeing that movie when I was only five. Years before, I had fallen in love with Frank Sinatra and his voice. The very thought of seeing *Anchors Aweigh* that night, this time with my good friends, made me feel even better.

The movie stayed with me throughout all of Monday. I kept humming *Anchors Aweigh,* with the image of Frank Sinatra dancing with Gene Kelly in my head. My mother had never seen the film, so we planned to go together the following night.

Right after school, I rushed to the phone booth in Mimi's to call the telephone company. The appointment was made to have phone service installed a week from tomorrow, on Tuesday, my mother's day off. She would have to sign for the installation, even though I was going to pay.

My mother and I arrived to see *Anchors Aweigh* early Tuesday night in order to get a good seat in the smoking section. We almost finished a large tub of popcorn as I anxiously waited for the lights to dim; it seemed like forever. During the movie, as my mother took long drags on her Pall Malls, she'd give my hand a squeeze every time Sinatra came on the screen. When he tenderly sang *I Fall in Love Too Easily,* I had to take my hanky from my pocket. When I saw my mother dabbing at her eyes, too, I reached for her hand.

On Tuesday of the following week, I thought the hands of the school clock would never move to three. When they finally did, I jumped up as the dismissal bell rang, dashed out the door, ran all the way home, and burst through the kitchen door, scaring Granny. Mommy had a big smile on her face and pointed to the bedroom. It was there—a beautiful, shiny black phone! I picked up the receiver, but someone was talking on it. My mother explained that we had a party-line, in fact, we had a two-party line. I'd have to wait until the people finished their conversation before I could make a call. I waited impatiently for a few minutes and when I picked it up again, a female voice snapped, "All right, all right, I'm getting off." Then I heard a click.

I immediately dialed Aunt Helen, who was thrilled that we could now talk to each other. Granny spoke next and was almost as happy as I was. Now I could phone Aunt Mae, Aunt Jean, my sister Louise, and my little niece Helen. Best of all, I could call my friends. I had been the only one that didn't have a phone. Sissy had moved to Lake Parsippany at the end of the summer—I could call her as well.

I made many calls over the next few weeks. Sometimes when I picked up the receiver, one of the party line people was talking. I'd put my hand over the mouthpiece and listen to their conversation; mostly it was boring but it was still fun to eavesdrop. However, when talking to one of my friends, I listened for a click—I didn't want anyone listening to us. I so wished we had a phone when my father was alive.

I realized it was up to me to take care of myself. I knew my mother loved me very much and I loved her in equal measure; she was the sweetest person in the whole world but helpless and childlike in many ways. My brother Ronnie was close to my heart and we loved each other, but he was out there in the world trying to take care of himself. I felt very peaceful, grown up, and in control of my life. Whenever I needed comfort, Frank Sinatra's voice would always be just a record away. I knew I would be fine.

CHAPTER 59

Fast Forward

When did I start living for myself? Certainly it was not when I graduated from East Side High School, when at my insistence and after quite a search, I moved my mother and me from my grandmother's to a modern apartment on Barbara Street, lined with Elm trees, a few houses in from Wilson Avenue. It seemed like the beginning of a whole new life. When fully decorated with the three rooms of furniture we bought on credit, the place was lovely. I thought the upgrade in our living conditions would bring my mother contentment and she'd stop drinking. I was wrong.

Furthermore, I had committed myself to sharing monthly expenses that my mother couldn't handle alone. Though I had worked hard to earn a scholarship to Newark State Teachers College, I couldn't afford to begin that fall. The scholarship committee granted me a one year extension, during which time I intended to work full time and save enough to start the following year. In the meantime, I began acting classes and commuted to New York City three nights a week after working from 9 to 5 at the Federal Pacific Electric Company in Newark. College was put on the back burner.

When Child's restaurant closed, my mother, then age fifty-four, began a counter job at Dingleman Donuts. Since her tips there were so much better than at Child's, she could now handle all the bills on Barbara Street by herself. Finally, at age twenty-six, I moved to New York City to pursue my acting career. Though I felt guilty about leaving my mother, I finally thought I was beginning to live life for myself.

I loved acting and, for the next fifteen years, I earned a living as an actress, supplementing my income with waitressing and other odd jobs. During that time, I married an actor and gave birth to my daughter, Christina, who embodies the very best of everyone that I have ever loved. When Christina was ten, some twenty-five years after I graduated from high school, I began matriculating at Marymount Manhattan College.

At sixty-eight years of age, my mother was laid off. It was difficult for her to manage on Social Security alone. She looked ten years younger than her age, and was hired as a lunchtime waitress in a bar near her apartment. Several months later, Dorothy, the owner of the bar, phoned me late one afternoon. She was concerned because, after her lunch shift, my mother had been sitting quietly on a bar stool for a very long time. Dorothy repeatedly asked her if she was all right and although my mother kept insisting she was, Dorothy said she did not look well and her speech was slurred. I suspected a stroke and asked her to please call an ambulance, and I would leave for Newark immediately. After phoning Ronnie, who was working in New York City, we went together directly to St. James Hospital. Our mother had indeed suffered a stroke that paralyzed her right side and affected her speech.

The next year was rough for both of us. After being in a rehabilitation facility for several weeks, my mother was released. Determined to recover, she worked very hard in her apartment with a visiting physical therapist. I also arranged for an aide to assist her for a few hours three times a week. At the time, my husband was ill and my daughter was young, plus I was working, attending college, and making the trip back and forth from New York to Newark at least twice a week to oversee my mother's care.

Almost achieving full rehabilitation over that next year, and finally able to descend the stairs by herself, she suffered another massive stroke. While comatose in the intensive care unit at St. James Hospital, the doctor informed me she would probably not live through the night. The nurse said the monitors indicated she was responsive to my voice. Therefore, all night long I pleaded, "Please don't die. I love you so much, Mommy." In the morning, she came out of the coma—she came back to me! However, the stroke left her completely incapacitated and in need of constant assistance, so it was now necessary for her to reside in a nursing home. After several New Jersey nursing homes, I was finally able to get her transferred to Kateri, a home in New York several blocks from my apartment.

I vividly remember the day at Kateri when I pushed my mother's wheelchair past a full length mirror. Suddenly, she let out a wail when she saw the reflection of an old, emaciated, gray-haired woman that bore no resemblance to Eva-Sonia-Tommy. Inarticulate sounds escaped from her throat as she looked in horror at her image and wept. Weeping with her and for her, guilt flooded through me since I had begged her not to die and now she lived in this limbo between life and death.

Though only in my forties, I was gripped by fear: the years fly by too quickly. A scene flashed through my mind of my beautiful mother and me smiling at each other, high up on the swings at Olympic Park, spinning round and round until the breeze caused her white gardenia to loosen from her hair and fly to the ground. I was brought back to reality when my mother made a fist and raised her arm—as she kept nodding. I knew that she was cheering me on to *LIVE!* I nodded and kissed her cheek in affirmation.

For the next two years, I visited her everyday until her death on July 10, 1984, at age seventy-one. That day I sat for hours with her washed, naked body wrapped in a sheet until the funeral director came. I watched as he gently tucked her into and zipped up the body bag. She was at peace and so was I.

Epilogue

One night when I was thirty-four, I was filling in as a waitress for a friend at Jilly's bar, known to be a Frank Sinatra favorite. The Chinese cook didn't show up that night. I overheard the manager say, "If Frank comes in, we'll have to tell him there is no Chow Mein."

At 2 a.m., I was alone in the tiny kitchen washing glasses, when the shutter doors swung open and there stood an extraordinarily handsome, tanned man with the deepest blue eyes looking straight into mine, giving me the biggest smile and the warmest, "Hi."

It took a few seconds before I realized…it was him! Frank Sinatra himself—not five feet away from me! I felt the blood rush up the back of my neck. Finally finding my voice, stepping forward, I heard myself speak.

"There is no Chow Mein," I stammered, shaking my head regretfully.

"Huh?"

"We don't have any Chow Mein."

Looking confused, he nodded. The doors swung shut behind him and he was gone.

I often play *I'll Be Seeing You,* one of my all time favorites. As I sing along with Sinatra, I think of all those I have loved and lost…

"I'll be seeing you, in all the old familiar places."

Postscript

Decades later...

So many of my early readers have asked what became of everyone who has lived within these pages, I decided to respond, in brief, to their inquiries.

After the Army, while working in a full time job, my brother Ronnie earned his high school equivalency and went on to college, earning a Masters in Education. Though he loved teaching, he eventually left the profession because of the bureaucracy. He then achieved great success in educational publishing first as Vice President of Marketing and Sales, and then as Vice President of Product Development. Ronnie is still married to his first sweetheart, Felicia, and they live in New Jersey. They have two adult children, Jennifer and Mark, and six grandchildren.

Little Billy, who stopped "blowing his bugle" long ago, grew up to be a wonderful man and a very successful engineer. Billy also lives in New Jersey and is happily married to his wife Linda. They have two adult boys and several grandchildren.

My Aunt Helen and Uncle Bill became snow birds; they stayed in Picky Pine in the summer and Fort Lauderdale, Florida in the winter. When Uncle Bill developed prostate cancer, I went to Picky Pine many times to give Aunt Helen a hand in caring for him. He was quite humble and thankful. We never spoke of the incidents. After his death, Aunt Helen sold the big house in Carmersville and lived in Picky Pine, the original the little house, continuing to go back and forth to Florida. In her last years, Ronnie became her caretaker until he could no longer manage to keep her in his home. Because she had advanced Alzheimer's, she spent the last few months of her life in a nursing home. When I saw her shortly before she died, she didn't recognize me. Her beautiful blue eyes looked into mine without any recognition.

Once my mother and I moved out of my grandmother's apartment, I began to really appreciate Granny and all she had done for us. I visited her often on Jackson Street, where she lived alone for many years until she became ill. When Billy was grown, Aunt Mae shifted her caretaking to my grandmother and moved in with her on Jackson Street until my grandmother's death.

Shortly after Granny passed away, Aunt Mae had applied for—and was thrilled to be accepted into—a lovely, brand new senior citizens housing development. She enjoyed living there for several years until she developed heart trouble. Billy and his wife Linda took her into their home, where she resided until her death.

After Billy married, Aunt Jean retired from Hayne & Company and worked part time at an A & P supermarket near her apartment in Kearney. When she became ill several years after Aunt Mae died, Billy and his wife also took her into their home, where she lived until her death.

My mother's old friend, Eva Prokapchak, bought a piece of property in Carmersville near Picky Pine. She became a very close friend of Aunt Helen's. It was nice for me to see her often over the years. The original Picky Pine house and the other back house were left to my brother Ronnie in my Aunt Helen's will. His son Mark bought them and expanded the back house, where he still lives with his wife Lauren and their two daughters.

My sister Louise and I grew close over the years and Helen, my niece, is also my good friend.

I've kept all the letters from my father and mother.

Mugsy stays in my heart until this day. Remembering him and memorializing his death in these pages caused me to mourn his loss once again.

Kathy Wilson's background includes many years in the theater both as an actor and teacher. As an adult she attended Marymount Manhattan College, earning a degree in Communication Arts. She then taught numerous writing courses at MMC for both Continuing Education and the Center for Learning and Living. Active in the Poets and Writers Workshop for over a decade, she published a chapbook, and read many of her essays for their annual Intergenerational Readings at Barnes and Noble. Her poetry was published by the International Library of Poetry. Kathy has lived on the Upper West Side in New York City all of her adult life.

CPSIA information can be obtained at www.ICGtesting.com
Printed in the USA
BVOW05s2319061115

425645BV00002B/138/P